D1811050

TIBET, SELF, AND THE TIBETAN DIASPORA

BRILL'S TIBETAN STUDIES LIBRARY

EDITED BY

HENK BLEZER
ALEX MCKAY
CHARLES RAMBLE

VOLUME 2/8

TIBET, SELF, AND THE TIBETAN DIASPORA

Voices of Difference

PIATS 2000: Tibetan Studies: Proceedings of the Ninth Seminar of the International Association for Tibetan Studies, Leiden 2000. Managing Editor: Henk Blezer.

EDITED BY

P. CHRISTIAAN KLIEGER

BRILL
LEIDEN · BOSTON · KÖLN
2002

Publication of the Proceedings of the Ninth Seminar of the IATS was made possible through financial support from the Gonda Foundation (Royal Dutch Academy of Sciences—KNAW) and was facilitated by the International Institute for Asian Studies (IIAS)

This book is printed on acid-free paper.

Die Deutsche Bibliothek - CIP-Einheitsaufnahme

Klieger, P. Ch. (ed.)
Tibet, Self, and the Tibetan Diaspora. PIATS 2000: Tibetan Studies:
Proceedings of the Ninth Seminar of the International Association for
Tibetan Studies, Leiden 2000. Managing Editor: Henk Blezer / edited
by P. Christiaan Klieger. – Leiden ; Boston ; Köln : Brill, 2002
   (Brill's Tibetan studies library ; Vol 2/8)
   ISBN 90-04-12555-8

Library of Congress Cataloging-in-Publication Data

Library of Congress Cataloging-in-Publication Data is also available

On the cover: Prayer-flags at Skor ra in Dharamsala (H.P., India; Blezer 1996)

ISSN   1568-6183
ISBN   90 04 12555 8

© *Copyright 2002 by Koninklijke Brill NV, Leiden, The Netherlands*

Cover design: Cédilles / Studio Cursief, Amsterdam
*All rights reserved. No part of this publication may be reproduced, translated, stored in
a retrieval system, or transmitted in any form or by any means, electronic,
mechanical, photocopying, recording or otherwise, without prior written
permission from the publisher.*

*Authorization to photocopy items for internal or personal
use is granted by Brill provided that
the appropriate fees are paid directly to The Copyright
Clearance Center, 222 Rosewood Drive, Suite 910
Danvers MA 01923, USA.
Fees are subject to change.*

PRINTED IN THE NETHERLANDS

CONTENTS

LIST OF ILLUSTRATIONS

INTRODUCTION

THE QUEST FOR UNDERSTANDING
THE MODERN TIBETAN SELF

P. CHRISTIAAN KLIEGER (CALIFORNIA ACADEMY OF SCIENCES)

Tibetans, viewed by some as prisoners of paradigms imposed from
without, may nevertheless construct convenient sounding boards
from which discordances about the current trends in real-life Tibetan
expression may be played. As colourful and engaging that they are,
the restrictive orientalist paradigm has tend to reduce the rich field of
Tibetan expression to an essentialist trope. Despite many elegant
attempts, such reductionism is itself a prison, ironically as dark as
Shangri-La is bright. The ten papers presented in this volume attempt
to provide an example of the colourful and lively range of Tibetan
self-expressions that presently exist within the modern homeland and
in exile. The scholars here represent the fields of anthropology,
sociology, literary studies, history, and political science. Four of the
papers are based in studies in the modern Tibet Autonomous Region,
five of the papers are grounded in the Tibetan diaspora, and one
paper deals with both classical Tibetan history and current affairs
along both cultural trajectories. The papers were presented at Leiden
University in June 2000 at a symposium on the Tibetan Self for the
9th Seminar of the International Association for Tibetan Studies.

For Tibetological scholarship over the last two generations,
indeed for over two centuries, Shangri-La has provided a convenient
model from which contemporary praxis may be compared. Most
scholars have used it as a sensitive gauge from which the deadly
poison 'change' can be measured in Tibetan society. The Tibet of
Shangri-La is nothing if it does not represent the golden parapets of
the highest achievements of this realm. For within Shangri-La lie the
power of epiphany and the power for individual transformation. Over
the last six or seven years, the Tibetological deconstructionists have
largely succeeded in torching Shangri-La, a virtual Götterdämme-
rung that has both Dharamsala and Beijing image-makers muttering

tales of woe. Can Tibet and Tibetan self-expression survive without these ideals? Or perhaps there are other ideologies that conceptualise what it is to be Tibetan. Many of these papers show some of the variety in the concept of the Tibetan self from the point of view of the actors rather than the observers. Others look at the Chinese perspective towards their restless colony.

Far from being devoid of content, 'anti-Shangri-La', that mode of analysis that may be traced to the tribe of deconstructionists emerging from the 1996 "Mythos Tibet" conference in Bonn, is ripe with novel potentialities. As happens in many post-paradigmatic arenas, there is a greater possibility in this case that new concepts of the Tibetan self-image may be recognised in Tibetological scholarship as authentic. Herein lies the point: although Tibetans have been expressing themselves throughout their own long history, both Tibetan canonical, indigenous societal, and Western ideological expectations have tended to exclude varieties of self-expression that did not suit particular orthodox norms. It is far easier to examine the great variety of contemporary Tibetan self-expression now that Shangri-La is presently unfashionable. Perhaps in its place more of the 'real-politik' of occupied Tibet and the societies of the diaspora, full of their contradictions, paradoxes, and ironies will become more evident—all markers of the living culture the Tibetan people still construct.

For both homeland and exile Tibetans, self-identity is perhaps more consciously articulated here than within societies that have not been explicitly given a death sentence by others. In both Shangri-La and Chinese centrist philosophies, Tibetan culture is supposed to vanish as a natural and evolutionary outcome of regional modernisation. Of course, no group of people relish the thought of becoming extinct—the strategy for Tibetan people in general, at least since the occupation in the 1950s, is to perpetually define oneself as different from the powerful 'Others' encroaching upon their territorial, political, and religious borders. The public representation of Tibetan self, delivered through various literary vehicles, or by linguistic competence, body decoration, landscape planning, individual deportment, etc., constitutes the basic theme of this collection of papers.

Dibyesh Anand confronts Shangri-La head on in his analysis of Dharamsala as "Little Lhasa." Having been firmly planted on the New Age, Dharma, and otherwise alternative Western tourist beat for over 25 years, Dharamsala (and particularly its Tibetan village of McLeod Ganj) may in some sense be the most vigorous proponent of Shangri-La in existence. With a close second perhaps existing in Kathmandu, Dharamsala unabashedly markets itself to tourists (Western, Indian, and other Asian) as more authentically Tibetan than modern but occupied Tibet itself. This is due to the holistic font of legitimacy emanating from the Dalai Lama and the institutions that he has established in exile. Dharamsala displays a deeply ironic landscape, in that its claim to Tibetan legitimacy exists among scores of tourist souvenir shops, hotels, chai huts, and cake and donut restaurants, none of which ever existed in traditional Tibetan cities. N'er a yak has set foot in McLeod Ganj, yet Dharamsala is a place where memories and nostalgia for a lost way of life are perpetuated as no other.

Anand examines the coincidental irony of the word *dharamsala* as a place of temporary rest, a point of retreat. The Dalai Lama's place on the top of the hill, with Namgyal Monastery and the Tshulha-khang nearby, with the people's village down the road, neatly reproduces the landscape of Lhasa itself. Circular paths around important Tibetan exile institutions model the great Ling Khor and Bar Khor of the Tibetan capital. Such simulation is powerful and highly useful as a mnemonic of the golden days of pre-1959 Tibet.

Two papers discuss the Chinese presentation of the Tibetan Self through newspaper biographies and obituaries (Garratt) and through the Chinese language poetry of the contemporary Tibetan poet Yi dam Tshe ring (Maconi). Contemporary Chinese literary activities at least since the cultural revolution have developed an idealisation of Tibetan culture independently of Shangri-La, yet it is remarkably similar. The genre of the 'colourful Tibetan minority', with their traditions of superstition, shamanism, tantrism, and other esoteric practices, are charged with an approach-avoidance barbarism that clearly represents the exotic=erotic orientalist posit.

Garratt illustrates the use of the media for not just reporting the death and discovery of important *tulku*, but how the State is considered by the Chinese government as an essential instrument in the confirmation of the successful candidates. This is seen with the recent examples of the 17th Karmapa and 11th Panchen Rinpoche discoveries, and with other newsworthy events in the religious affairs of Tibet. Garratt's work, by presenting a Chinese depiction of

Tibetan 'Other' shows an idealised alternative to Western-based Shangri-La. The general tone of the Chinese press releases on Tibetan *tulku* follows a rather matter-of-fact description of the discovery of the reincarnation, his life, and religious curriculum vitae. If anything, such press coverage tends to convey the message that Tibetan religious life is thriving under Chinese patronage.

Garratt's paper shows how the Chinese press coverage to report on the discovery and demise of Tibet's famous *tulku* is used for enhancing the position of the state. He suggests that China is afraid of traditional 'hard power' resources found in the traditional Tibetan system, and views this as a threat to continued Chinese rule in the region. By supporting the selection process, not to mention particularly candidates for certain political expediency, China demonstrates that it has a vital role to play in traditional Tibetan religious affairs and in the long-term future of Tibet.

That Beijing is meddlesome with the process of selection of Tibetan reincarnates is not necessarily a new idea—the Manchus, from Nuhaci to Pu Yi, were always most active in the affairs of the Tibetan system of *tulku* selection. So too were the rulers of the Yuan dynasty of the Mongols. Such essential rights were not so much the prerogatives of a universalistic, Confucian-based Son of Heaven, but the more Inner Asia flavour of the emperor as the Great Khan.

Garratt suggest that the interest seen in the Chinese press for Tibetan matters is indicative of an attempt to subsume a major aspect of Tibetan uniqueness, and thus one of the foundations for Tibetan national identity.

Maconi's paper on the poet Yi dam Tshe ring presents the writer's work on Tibetan national identity. She demonstrates that Tibetan 'post-Liberation' literature shows that presently two cultures co-exist within a single social context: Tibetophone writers who were raised with Tibetan as their mother tongue; and the younger generation of Sinophone writers, largely from poor backgrounds, who were schooled in Chinese language. Maconi demonstrates that the relationships between the two are complex, sometimes antithetical, but that nevertheless they can demonstrate interesting evidence of literary and linguistic hybridisation.

Antonio Terrone appraises the *gter ston* tradition of Tibetan autobiography. He provides an exploration into some of the features that characterise the charismatic personality of a contemporary tantric layman. This is at the heart of the phenomenon of 'treasure discovery' operating nowadays in Tibet itself. While outlining this process, he provides tentative hypotheses as to how treasure discovery may be considered an active force in the process of revitalisation of religious practices in Tibet. He also provides a fascinating look at how religion and individual identity operates with traditional and continuing Tibetan society.

In a different literary genre, Laurie Hovell McMillin examines Tibetan autobiographies written in English. Historically Tibetan culture has been rich with traditional life stories, *rnam thar* (biography) and *rang rnam* (autobiography). In exile, a new form of autobiography has appeared. McMillin's paper tells us something about the way that Tibetan self-identity interacts with Western expectations. For one, there is a question of authenticity. Tibetan refugee writers are often considered by Western audiences as the true representatives of Tibetan culture, not those who live in Tibet, especially those that show any form of hybridism or political compromise. Thus the 'authentic' Tibetan individual is the refugee one, for he or she has been blessed by the continuing presence of the Dalai Lama. The diasporic Tibetan people themselves reach a form of apotheosis through their immediate connection with their exiled leader. This can be seen clearly in many autobiographies written for the Anglophone press in the West.

George Dreyfus examines the historical and present status of Tibetan nationalism, a relationship between the self and the once-and-future state of Tibet. He sees Tibetan nationalism as basically religiously defined, one that is considerably different from the orthodox Western definitions of nationhood. Regarding the construction of the notion of the Tibetan nation, Dreyfus takes exception with the broadly-held notions that 1) in non-Western countries, modern nationalism is a foreign import; 2) it is necessarily secular: and 3) that it is orientalist in its basic assumptions. Dreyfus thus flatly dismisses Shangri-La as a component of indigenous Tibetan Nationalism, including the exile version of the Tibetan government-in-exile. Dreyfus argues that the Tibetan nationalism most widely articulated by the Dalai Lama didn't suddenly drop down upon the world stage in 1959 merely to be co-opted by subsequent Western interaction. It is much more complex. The modern Tibetan state was first expressed, perhaps, by the 13th Dalai Lama in his proclamation of 'independence' in 1913. Much later, organised movements such as the 'Four Rivers, Six Ranges (*chu bzhi gang drug*) movement helped galvanise opposition to Chinese occupation in the 1950s. This led directly to the 1959 Lhasa Uprising.

Religious nationalism is exemplified according to Dreyfus in the Tibetan national hymns, which are essentially prayers. One is reminded of Tambiah's well-known work on Buddhist universalism and of the ideals of the old Holy Roman Empire that promoted a unified Christendom. Yet one is intrigued by the interplay of this universalism with an ethnic particularism evident in Tibetan nationalism. Dreyfus suggests that Tibetan nationalism has long historical precedence, contrary to the popularly accepted notion that Tibetan nationalism is largely a product of Dharamsala propagandists and their internalisation of orientalist motifs.

In further reference to the Tibetan Self, Dreyfus notes the complex matrix of individual karma and the persona gods ('*go ba'i lha*) that help constitute a sense of individual being. This is in marked contrast to the more canonical Buddhist sense of identity that teaches the ultimate non-existence of the self.

Emily Yeh offers a particularly interesting perspective on being Tibetan. An American scholar of Chinese heritage, Yeh brings a strong reflexive perspective to how Tibetans in both the homeland and in the diaspora in San Francisco, California, attempt to categories her and each other. 'Looking' Tibetan appears to be an all-important means of establishing solidarity in Tibet among the citizenry, even though Yeh's research suggests that neither dress, linguistic competence, nor behaviour alone necessarily produces mutual recognition. Indeed, her research suggests that the Tibetan Self is envisioned as an intuitive process, as defined by actors. Tibetan informants reported that they often recognised each other by assessing the sum of many characteristics, some of which include language, physical type, deportment, dress, etc. No one particular feature seemed more efficacious than others. Yeh shows, by means of comparison, that Tibetan refugees living in San Francisco Bay Area also ascribe Tibetan identity both by means of active negotiations and through intuitive realisation. An ethnic border exists, in classic Barthian fashion, while personnel may cross at will. This apparent characteristic of Tibetan identity seems to lie at a considerable distance from the 'Cheshire Cat' variety of ethnic affiliation found in the work of Leach and Moermann. In the latter, entire groups may change the content of their expressive and material culture while maintaining a strong sense of group affiliation. Tibetan identity categories are thus rather essentialistic—one notes the experiences of Charlene Makley who was stunned not to be recognised as a woman in A mdo, even though her physical appearance, dress, etc. would most likely be considered elsewhere as feminine. Makley was not recognised as a woman for her behaviour, as lone foreigners travelling through the villages, such on trading mission, would be exhibiting male gendered behaviour. Yeh, on the other hand, was often perceived as a Tibetan woman, and other times as a foreign woman. Her treading over Ockham's razor provides a fascinating insight into the deep construction of Tibetan identity.

Jan Magnusson describes 'soft power' resources that Dharamsala has commandeered to achieve a high level of moral prominence on the global state. His Holiness the Dalai Lama, far from appearing as a deposed orientalist potentate of Shangri-La, creates a charismatic atmosphere of irony by expressly conveying his humanity. That 'humaneness' can be equated with compassion, and this compassion of course is a principle attribute of Avalokiteshvara, incarnate in the lineage of the Dalai Lamas. Thus the Tibetan leader is rocketed to the high moral ground in the ideological battle with China over Tibet. The Dalai Lama succeeds just by being himself. This is a type of 'soft power'. Similarly, the appeal to the world community to make Tibet a zone of peace, and ecological preserve, a historical 'park', etc., is an innovative commandeering of the traditional ideal of active Buddhist *ahimsa*. The traditionally strong position of women in Tibetan society melds seamlessly with Western feminist ideals to construct yet another soft power resource for the positing of Tibetan aspirations for a global audience. The use of the 'golden age' imagery for political purposes by the Tibetan government-in-exile is pure Shangri-La in action. One could note in Magnusson's work the primary modus operandi of the Dharamsala spin-pundits an attempt to make Tibetans seem 'worthy' of self-determination to the outside world. The message is that Tibetans deserves their own country (or true autonomy) because they are natural conservationists, feminists, and peace-loving humanitarians. They merit their own freedom, not so much through natural rights of self-determination, but by commandeering inarguably noble, popular, and modern global ideals.

Magnusson also discusses reverse orientalism in Tibetan society, which is defined as "seeking to valorise for the self what in the former system had been devaluated as other" (Abu-Lughod, 1991:144). This is perhaps the phenomenon as the Western transformation of the Tartar 'Other' as the Scourge of God to none other than the embodiment of the divine itself.

While democracy too is slowly taking root Tibetan refugee society, Dharamsala eschews some liberal causes popular in Western and westernising societies—sexual orientation, for example, is a topic not usually discussed at all, much less being a soft power resource for burnishing the cause of Tibetan freedom. Soft power, then, would appear to be quite selectively chosen by the Tibetan government-in-exile. Such activities are then quite consistent with the hyperconscious attempts to keep the best of Tibetan culture alive.

One does not usually think of marriage pattern or type as a conduit of self-identity. Nellie Grent present a much-welcomed paper on the continuation of polyandrous marriage among Tibetan exiles living in Dharamsala. It is a common-sense assumption that polyandry was among the first social practices of old Tibet to have disappeared in the diaspora. Being relegated as an exotic cultural trait particularly sensitive to assimilative pressures, polyandry had seemed to disappear unnoticed and apparently unmourned. Klieger's current work on marriage ideals in urban refugee society (this volume) also indicates that monogamy, love matches, and the establishment of nuclear families are by far the most popular marriage and residential practices among the younger generation of Tibetans in exile. But Grent demonstrates that polyandry has not disappeared; in fact, it still continues as a marriage option at least in Dharamsala. The question then arises if it is possible that polyandrous practice continues in exile, because as a host of other practices in the diaspora, it is considered 'traditional' to keep it. Not necessarily of the active, hyper-conscious, and proselytising type of Dharamsala presentation of the Tibetan self, the continuation of polyandry in exile may present a subtle signal to the group and 'Other' that many traditional Tibetan ways indeed continue.

Klieger's paper on Engendering Tibet examines some of the interplay between gender and nationalism as it constructs notion of the Tibetan Self. It is base on survey data from two urban Tibetan refugee communities in Delhi. Over 250 second generation exiled

Tibetans (aged 18–35) filled out questionnaires, which were followed by 30 in-depth interviews chosen from among those respondents who had volunteered to be interviewed. Tibetan sociology majors from area colleges were hired to distribute the survey of 47 questions on family background, work and career, Tibetan activism, gender, marriage patterns, etc, and to collect interviews that focused on these themes.

The particular age cohort was chosen in the hopes that aspects of culture change and variation from the diaspora ideology of Dharamsala could be seen. Furthermore, Klieger was interested in the urban experience of exile, as apart from the rural exile of the majority of Tibetans in South Asia.

From the data collected, it seems evident that while the maintenance of Tibetan identity for the conceivable future is of paramount importance, the content of perceived traditional Tibetan life ways, such as marriage patterns, post-marital residence choice, work and dress, are changing. These aspects of life, according to the great majority, are of substantially less importance than the essential 'Tibetan-ness' as a category of inclusiveness and *nang pa* solidarity. Like in Yeh's paper, Tibetan-ness is quite a concrete thing, but very difficult to conceptualise and describe. The results of the survey also support Dreyfus' concept of the operation of an active Buddhist twist to modern Tibetan national aspirations. In both Majnukatilla and Rohini refugee settlements in Delhi, active Buddhist national expression is articulated not necessarily through religious proselytising, but through the utilisation of an active display of compassion and politeness, and the telling of the story of Tibet to outsiders.

CHAPTER ONE

A GUIDE TO LITTLE LHASA IN INDIA: THE ROLE OF SYMBOLIC GEOGRAPHY OF DHARAMSALA IN CONSTITUTING TIBETAN DIASPORIC IDENTITY[1]

DIBYESH ANAND (UNIVERSITY OF BRISTOL)

Until the last decades of 20th century, preoccupation with religion and history contributed to relative neglect of issues of contemporary identity within Tibetan studies. Prevalence of missionary, diplomatic, journalistic, and traveller's views[2] within western popular culture too had an impact on the academic study of Tibetans as essentially political question of what it means to be a Tibetan was ignored. Even as scholars, following Charles Bell (Bell, 1924:22), recognised a distinction between 'political' and 'ethnographic' Tibet, the signifier Tibetan was usually seen in terms of ontological essentialism.[3] This often led to a papering over of socially constructed and politically contested nature of Tibetan diasporic identity (the primary concern of this paper), or Tibetan-ness as it may be conveniently called.[4]

---

[1] The paper is based on my field trip to Dharamsala that was funded by a travel grant from the British Academy Society for South Asian Studies. At Dharamsala, I gained a lot from conversations with Topden Tsering and Thupten Samphel at Department of Information and International Relations (DIIR). However, the responsibility of all the comments made here lie solely with me. My thanks to P. Christiaan Klieger, Robbie Barnett, and many others at the IATS Conference for giving me valuable comments on the paper.
[2] This borrows from Tsering Shakya's discussion of five major views held within Tibetan studies—the four mentioned here along with social scientific approach. See Shakya (1994:1–14).
[3] This approach is exemplified in Ekvall's pioneering work where he identified five common cultural traits through which Tibetans define themselves. These were religion, folkways, language, race (human lineage), and land (Ekvall, 1960).
[4] For exceptions see, for instance, Nowak and Klieger. Nowak in her study points out that innovative ideological strategies are deployed by Tibetan refugee youth while expressing their identity (Nowak, 1984). Klieger in an analysis of past

However, since the 1990s the situation is changing as more and more scholars of Tibetan diaspora are giving up essentialist notions of culture and identity, and interrogating Tibetan-ness as a contingent product of negotiations among several complementary and contradictory processes. These processes may be looked at in terms of different pairs of contrastive dynamics. Some of these are: imperatives of a culture-in-displacement and the need to present an overarching stable identity; interaction with host societies and an avoidance of cultural assimilation into hegemonic cultural formations there; emphasis upon tradition as the defining character and the need to present exiled Tibetans as 'modern'; desire to present Tibetan culture as unique while at the same time highlighting its universal features; interaction with sympathetic western audience and emphasising difference from occidental cultures; and finally, the desire to project a sense of continuity with the past while distancing from oppressive elements of history. These dynamics impact upon theory as well as praxis of Tibetan-ness at several overlapping and hierarchical levels.

One increasingly comes across works dealing Tibetan diaspora that is in line with wider disciplinary developments in humanities and social sciences. My attempt is to complement these efforts at studying Tibetan identity and culture, while at the same time hoping to provide some new insights on how to theorise them. An underlying assumption here is that instead of rejecting theories in the name of objective empirical studies, a better approach is to be self-conscious about one's own enterprise. My contention is that drawing upon critical social and cultural theories and deploying them contextually is a better approach than shying away from them in the name of theoretical imperialism.[5]

---

as well as present Tibetan history argues that the "patron/client dyad is a warp and weft upon which ideas of Tibetan identity are woven" (Klieger, 1994:22).

[5] Often well-intentioned scholars avoid using western theoretical ideas in the case of non-West in general and Tibet in particular since history is replete with examples of similar moves to the detriment of local people. However, moving towards a purely empirical study is not the right solution since this idea of pure empiricism is the most hegemonic of western paradigms. It is complicit with dominant regimes of patriarchal and racialised power. So, in my opinion, it is better to adopt the critical theories' idea of theorising everything (even though these have originated in the West, they question the assumption of superiority of the West and thus leave room for alliances with 'progressive' ideas from non-Western world) since it reveals all practices as political, and therefore contestable. On the other

In this context, here, I interrogate the role played by symbolic geography of Dharamsala[6] in circulating particularised meanings of Tibetan-ness, especially those connected to the theme of preservation of traditional culture and return to homeland, and the desire to project a sense of continuity in changing external environment.

A focus on Dharamsala as a place will be complemented by a 'play' with the root word *dharamshala*[7] in order to tease out various possible alternative narratives of Tibetan-ness. My contention is that the symbolic geography of the place along with a particular implication of the word *dharamshala* supports the dominant story preferred by the exile elite and their non-Tibetan supporters (the 'salvage mentality' or 'Shangri-La paradigm' as they are often termed). Here the emphasis would be on the projection of Dharamsala as the "Little Lhasa in India",[8] a temporary home preserving a historical culture in its pure form before an inevitable return to the original *homeland*. However, an alternative reading of Dharamsala/*dharamshala* may provide a different story, one that affords a theoretically sophisticated conceptualisation of Tibetan-ness and therefore challenges the

hand, approaches that deny role to theory often operate on unconscious theoretical assumptions that are left un-interrogated. But in giving my preference here, I do accept certain degree of subjectivity and arbitrariness involved in my research agenda.

[6] The place name is spelt either as Dharamsala or Dharamshala. But the Government-in-exile, following Indian government surveys, uses the former spelling. Throughout the essay I shall use this spelling when I have to designate the place (unless otherwise specified) and *dharamshala* when I intend to only use the word. Dharamsala is a common name used for Dharamsala proper (the Kotwali Bazaar area) or the Lower Dharamsala, McLeod Gunj (also spelt Mcleodganj and McLeod Ganj) or the Upper Dharamsala, and Gangchen Kyishong (the complex of Central Tibetan Administration). Lower Dharamsala is a predominantly Indian area. While many Tibetan establishments are located here, there are many more in the vicinity of Dharamsala (for instance the Norbulingka Istitute). Dharamsala is used as a generic name for all. Location wise, it can be characterised as a hill station in the north Indian state of Himachal Pradesh.

[7] The place name Dharamsala comes from the Sanskrit word *Dharmashala* comprising of two parts—*dharma* ('religion') and *shala* (house). However, popular Hindi usage of *dharamshala* (note the slight difference in the spellings with an 'a' added here to highlight different pronunciation) gives it different meanings, something that shall be discussed later in this essay.

[8] There is an issue of temporality of the projection as Little Lhasa too. Though the 'Little Lhasa' was put on the map of global tourism mostly after the mid eighties, the name had come to be associated with McLeod Gunj from the sixties itself (see the passing reference to it in Avendon, 1984:103).

dominant story. Such reading not only looks at identity as always already in process, but also affirms the diaspora experience as something more than a temporary aberration. The two different narratives of diasporic Tibetan identity I posit are not strictly contradictory since they can be re-theorised together productively in a postcolonial vein of combining deconstructive attitude with agential politics of identity.[9] They highlight several things within discourses of Tibetan-ness at once—the politics of place as well as the place of politics; the social construction of space as well as spatialised social relations; and, the rhetoric of essentialism as well as strategic essentialism.

Before going into any further discussion, I should clarify the choices I make here. Why Dharamsala and not any other, even bigger, Tibetan settlement elsewhere? Why symbolic geography and not cultural geography? Focus on Dharamsala does not deny important role played by several other places in Tibetan diaspora. However, I chose Dharamsala since it plays a very crucial role in acting as a symbolic nerve centre from which articulations of Tibetan-ness emerge. Not only do these articulations affect international media's perception. More importantly, they are reabsorbed into the exile community's self-perception. Thus, instead of representation being merely reflective of identity, they are constitutive of the very entity they seek to represent. Another reason for the choice Dharamsala for my study is the fact that its name offers exciting possibilities for my purpose. My preference is for the term symbolic (and not cultural) geography since the primary emphasis here is on theorising Tibetan-ness by drawing upon Dharamsala the place as well as the place name. Symbolic geography is more conducive to conceptualisation of identity and politicisation of space as compared to cultural geography, which deals more with spatialised nature of cultural formations.

---

[9] As Radhakrishnan points out, "the deconstructive attitude, in conjunction with the agential politics of identity, makes it possible for movements to commit themselves simultaneously both to the task of affirming concrete projects of identity on behalf of the dominated and subjugated knowledges and to the utopian or long-term project of interrogating identity-as-such" (Radhakrishnan, 1996:xxiii).

SYMBOLISM OF DHARAMSALA: A CONTESTED TERRAIN

Conventionally, identity was seen as primordial and natural, culture as organically rooted in a particular geographical space, and place as inert space over which history is enacted. With specific reference to the place of 'place' in human life, it was seen as providing "an inert, fixed, isotropic backdrop to the real stuff of politics and history" (Keith & Pile, 1997:4). In this vein, Dharamsala would only be seen as a static stage for theatrics of Tibetan diasporic culture and politics. However, this notion of fixity hides the fact that the geography of Dharamsala has had a changing symbolic role for Tibetan diaspora. A movement from a poor refugee settlement to one of the most popular tourist destination, a change from a small, dilapidated village to a cosmopolitan small town—all these are indicative as well as constitutive of changes within Tibetan exile community. The questioning of the edifice of conventional geographical imagination by a 'cultural turn' within the field makes to possible to study Dharamsala's symbolic geography. For, place and space are now seen in social terms—not only do they shape social relations, more importantly, they themselves are discursively constituted by social forces.

Spatialities, a term that recognises social construction of space and place, can be invoked to study how landscapes themselves are laden with multiplicities of meaning. "Spatialities have always produced landscapes that are loaded with ethical, epistemological and aestheticised meanings" (Keith & Pile, 1993:26). Therefore it is not surprising that the spatiality of Dharamsala has come to acquire multiple layers of meaning, not always in harmony. While for some it is a place of refuge from oppression (the Tibetan refugees), for others it is a centre of seditious activities (the Chinese government). For some it is a vital opportunity for material advancement (local Indian), for others it is a spiritual refuge from the crass materialism of modern western societies (many western tourists). For some it is a centre of pilgrimage (the Tibetans as well as non-Tibetan Buddhists), for others it is a mere site of curiosity (many Indian tourists). All these ascribed meanings, some complementary and some contra-dictory, simply go on problematise any simplistic and (w)holistic reading of what I prefer to call the 'symbolic geography' of Dharam-sala. Rather than treating such tensions and contradictions as regret-

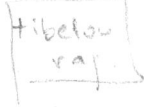

table, the malleability of symbolic role of landscape (i.e. symbolic geography) as a weakness, they should be seen as productive of wider Tibetan diasporic identity-in-process.

The importance of recognising complexly intertwined and mutually constitutive relationship between imaginary and material geography cannot be overemphasised. For instance, while discussing city and post-colonialism, Jacobs points out that "Imaginary and material geographies are not incommensurate, nor is one simply the product, a disempowered surplus, of the other" (Jacobs, 1996:158). Instead of treating symbolic in opposition to actual geography, I suggest a richer conceptualisation of study of politics of place, which recognises that there is no *actual* that can be accessed independently of out subjectivity, that there is no category of *natural* that is not mediated through culture. This would facilitate an understanding of the spatialised politics of identity as well as the identity politics of space. The former might include a consideration of how particular-ised imagining of a unified *homeland* of Tibet shapes discourses of Tibetan-ness. A discussion of the identity politics of space might, on the other hand, consider how different groups including Tibetan government-in-exile, ordinary Tibetan refugees, Tibetans inside Tibet, the Chinese, the western sympathisers, and the local Gaddis ascribe their own meaning to the place of Dharamsala.

Recognition that all geographies have acquired contested and contestable meanings through continuous processes of individual and collective imagination, however, does not preclude a consideration of physical and structural factors at play. For instance, talking of the locational factor first, though the residence of the Dalai Lama and the existence of the Government-in-exile are among the more important factors, the physical location of Dharamsala in the hills of Himachal Pradesh too has facilitated its projection and promotion as Little Lhasa. It is difficult to imagine some other place in the plains of India being promoted as the same. One often comes across travel writings that emphasise the relative inaccessibility of Dharamsala. This resonates with the reputation of Lhasa as the *forbidden city* at the *roof of the world*. In a certain sense, Dharamsala acts as an accessible substitute for those travellers (often white, Western)[10]

---

[10] There seems to be a difference of motive for travelling to Dharamsala between (White) Westerners and others. The influence of a Shangri-La paradigm is less noticeable in the case of Japanese and Korean visitors (for whom Dharamsala is a

whose imaginations have been influenced by earlier writing of Imperialist adventurers, 'the trespassers on the roof of the world' (to evoke the title of Hopkirk's book). Thus, the mountainous terrain of McLeod Gunj and its distance from any big city contributes to the symbolic geography of Dharamsala. Of course, there are logistical and practical problems because of such location and the Government-in-exile recognises it. At the same time, I believe, it would have been slightly more difficult for Tibetans to pursue a strategy of limited acculturation had Dharamsala been near some big city.[11]

Regarding the structural factors at play, the most important is the imperative of refugee status. The locations of Tibetan settlements have been decided entirely by Indian central and state governments. For instance, The Dalai Lama shifted from Mussoorie to Dharamsala on Jawaharlal Nehru's advice in 1960. An abandoned British hill station, McLeod Gunj was offered as a suitable quiet place for the Dalai Lama.[12] The transfer of Central Tibetan Administration (the Government-in-exile) followed him soon. Unlike in Lhasa where the three big monasteries of the Gelukpa order were close to the Dalai Lama's seat, in India these monasteries have been re-established in far off place, due to limitations of land available to them for settlement. It is safe to assume that the Tibetan government-in-exile would have preferred to re-establish them in Dharamsala or some

---

often only a constituent part of Buddhist pilgrimage circuit in India, a minor part) or the Indian tourists (for whom it is a replacement for crowded hill stations like Simla). This is not to say that all the westerners who come here are affected by Shangri-La myth (since many come here for the same reasons as they visit Kullu, Manali, or Goa) or that all non-Western tourists are free from it. The wide distinction I have made is a result of my general observation, which may be highly limited and selective.

[11] Assimilation of minorities into the mainstream Indian culture is usually more common in big cities than in some remote small town. This may be because while Indian cities are increasingly developing a relatively homogenous culture informed by Bollywood as well as cable television, remote towns are yet to have a similar level of impact. The hegemony of popular Indian culture (itself a contested construct) is still patchy in remote places with their own different lifestyles and therefore there is more legroom for distinct cultural formations. Of course, this does not deny that enclaves within big cities too zealously maintain their cultural boundary. But they always have a more difficult task in hand.

[12] The crucial role played by the Nowrojee family (the biggest proprietor here) in encouraging the development of Little Lhasa needs to be kept in mind. The Nowrojee store's pivotal location at the McLeod Gunj bus stop stands as a silent symbol of this role.

nearby location had it the resources and legal rights to do so. The refugee status of Tibetans in South Asia prohibits them from owning immovable property apart from those offered by the host government. So, any consideration of the symbolic geography of Dharamsala would need to keep these physical and structural factors in mind too.

At the same time, here we may concentrate more on the imaginative and creative negotiations of Tibetans with these uncontrollable factors that go on to constitute Dharamsala's spatialities. This would entail recognising Tibetans not as mere victims, but having agency of their own, which they exercise in circumstances laden with asymmetrical power relations. It would not be sufficient to take on board the idea that place is always a social construction, if it is not followed by a politicisation of identity question results from this recognition.

Before dwelling more on Dharamsala and the politics of identity, it should be pointed that the place that is commonly designated as the Little Lhasa is actually McLeod Gunj. As the Himachal Pradesh Tourism Department board reads: "Welcome to Mcleodganj, the little Lhasa in India." This name too is pregnant with many meanings that may be explored further (something not feasible within the space of this essay)—British imperialism, development of hill stations as places of refuge for Imperial class, indigenisation of name, etc. It can be read as indicating the important role played by British Imperial practices in framing the various aspects of Tibetan question. The distinction between Lower and Upper Dharamsala also reflects a gap between local population and the refugees. While Tibetans here have generally managed to create their own niche in the wider society, the assertion of difference also leaves the potential open for conflict if the locals perceive the refugees as source of problems.[13] It should be noted that the Government-in-exile promotes the name Dharamsala, and not McLeod Gunj, as the Little Lhasa. This may be because Tibetan institutions and establishments are spread throughout the vicinity of Dharamsala. But how far the name Dharamsala itself may have inspired it is an open question for the literal meaning of

---

[13] Though it is rare for such tensions between Tibetans and local Indians to burst out in full-fledged rioting, the resentment of the locals against Tibetans perceived as wealthier is evident. I say this from my personal experience of talking to many 'Indian' taxi drivers and shopkeepers. Since for them I was an insider (with Indian nationality), they often expressed their anxiety about the Tibetan 'others'.

Dharmashala—"the house of God/dharma"—resonates well with the fact of location of the Dalai Lama's residence and several religious institutions here. Indirectly, the choice of name with its association with spiritualism and faith makes it more appealing to the western tourists too.

DHARAMSALA AS A TEMPORARY HOME: THE DOMINANT STORY

What are the specific ways in which politics of place as embodied in Dharamsala inform discourses of Tibetan identity? By drawing upon the usage of the word *dharamshala*, we can theorise Tibetan identity discourse in broadly two ways. *Dharamshala* in popular Hindi usage refers to a "temporary home." The first way, which has a wide currency among Tibetan government and nationalists as well as non-Tibetan supporters of the Tibetan cause, looks at the experience of diaspora as a temporary and regrettable phenomenon. And indeed, the place Dharamsala is seen as a temporary home with the final destination being the original homeland of Tibet. The exile is seen as a break in the evolution of an ancient civilisation in Tibet, a time when it is vital to preserve a pure form of this civilisation since it is itself under erasure in the original home. In journalistic and travel writings, one often comes across eulogy to a lost Shangri-La in Tibet (particularly Lhasa) and observations on how forces of modernity infused by the Chinese have spelt doom for the Tibetan culture. Such observations stand in contrast to those about the Tibetan communities living in South Asia, particularly in the area surrounding Dharamsala. In this case, though the cosmopolitan and eclectic cultural scene of McLeod Gunj is recognised, often the emphasis is on the success story of Tibetans in preserving their culture. "Working hard to rebuild their lives and preserve their distinctive and timeless culture and lifestyle, these people, from difficult beginnings, have become arguably the most successful refugee community in the world whilst continuing the non violent struggle for Tibet's freedom in exile" (Barker, 1999). Tibetan identity maintenance is seen as a functional expression of this culture.

In this scenario it is not surprising that Dharamsala is projected as the Little Lhasa in India and several dynamics go on to support such projection. Not only is this the residence of the Dalai Lama and (therefore) a place of pilgrimage for many Tibetans and non-Tibetan

Buddhists, but also the focus for the individual, communal, and institutional practices of Tibetan culture. Earlier pilgrims used to visit Lhasa, which for them was a source of refuge from everyday of life with hope of good in next life. Now refugee status is often seen as a sort of pilgrimage where a *darshan* of the Dalai Lama in Dharamsala is a compensation for hardship. Therefore, it comes as no surprise that the new refugees are first stationed in Dharamsala, helped to meet the Dalai Lama and only then sent to some resettlement camp.

This projection also provides legitimacy to the claims that the Central Tibetan Administration is a government-in-exile, a continuation of the pre-1959 Lhasa government, and therefore the rightful representative of all Tibetan people. Politically too, the projection provides added legitimacy to the political struggle for self-determination in Tibet. Dharamsala is thus perceived as the temporary capital of entire Tibetan world and the *Tibet movement* (the transnational network of support groups that work towards preserving the culture and assuring the survival and human rights of the Tibetan people). Conscious efforts have been made to recapture, what has been called the spirit of the *Old Tibet*, by recreating, for instance the main temple of Tsuglakhang. Symbolic representation of Dharamsala as Little Lhasa, as Thupten Samphel of the DIIR pointed out, is to convey that what has been destroyed is being recreated (Personal Interview, January 2000). This idea of recreation of a civilisation and preservation of culture is the single most strand of Tibetan *identity problematique* and is conspicuously evident in Dharamsala's geography.

The institutionalised expression of the theme of preservation of culture is best found at the Norbulingka Institute, which is dedicated explicitly to the preservation of Tibetan culture in both its literary and artistic form (See Figure 1.1). Activities and publications of the Institute give a distinct impression of how a unique ancient culture needs to be preserved from a possible extinction. For instance, in the Norbulingka's Centre for Arts, the skills preserved and passed on through training and apprenticeship include: statue making, *thangka* painting, applique and tailoring, woodcarving, carpentry and metal craft. It is emphasised that the practice of making traditional works of art such as religious statues and *thangkas* only in response to the

FIGURE 1.1: Preserving Tibetan Culture: The Norbulingka Institute. D. Anand.

customer's order is a continuation of earlier practices where patrons would personally commission artists to do such work. Norbulingka is keen "to preserve the relationship between patron and artist free from the taint of commercialisation" (Norbulingka Institute, 2000).

Even the Dalai Lama considers the aspect of preservation to be the single most important achievement of the exile community. He points out that the pure form of culture is now found outside and not inside Tibet (Powell, 1992:384). This idea that Tibetan culture in diaspora is more authentic than one prevalent in Chinese controlled Tibet is supported by few factors. One of them is the passing down of cultural authority though practice of reincarnation. Significant part of Tibetan culture and religion has been embodied within reincarnate lamas, the most important being the Dalai Lama himself. And many of them left Tibet and became a part of the diaspora. The struggle between the Dalai Lama and Beijing over reincarnation of the Panchen Lama reinforces the Dharamsala establishment's desire to prevent this process from getting into wrong hands. While outside (read Chinese) influence is resisted, there have been instances where the practice has been deployed to incorporate individual ethnically non-Tibetans as a *nang pa* (the Buddhist 'insider'). One may recall here the recognition of Steven Seagal as a reincarnation of the 17th century hidden treasure revealer Chungdrag Dorje of Palyul Monastery by Penor Rinpoche.

The idea of true cultural authority in exile rather than within Tibet is also supported by the presence of some great mastercrafts*men*[14] who had been trained in their art on Old Tibet (a reference to pre-1959 Tibet) and then moved to exile. These artists are regarded as 'precious' since they are seen as having direct experience of authentic Old Tibet. Moreover, the exile elite has tended to favour certain strands of Tibetan culture as more authentic and therefore worthy of patronage. Here, the ultimate cultural authority has come to be associated with the Dalai Lama himself (for a discussion of how Dharamsala assumes a canonical role in religious art, see Harris, 1999).

An interrelated thematic aspect of symbolic geography of Dharamsala is the role of memory in housing distinct Tibetan identity. The names of many establishments in Dharamsala resonate specifically Tibetan idioms. Here I am not talking only of Tibetan governmental and non-governmental institutions, but also the commercial establishments. If, for instance, one walks up the Jogibara Road from the Amnya Machen Institute to the right and Gaden Choeling Nunnery to the left, one would find names such as Amdo Cha-Chung Restaurant, Lhasa Tailors, Café Shambhala, Tsongkha Restaurant, Drepung Loseling Guest House, Tibet Lhoka Café, etc. Similarly, on the Bhagsu Road starting from the bus stop, one comes across Potala Tours & Travels, Dhompatsang Boutique and Handicraft, Rangzen Café, Tara Café, and Tashi Kangsar Travel Lodge to name a few. Then there are names that specifically deploy ideas of loss and longing such as the Tibet Memory Restaurant, Lhasa Tailors, Lhasa Hotel, and Hotel Tibet (the hotel belongs to the Government-in-exile). At one level it may be possible that an important factor influencing the naming practice could be the nostalgia for Tibet and the desire to create familiarity in strange places. If you

---

[14] The emphasis, crafts*men*, is deliberate in order to highlight the gendered character of traditional cultural practices and their reinforcement by preservation ethos. For instance, in the Norbulingka I was told that statue making as well as thangka painting is not meant for women. Not surprisingly, most women were concentrated in sections such as tailoring.

don't find Tibetan names in the Little Lhasa, where else can you expect to find them?

CULTURE AND POLITICS OF PLACE: SOME CONCEPTUAL PROBLEMS WITH THE DOMINANT STORY

However, this dominant story of 'Little Lhasa' as a temporary station where Tibetan culture is being preserved is highly problematic, both practically and theoretically. While in practical terms this simple story is complicated by the experiences of living as refugees, the unproblematic acceptance of a stylised understanding of the basic concepts of identity and culture renders it open to serious theoretical challenges.

Let us first take the theme of the preservation of Tibetan culture. Without belittling the attempts at maintaining distinctive traditions of creative and artistic expression, at a theoretical level, this over-emphasis on preservation should be seen as problematic. This takes a sanitised view of what culture means. Culture is seen as a thing out there that can be identified, mapped, practised, and preserved. Such conceptualisation of culture essentialises and naturalises what is so-cially and politically constructed and contested. It ignores the fact that culture is a "dynamic mix of symbols, beliefs, languages and prac-tices which people create, not a fixed thing or entity governing hu-mans" (Anderson & Gale, 1992:3). Cultural identities, far from being eternally fixed in some essentialised past, are actually subject to the continuous play of history, culture and power. Tibetan culture is as much a process as it is a product of particular historical processes. An explicit recognition of this would certainly challenge the dominant tendency to make exilic 'Tibet' fit the Shangri-La paradigm (Tibet as a utopia and Tibetans as essentially good, spiritual, and otherworldly), something that could lead to the Tibetan culture remaining on, what Harris writes as, "a life-support system in perpetuity" without much chance of self-regeneration (Harris, 1999:197).

The significance of commodification and tourism on particular expressions of *authentic* Tibetan culture is an area that calls for further exploration. Here Wood's discussion on touristic ethnicity is highly relevant. He argues that tourism affects not only the ways in *which* ethnic identities are asserted, but also *which ethnic markers* are chosen to symbolise group membership and culture (Wood,

1998:222). The role of tourism can be seen in the issue of intentionality behind the projection of Dharamsala as the Little Lhasa. We must keep in mind that it is not only the Government-in-exile that does so, but the Himachal Tourism Department too promotes it as so. While for the Tibetans it may reflect a desire to assert continuity from the pre-1959 Lhasa government, for the Himachal government it is yet another tourist destination.

Even the names of most establishments in McLeod Gunj, particularly the commercial ones, highlight the importance of tourism and the desire to appeal to outsiders' idea of Tibet as a Shangri-La. For instance, on the Jogibara Road this is exemplified in names such as Yak Restaurant, Snow Land Restaurants, Hotel Shangri-La, Snow Lion complex (hotel, restaurant, and medical store), Travel Tibet Tailoring Shop, etc. The fact that many of such establishments are owned by local Indians goes on to show that primary motive for such naming practice is to appeal to the tourists. In fact, this dynamic is also underlined by the presence of other shops with names that are unabashedly orientalist such as Dreaming Oriental Carpet Cottage Handicrafts, Royal Asia Art, Heaven Art, Rising Horizon Café, etc. It is hard to imagine the old city of Lhasa having place names such as Shangri-La, Snow Lion, or Yeti before its incorporation into international tourism network. To make a somewhat artificial distinction, while the names such as Amnye Machen Institute, Gangchen Kyishong, Lhagyal Ri, etc. (used in non-commercial establishments) reflect Tibetan desire to recreate a familiar environment, other more orientalist names such as Shangri-La and Snow Lion (mostly in commercial establishments) pander to the exoticised representations of Tibet.

While challenging the dominance of salvage mentality in the di-aspora, we must recognise that the preservation ethos is not hegemonic. Counter hegemonic spaces are available in Dharamsala for innovative and more contemporary practices of culture. At the same time it should be recognised that even these practitioners do not see their role in opposition to traditional culture but as complemen-tary to it. For instance, though the catalogues and brochures of Nor-bulingka 'forget' to mention this, they have a section where young artists work on contemporary themes (Figure 1.2). Moreover, even the traditional cultural practices are often laden with contemporary

Figure 1.2: A Doll with 'Free Tibet' Badge, Norbulingka Institute. D. Anand.

Figure 1.3: Political Backdrop to Art, Norbulingka Institute. D. Anand.

political meanings. The Namgyalma Stupa in the centre of McLeod Gunj, erected during the sixties as a memorial to the Tibetans who lost their lives fighting against the Chinese, is the best example of this. Then there are the dolls made in traditional style at Norbulingka that carry *Free Tibet* badges. The political context of occupation and coercion is always present even in the space provided for traditional art and crafts (Figure 1.3). Therefore, we must consider not only the way politics affect the work of art, but in what sense an artwork may itself constitute a political act or statement, rather than being conceived merely as the result of a political intention (Millon & Nochlin, 1978).

Rather than seeing culture as informing politics and vice versa, the entire category of culture has to be understood as political. For instance, the very desire of preserving a culture under threat is an act of resistance to dominant forces of modernity as well as to the Chinese statecraft. It is also difficult to miss the centrality of the Tibetan political cause in McLeod Gunj's landscape as 'Free Tibet', 'Boycott Chinese Goods', and similar stickers and posters are glaringly visible. The symbolic geography of Dharamsala in this sense is a geography of resistance as much as it is a geography of regeneration. Theories lag behind practices of Tibetan identity when it comes to recognising that cultural is political. Integral part of Dharamsala's geography is the festivals and various other events occurring throughout the year. Rather than seeing the festivals as merely reflecting religious beliefs or political ritual, they may be studied to reveal the techniques and dynamics through which the narratives, symbolic spaces and the collective fantasies of communal identities are reproduced and regulated among the Tibetans and their supporters. One recalls here Richardson's observations on great ceremonies of Lhasa- although full of colour and spectacle, they were not mere pageantry but were essential rites for the wellbeing of church and State (Richardson, 1993). Some such festivals that are replete with multiple meanings are Losar, Tibetan Uprising Day (March 10), Dalai Lama's birthday on July 6, Democracy Day of Tibet (September 2), the commemoration of the awarding of Nobel Peace Prize to Dalai Lama (December 10). We may investigate in Dharamsala's culturoscape (its symbolic geography), the relevance of Connerton's observations that "the ritual performances and commemorative ceremonies are important in building up collective memory, which in turn is crucial for the development of a sense of home" (Kong & Yeoh, 1997:217).

Finally, we come to the important question of purity versus hybridity in cultural life. While no one can deny that, given the situation inside Tibet, promoting unmitigated hybridity is not a viable strategy for Tibetans, cross cultural influences on Tibetan people living in diaspora may be recognised and affirmed. Mcllo Restaurant selling Indian, South India, Chinese, and Continental food; Tibtronics Cybercafe; Tea O'clock Cafeteria next to Malabar Restaurant, Green Cybercafe and Hotel near Nick's Italian Kitchen—all these are reflective of a 'cosmopolitan' culture evolving particularly in McLeod Gunj. They also illustrate the heavy influence of Western and Indian popular culture on the landscape of McLeod Gunj.

In their struggle for living, Tibetan refugees in Dharamsala and elsewhere in South Asia negotiate with popular culture of India and therefore it should come as no surprise that Bollywood has a very significant influence on the lifestyle of many Tibetans. Everywhere I went, I found a striking similarity between Tibetan songs and songs from popular Hindi films as well as Western pop music. The Dharamsala establishment often expresses anxiety over this dilution of Tibetan culture especially amongst the new generation of Tibetans. However, such observations while complicating the notion of preservation of a 'pure' culture, do not militate against a more sophisticated conception of Tibetan culture. This new generation may not practice authentic versions of culture, but their creative negotiations with dominant cultures around them do not hamper their politicisation. On the contrary, the ability to simultaneously negotiate and resist varied cultural practices makes the common Tibetans well placed to carry forward their political movement in a rapidly changing world. How do we then address this gap between theory and praxis of Tibetan identity? This can be done via a different strategy of reading the Tibetan *identity problematique*.

CHALLENGING THE DOMINANT PARADIGM: READING CULTURAL
IDENTITY IN TERMS OF ROOTS AND ROUTES

The space for a different reading is afforded by the word *dharamshala* itself. As pointed out earlier, the word indicates a temporary home and this temporariness has been a central motif in Tibetan diasporic identity discourses. Tibet, the original homeland, is foregrounded as the final destination in these discourses and it also permeates the material as well as the performative cultural expressions of the Tibetans in diaspora. While focusing on the stations, such a reading ignores the crucial element of the travel itself. *Dharamshala* is not only a temporary home, but a temporary stop on the way to somewhere else. One does not travel from home to *dharamshala* to return back to the home. Rather, it is a temporary shelter to facilitate travel from one place to some other place. If instead of focusing solely on the theme of *return*, we care to look at the process and experience of journey itself, we may be better placed to appreciate the conundrum of Tibetan identity-process.

As Clifford rightly points in different context, "practices of displacement might emerge as *constitutive* of cultural meanings rather than as their simple transfer or extension" (Clifford, 1997:3). In terms of its cultural analogy, instead of concentrating solely on the essence, the *roots* of Tibetan identity, we should look at the processes that constitute a pan-Tibetan exilic identity, the *routes* travelled. Adoption of such view allows us to appreciate ambiguities involved in the project of preservation of culture as well as the changes that come about in the life of a community of people. While understanding the need to espouse one's cause in terms of an essential identity, the contingency of such claims is not papered over—and herein lies the strength of the alternative theorisation.

Let me now clarify how this different reading strategy might look and how it can seek to contextualise a politics of place and identity. Here I wish to make six interrelated points. Firstly, instead of framing an artificial opposition between the roots of culture and the routes of culture, we may look at them as complementary. For, this false dichotomy is sustained only by the conventional view of culture as rooted in a particular place. On the other hand, if we look at the roots as contingent foundations that are always already contested, we can begin to appreciate the complementarity.

Secondly, recognition of the contingent nature of identity does not preclude identity claims marshalled by Tibetans for their cause. It simply draws attention to strategic nature of such claims. This position is possible if one adopts a discursive approach to identity question. In contrast to *naturalism* of old definitions, discursive approach sees identification not as an artefact or an outcome but as a construction, a process never completed—something *always in process*. With determinate conditions of existence, including the material and symbolic resources required to sustain it, identification is in the end conditional, inevitably lodged in contingency. "Identification is, then, a process of articulation, a suturing, an over-determination not a subsumption" (Hall, 1996:3). We need to recognise that its popular usage notwithstanding, the concept does not signal a stable core of self, unfolding from beginning to end through all vicissitudes of history without any substantial change. On the contrary, we should accept that identities are increasingly fragmented and fractured; they are never singular but multiply constructed across different, often intersecting and antagonistic, discourses, practices and positions. Butler's idea of *performativity* is helpful here. As she succinctly puts it, "Identity is performatively constituted by the very 'expressions' that are said to be its results" (Butler, 1990:25). Applying this idea to the Tibetan case, we may see Tibetan identity as constituted by particular processes and practices, and not as some universal, timeless fixed thing. This would entail questioning the overemphasis on the preservation rhetoric within Tibetan diaspora.

Rather than seeing the identity question as one of simple historical investigation, it should be dealt in terms of deployment of the resources of history, language and culture in the process of becoming rather than being. The idea of symbolic geography encapsulates such discursive approach since instead of considering the ideas of locality and community as naturally given, it focuses on social and political processes of place making in Dharamsala. Discursive approach does not deny any act of communal political activism. It only reveals it as contingent, as strategic rather than something unambiguously natural. Venturino argues that the Tibetan claims to "an essential identity, while demonstrably imaginary, constructed, and teleologi-cal, are no less *essential* in that they serve as foundational claims that operate politically, socially, and, for many, spiritually" (Venturino, 1997:108). While one can appreciate such common practice of espousing one's claim in un-interrogated and essentialist terms, as academicians we should distinguish between these political claims and their theoretical underpinnings.

Thirdly, connected to the issue of discursive approach to the identity question is an explicit recognition of constitutive role played by (especially Western) representations. The 'Mythos Tibet' has had a real impact on the symbolic geography of Dharamsala. The desire to secure patronage from sympathetic outsiders,[15] elicit support for the Tibetan political cause, and make living through commercial processes—all these forces have contributed to self-reflexive adoption of western representations of Tibetans as a part of Tibetan-ness. Image has translated into identity. The representations of Tibetans as inherently religious and spiritual have certainly contributed to mushrooming of Yoga classes, Retreat centres, and Meditation Schools in Dharamsala. At the same time, we must keep in mind the fact that the Tibetan exiles are not unique in that representations have major effect on identity practices. As Huber argues, recent reflexive notions of Tibetan culture and identity witnessed in exile should be understood as recent products of a complex transnational politics of identity within which populations such as the Tibetan exiles are increasingly representing themselves and being represented by others (Huber, 1997). One such identity discourse, which Huber highlights is connected to environmentalism. Presence within Dharamsala of Green Hotel and Green Cyber Café, Vegetarian Health Food, etc. may be taken up as a conscious desire to appropriate this particular discourse as a part of identity formation. The symbolic geography of Little Lhasa questions the premise that Tibetans are innocent victims—'prisoners of Shangri-La'. Instead, even while recognising unequal power relations, one must recognise that the Tibetan exiles possess agency and subjectivity.[16]

Fourthly, an integral part of Dharamsala as well as Tibetan diasporic identity is the crucial role played by the personality as well as figure of the Dalai Lama. His smiling face adorns almost every establishment here, including the shops owned by the non-Tibetans.[17] More than anything else, it is his residence here that contributes to transformation of Dharamsala into Little Lhasa. He has a central

---

[15] For a discussion of different ways in which Westerners are incorporated as patrons, see Klieger (1994).

[16] This is something that has been done effectively by contributors to *Tibetan Culture in the Diaspora* (Korom, 1997).

[17] Apart from Indian Banks, the only exception I found was a shop selling *Desi Sharaab* (local alcohol) on the Jogibara Road.

position as a symbol of Tibet among Tibetan refugees as well as in the international media. Bishop's observation about Potala palace in Lhasa, its remarkable polyvalence as a *complexio oppositorium*,[18] can also be applied to the place of the Dalai Lama in Tibetan diasporic discourses. As Nowak pointed out, he is "neither wholly transcendent (and thereby out of this world) nor wholly immanent (enmeshed in temporalities like the rest of us), but an ambiguous symbol imbued with the qualities of both" (Nowak, 1984:30). The XIVth Dalai Lama has come to acquire an unprecedented position. He combines the role of the supreme leader of the entire Tibetan Buddhist community with being the chief spokesperson of Buddhist Modernism. He is as much a world spiritual leader as the undisputed leader of Tibetan political cause. This mix of uniqueness of culture with universalism and of a national cause with transnationalism is also underlined within Dharamsala's symbolic geography (Lopez, 1998:181–207).

Fifthly, though for the Tibetans the memory, the ideal and the image of *the land* from which they have been exiled have been a portent force in the struggle for national recognition, the notion of *return to the homeland* is problematic. This problematisation should not be seen in terms of pessimistic scenario where original Tibet has been destroyed and can never be retrieved. Instead, it guards against any naïve imagination of a particularised space-time projection of Tibet as a timeless construct. We can examine this theme of return to homeland as something that is common to many exiled communities. To place the issue of Tibet in a comparative perspective we may compare the imagination of Tibet as a homeland with the experiences of another community of refugees—the Palestinians. In both the cases one sees how the longing for home has changed over time from return to specific villages and particular dwellings to an emphasis on a collective national return to *the homeland* conceived more abstractly. Talking specifically about the Palestinians, Bisharat points out that in exile, there thus occurs a displacement of a community, once understood as being rooted in particular localities, to the level of the nation. Homeland is conceived as a moral as well as geographical location (Gupta and Ferguson, 1997:19).

---

[18] He borrows this term for 'a complex mix of opposites' from Jung (Bishop, 1999).

Lastly, the adoption of a different reading strategy also fore-
grounds the idea of Tibet as, what I prefer to call, a *Re-imag(in)ing
construct*. Following Anderson's theory of nations as imagined
communities (Anderson, 1983), Tibet can be seen as an imagined
construct. However, the use of the form *imagining* rather than
imagined indicates that the process of imagination is a continuous
one. And then, since the Dharamsala establishment plays a crucial
role in shaping this imagining process according to some particular
images and representations, I put 'in' under parenthesis. The process
is as much one of imaging as it is of imagining. The prefix 're' is to
counter any sense of simplistic linearity associated with the process
of imagining Tibet as a nation.

However, this theorisation of Tibet as an imagining discursive
construction does not deny the real desires and feelings of the people
towards this construct. Instead, it promotes a historicisation and
politicisation of such desires and feelings. It calls for some special
attention to be given to the ways spaces and places are made,
imagined, contested, and enforced. One needs to accept that given
the limited vocabulary available to Tibetans to espouse their cause in
international arena, use of the somewhat old-fashioned concept of
nationalism is perfectly understandable. As Kibreab points out, in a
world where rights such as equal treatment, access to sources of
livelihoods, rights of freedom of movement and residence are
apportioned on the basis of territorially anchored identities, the
identity people gain from their association with a particular place is
an indispensable instrument to a socially and economically fulfilling
life (Kibreab, 2000:384–428). Though an imagined construct, Tibet
has *real* impact on lives on many people, and this itself provides
legitimacy to those struggling for self-determination for the Tibetans.
My theorisation based on adoption of a discursive approach does not
make this struggle problematic. At the theoretical level it calls for a
reconceptualisation of basic themes involved in articulation of
Tibetan identification process as encapsulated within Dharamsala's
symbolic geography. And at the level of political praxis, it simply
warns against any naïve ideas about nationalism, return to homeland,
etc.

CONCLUSION: AFFIRMING TIBETAN-NESS THROUGH ITS PROBLEMATISATION

As a way to conclusion, I would like to clarify that the reading based on a different understanding of the word *Dharamshala* should not be seen as an alternative to the more common story outlined earlier in the paper. For the political practices embedded within Dharamsala's symbolic geography defy any clear categorisation in either of the two conceptual frameworks. My preferred approach appreciates the practical need for espousing the Tibetan identity in essentialist terms. At the same time it highlights the need to recognise the contingent and strategic character of these claims at a theoretical level. Sophisticated theorisation of Dharamsala in terms of symbolic geography facilitates such a two-pronged approach, while at the same time recognising the arbitrariness involved in any distinction between theory and practice.

BIBLIOGRAPHY

Anderson, Benedict. 1983. *Imagined communities: reflections of the origin and spread of nationalism.* London: Verso.

Anderson, Kay and Fay Gale (eds.). 1992. *Inventing Places: studies in Cultural Geography.* Longman Cheshire & Wiley Halsted Press: Melbroune.

Avendon, John F. 1984 (1979). *In Exile from the Land of Snows.* London: Michael Joseph.

Barker, Diane. "Free Spirits: Tibet in Exile." Photo exhibition, http://www.friendsoftibet.org/diane.html.

Barnes, Trevor J. and James S. Duncan (eds). 1992. *Writing Worlds: discourse, text & metaphor in the representation of landscape.* London & New York: Routledge,

Baumann, Martin. 1997. "Shangri-La in Exile: Portraying Tibetan Diaspora Studies and Reconsidering Diaspora(s)," *Diaspora,* 6 (3): 377–404.

Bell, Charles. 1924. *Tibet, Past and Present.* Oxford: Clarendon,

Benko, Georges and Ulf Strohmayer (eds.). 1997. *Space and Social Theory: Interpreting Modernity and Postmodernity.* Oxford & Malden, MA: Blackwell.

Bishop, Peter. 1999. "Reading the Potala," in Toni Huber (ed.), *Sacred Spaces and Powerful Places in Tibetan Culture: a Collection of Essays.* Dharamsala: Library of Tibetan Works and Archives, 367–85.

Blunt, Alison and Gillian Rose (eds.). 1994. *Writing Women and Space: colonial and Postcolonial Geographies.* London & New York: The Guilford Press,

Butler, Judith. 1990. *Gender trouble: feminism and the subversion of identity.* New York: Routledge.

Carter, Erica, James Donald and Judith Squires (eds.). 1993. *Space and Place: theories of Identity and Location.* London: Lawrence & Wishart.

Chambers, I. 1994. *Migrancy, Culture, Identity.* London: Routledge.

Clifford, James and George E. Marcus (eds.). 1986. *Writing Culture: The Poetics and Politics of Ethnography.* London & Berkeley: University of California Press.

Clifford, James. 1997. *Routes: Travel and Translation in the Late Twentieth Century.* London & Cambridge MA: Harvard University Press.

Cloke, Paul, Philip Crang, and Mark Goodwin (eds.). 1999. *Introducing Human Geographies.* London & New York: Arnold.

Cohen, Robin. 1997. *Global Diasporas: An Introduction.* London: UCL Press.

Department of Information and International Relations. 1999. *Dharamsala: a guide to little Lhasa in India.* Dharamsala: DIIR.

Dreyfus, Georges. 1994. "Proto-Nationalism in Tibet," in Per Kvaerne (ed.),

Tibetan Studies: Proceedings of the 6ᵗʰ Seminar of the International Association for Tibetan Studies, Fagernes, 1992. Volume I. Oslo: Institute for Comparative Research in Human Culture, 205–18.

Ekvall, Robert B. 1960. "The Tibetan Self-Image," *Pacific Affairs*, XXXIII(4):375–81.

Gregory, Derek. 1994. *Geographical Imaginations.* Oxford & Cambridge, MA: Blackwell.

Gupta, Akhil and James Ferguson (eds.). 1997. *Culture, Place, Power: Explorations in Critical Anthropology.* London & Durham: Duke University Press.

Gyatso, Tenzin. 1998. *Freedom in Exile: the Autobiography of the Dalai Lama of Tibet.* London: Abacus. Second edition.

Hall, Stuart. 1996. "Introduction: Who Needs 'Identity'?," in Stuart Hall and Paul Du Gay (eds.), *Questions of Cultural Identity.* London & Thousand Oaks: Sage.

Hobsbawm, Eric and Terence Ranger (eds.). 1992 (1983). *The Invention of Tradition.* Cambridge: Cambridge University Press. Revised edition.

http://www.tibet.com.

Huber, Toni. 1997. "Shangri-La in Exile: Tibetan Identity Representations and Transnational Culture." Paper received from the author. English version of Huber, Toni, "Shangri-La im Exile: Darstellungen tibetischer Identität und transnationale Kultur," in T. Dodin & H. Räther (eds.), *Mythos Tibet: Wahrnehmungen, Projektionen, Phantasien.* Kunst- und Ausstellungshalle der Bundersrepublik Deutschland. Köln: DuMont, 300–12.

—— (ed.). 1999. *Sacred Spaces and Powerful Places in Tibetan Culture.* Dharamsala: Library of Tibetan Works and Archives.

Jackson, Peter. 1989. *Maps of Meaning: An Introduction to Cultural Geography.* London & Boston: Unwin Hyman.

Jacobs, Jane M. 1996. *Edge of Empire: Postcolonialism and the City.* London & New York: Routledge.

Keith, Michael and Steve Pile (eds.). 1997. *Geographies of Resistance.* London & New York: Routledge.

—— 1993. *Place and the Politics of Identity.* London & New York: Routledge.

Kibreab, Gaim. 1999. "Revisiting the Debate on People, Place, Identity and Displacement," *Journal of Refugee Studies*, 12(4):384–428.

Klieger, P. Christiaan. 1992. *Tibetan Nationalism: the Role of Patronage in the Accomplishment of a National Identity.* Meerut: Archana Publishers.

Kolas, Ashild. 1996. "Tibetan Nationalism: the Politics of Religion," *Journal of Peace Research*, 33(1):51–66.

Kong, Lily and Brenda S.A. Yeoh. 1997. "The construction of national identity through the production of ritual and spectacle: an analysis of National Day parades in Singapore," *Political Geography*, 16(3):213–39.

Korom, Frank J. (ed.). 1997. *Constructing Tibetan Culture: Contemporary Perspectives*. Quebec: World Heritage Press.

—— (ed.). 1997. *Tibetan Culture in the Diaspora: Papers presented at a panel of the 7th Seminar of the International Association for Tibetan Studies, Graz 1995*. Wien: Verlag Der Osterreichischen Akademie Der Wissenschaften.

Lavie, Smadar and Ted Swedenburg (eds.). 1996. *Displacement, Diaspora, and Geographies of Identity*. London & Durham: Duke University Press.

Lopez, Donald S. Jr., 1998. *Prisoners of Shangri-La: Tibetan Buddhism and the West*. London: University of Chicago Press.

Massey, Doreen. 1994. *Space, Place and Gender*. Cambridge: Polity.

McLagan, Meg. 1996. "Computing for Tibet: Virtual Politics in the Post-Cold War Era," in George E. Marcus (ed.), *Connected: Engagements with Media*. London: University of Chicago, 159–94.

Millon, Henry A. and Linda Nochlin (eds). 1978. *Art and Architecture in the Service of Politics*. London & Cambridge, MA: MIT Press.

Norbu, Dawa. 1992. *Culture and the politics of Third World Nationalism*. London: Routledge.

Norbulingka Institute, http://www.tibet.org/norling.

Nowak, Margaret. 1984. *Tibetan Refugees: Youth and the New Generation of Meaning*. New Brunswick, NJ: Rutgers UP.

Powell, Andrew. 1992. *Heirs to Tibet: Travels among the Exiles in India*. New Delhi: Bluejay Books.

Radhakrishnan, Rajagopalan. 1996. *Diasporic Mediations: Between Home and Location*. Minneapolis and London: University of Minnesota Press.

Richardson, Hugh. 1993. *Ceremonies of the Lhasa Year*. Michael Aris (ed.). London: Serindia.

Rose, Nanci Hoetzlein and Bill Warren. 1995. *Living Tibet: the Dalai Lama in Dharamsala*. New Delhi: Paljor Publications.

Shakya, Tsering W. 1996. "Introduction: The Development of Modern Tibetan Studies," in Robert Barnett and Shirin Akiner (eds.), *Resistance and Reform in Tibet*. Delhi: Motilal Banarsidass, 1–14.

Venturino, Steven. 1997. "Reading Negotiations in the Tibetan Diaspora," in Frank J. Korom (ed.), *Constructing Tibetan Culture: Contemporary Perspectives*. Quebec: World Heritage Press, 98–121.

Wood, Robert E. 1998. "Touristic Ethnicity: a brief itinerary," *Ethnic and Racial Studies*, 21(2):218–41.

World Tibet Network News, "Little Lhasa: Dharamshala: A Refuge from Shangrila." http://www.tibet.ca/wtnarchive/1999/4/3–2_4.htm, Saturday, April 3, 1999.

CHAPTER TWO

TIBETAN RELIGIOUS NATIONALISM: WESTERN FANTASY OR EMPOWERING VISION?

GEORGES DREYFUS (WILLIAMS COLLEGE)

In recent years, an impressive scholarly literature concerning nationalism in non-Western societies has emerged.[19] The dominant view in this literature, represented by Gellner, Anderson, and Hobsbawm, is that nationlisms in non-Western societies are exogenous phenomena, Western influences imported into these societies through the process of modernisation (Gellner, 1983). The nationalisms thus depicted are characterised as 'inventions of tradition' (Hobsbawm and T. Ranger, 1983) or 'imagined communities' (Anderson, 1983), artificial creations mythically retrojected into the past of human communities in order to legitimise their present political organisation. In this view, nationalism is always a secular movement arising out of the demotion of sacred language and the relativisation of faith. Nationalism represents, in Anderson's words, "a secular transformation of fatality into continuity, contingency into meaning" (Anderson, 1983:11). This view of nationalism is also often combined with a critique of orientalism, which view non-Western nationalisms as introjections of orientalist visions, further victimisations of these societies through the imposition of Western values that are mistaken to represent what is most valuable in these new nations.

Although there is much that is true and valuable in this dominant model, I believe that it overstates the case and misses important aspects of the nature of non-Western nationalisms. This view often seems to be held apriori without giving much attention to the historical developments of local nationalisms. In this essay, I will raise objections against three key elements in this model. The first is that

---

[19] A recent article listed no less than one hundred and sixty-two works on this subject published in the last ten years: R.J. Foster. 1991. "Making National Cultures in the Global Ecumene," *Annual Review of Anthropology*, 20:235–60.

nationalism in non-Western countries is a foreign import, an internalisation of ideas and practices that are alien to these countries and
hence do not suit them. The second is that nationalism cannot be
religious and must be secular. The third is the idea that the content of
non-Western nationalisms is provided by orientalism and that far
from being an original expression of the culture of these societies
non-Western nationalisms are little more than assimilations of colonial ideas.

In this essay I analyse these three points (the exogenous origins of
non-Western nationalisms, its secular nature, and the role of orientalism) in relation to some aspects of Tibetan nationalism, particularly the kind of religious nationalism advocated by the present Dalai
Lama. I argue that this kind of nationalism, while it clearly bears the
mark of external influence, is not a Western creation. I further argue
that it is mistaken to describe this nationalism as an internalisation of
orientalist ideas about Tibet. The depiction of Tibetans as emerging
on the world scene in 1959 without any national self-consciousness,
only to be captured by Western fantasies, distorts a situation that is
vastly more complex than the uni-directional influence often suggested by the dominant model of nationalism.

FROM PROTO-NATIONALISM TO MODERN NATIONALISM

It is true that Tibetans did not have a full-fledged nationalism before
1950. The reason for this is not to be found in the fact that Tibet was
not colonised by the West. The countries that developed some of the
most active nationalisms in Asia, Japan and Thailand were never
colonised and yet succeeded in their process of nation building.
Similarly, the reason for the failure to develop nationalism is not
Buddhism itself. Buddhist countries such as Burma and Sri Lanka
both developed, in different ways, their own national self-awareness.
As Melvyn Goldstein has shown, the reasons why Tibet failed to
develop in this way lie with the social structures of the Tibetan
society, particularly the dominant role of monasteries and the con-
comitant imposition of a rigid conservatism (Goldstein, 1989). Also
particularly disastrous was the deliberate choice made by the Tibetan
ruling elites during the eighteenth and the nineteenth centuries to
keep Tibet isolated from what was happening in Asia at that time.
This decision prevented Tibet from developing the kind of institutions, such as print capitalism, a well equipped army, a census, and

schools, that could have led to the development of a modern nationalism and a successful process of nation building.[20]

This failure to develop nationalism does not mean, however, that
prior to 1950 Tibetans did not have any sense of themselves as
belonging to a distinct country. As I have argued elsewhere (Dreyfus, 1994), at least in Central Tibet since the thirteenth or fourteenth
century Tibetans understood themselves as belonging to a country
defined in terms of the shared memories articulated by some of the
more important hidden treasures (*gter ma*) such as the *Maṇi bka'*
'bum, etc (see MacDonald 1969; Blondeau, 1984). These narratives
identify Tibet as an originally barbarous country civilised by Buddhism and transformed into the "pure land surrounded by snow
mountains" (*gang ris bskor ba'i zhing khams*) often referred to in
Tibetan prayers. This transformation was brought about by the
beneficent activities of Avalokiteshvara through his periodic manifestations throughout Tibetan history as Srong btsan sgam po, Padmasambhava, Atisha, and later the Dalai Lamas. In the *Maṇi bka'*
'bum, Avalokiteshvara is described as the deity with whom Tibetans
have a special relation. He is considered the progenitor of the Tibetan
race, helping Tibet throughout its history.

Such a sense of collective identity, which I have described following Hobsbawm as *proto-nationalism* (1990:46),[21] differs from a
full-blown modern nationalism. Nevertheless, it prefigures nationalism in several ways and explains the ease with which Tibetans have
stepped into nationalist modernity. In the next pages, I sketch out this
transition, which took place during the 1950s and has yet to be
explored fully, though it has started to receive the kind of attention it
deserves, particularly in the excellent work of Tsering Shakya
(1999). I show that the development of Tibetan nationalism is par-

---

[20] For an argument on the link between these institutions and nationalism, see
Anderson, *Imagined Communities*.

[21] The use of the term of *proto-nationalism* to describe such a pre-modern sense
of collective identity is not unproblematic. It can be taken, mistakenly, to imply that
modern nationalism is normative and that traditional senses of collective identity
should be seen as prefigurations of this more mature way of understanding
communities. The term can also be seen to suggest a kind of continuous existence of
a pre-modern sense of collective identity and its transfomation into a modern
nationalism. Though I am arguing for some degree of continuity between these
different senses of identity, I do not accept the idea of a continuous development. I
do think, however, that it is important to highlight the relevance of more traditional
senses of identity to the formation of modern nationalism, particularly in the case of
Tibet. This is what my use of the term *proto-nationalism* is meant to communicate.

ticularly interesting in that it exemplifies a form of nationalism that owes very little to Western influence, thus undermining the first assumption of the dominant model about the exogenous nature of nationalism in non-Western countries and the third about the role of orientalism in the formation of nationalism in Tibet.

The beginnings of a cultural movement such as nationalism are not easy to trace. In Tibet, perhaps the first relevant document is the Thirteenth Dalai Lama's proclamation upon his return from exile in 1913. In this proclamation, one can see an awareness of Tibet as a distinct country, defined by its culture and history. The Dalai Lama starts his proclamation by explaining his claim to sovereignty on the basis of a connection with Avalokiteshvara, which goes back to the time of the religious kings (*chos rgyal*). He also traces the history of the relations between China and Tibet from the Yüan dynasty to the present, concluding that Tibet is a separate country. He then moves to issue five prescriptions, several of them bearing little direct connection with nationalism: Buddhism should be preserved, its schools should live in good harmony, and officials should be honest. The Dalai Lama also makes two points that are more directly related to nationalism: Tibet should strengthen its defence and expand its economical basis by allowing people to cultivate vacant land (Goldstein, 1989:60).

These two points distinguish this proclamation from an earlier one that the Dalai Lama had issued in 1901. There, the Dalai Lama displays very little sense of Tibet as a separate country. His interest is in a Buddhist kingdom, which happens to be in Tibet but could be somewhere else. Hence, his prescriptions are essentially religious and moral: monks are urged to respect the discipline, officials to be fair, lay people to recite prayers and mantras and read the scriptures (see Chhodak, 1978:30-3).[22] The 1913 one differs. It is still concerned with religious and moral matters but contains the recognition of Tibet as a distinct country that is to be defended and developed. This is, perhaps, one of the first manifestations of modern nationalism in Tibet.

---

[22] This document may have been influenced by the ideas of Dorjeev, a learned Mongolian scholar who was favoured by the Dalai Lama. Dorjeev's ambition was to transform Central Asia into a Buddhist kingdom. Nevertheless, this document reflects traditional views about the socio-political organisation of Tibet as formulated by the ideology of the union of religion and politics, which we will examine below.

Another significant step was the formation in 1954 of People's Committees (*mi dmang tshogs 'du*) among low-ranking officials and traders (the kind of middle class among whom nationalism often develops). This movement of protest against the Chinese occupation was in part motivated by the realisation that the ruling elites had failed to confront the Chinese and by the desire to oppose more directly Chinese occupation. The activity of these committees was an interesting blend of traditional worship of local deities, anti-Chinese protests, and attempts to develop institutions such as the army and the mint (Shakya, 1999:144-7). The effects of this movement remained limited, though it contributed to the later rise of a resistance movement.

A second more significant step in the formation of Tibetan nationalism was the creation of the 'Four Rivers, Six Ranges' (*chu bzhi gang drug*) movement against the Chinese occupation organised by some of the rebel leaders from Khams. Shaken by the events taking place in Khams and the bad omen reported throughout Tibet, a group of traders from Khams living in Lhasa decided to collect funds from all over Tibet to offer a golden throne to the Dalai Lama. On the 4th of July 1957 the ceremony took place in the Nor bu Ling ka in Lhasa where a large number of people came together to express their allegiance to their leader and their defiance of the Chinese (Shakya, 1999:165-70). Offering a golden throne to the Dalai Lama was seen as a way to express and strengthen the bond between the Tibetans and their leader. It was an attempt to reaffirm the power of the Dalai Lama over the land of Tibet, land that according to traditional Tibetan narratives belonged to him by virtue of his being a manifestation of Avalokiteshvara. Finally, this was also an act of opposition against the Chinese occupation, which was perceived as the action of enemies of Buddhism (*bstan gra*, the beings that are to be eliminated by the dharma-protectors).

This date, 4th of July 1957, can be seen retrospectively as marking the birth of Tibetan nationalism, the awareness that Tibetans have of belonging to a single country. The offering of a throne, a traditional symbol of religious authority, was a way for Tibetans to affirm their allegiance to the entity thus defined. Shortly after, the 'Four Rivers, Six Ranges' was constituted formally as a movement of resistance to the Chinese occupation, thus transforming the local uprisings in Khams into a nationalist struggle encompassing Central as well as Eastern Tibet. This in turn led to the uprising of March 1959 and the tragic events that followed including the Dalai Lama's flight to India, which sealed the national awareness developed during the 1950s.

TIBETAN RELIGIOUS NATIONALISM

The particularity of the nationalism that emerged in Tibet in the 1950s is that it deploys traditional religious themes to define the nation. Instead of adopting the secular lingua usually associated with modern nationalism, this nationalism defines the Tibetan nation using traditional Buddhist values such as compassion, karma and the bond between Tibetans and Avalokiteshvara. The nation thus defined is not, however, traditional Tibet with its diversity of local cultural, social and political communities, but a modern country united by its opposition to Chinese oppression (see Tambiah 1976; Brow, 1990:1-6).[23] Such a country is conceived of as a horizontal community determined by boundaries, a reified entity to which all its members owe equal allegiance irrespective of their local affiliations. Hence it is a nation-state and the loyalty toward such an entity is a form of modern nationalism, with all the potential dangers this implies.

The religious nature of this nationalism is well captured by the anthems sung by Tibetans in exile to express their national aspirations, such as the "Prayer of Truthful Words" (*bden tshig smon lam*) and the National Anthem (see Klieger 1992:61). A particularity of both these songs, which are still used nowadays by Tibetans in exile for celebrations such as March 10th, is that they are modelled after traditional religious prayers. As such they contain traditional Buddhist motives such as the prayer for the continuation of the Buddhist teaching and the request to the *buddha*s and *bodhisattva*s to help the beings who are tormented by the unbearable suffering of karma. These anthems are not, however, just prayers but also contain political concerns, as when the author of the Prayer of Truthful Words refers to "the spiritual people of the Land of Snow who are being

---

[23] Tambiah characterises kingship in East Asia as galactic polity, that is, as a hierarchical structure focused on a symbolic centre. Such a state embraces a diversity of local arrangments organised hierarchically in relation to the centre. The horizontal character of nation states should not, however, be exaggerated. As James Brow remarks, hierarchical elements such as the British identification with the royal family continue to exist in modern states. Similarly, the unified character of the nation should not be overstated. The unity nation does not preclude the existence of local allegiances.

eliminated through every torture and tyranny by the barbarism of destructive forces lacking loving kindness." This clear reference to the actions of the PRC in Tibet expresses the nationalist opposition to Chinese occupation. And yet, the song never leaves the religious idiom, going on to say that these actions should not be seen through anger but with compassion. The people who destroy Tibet are worthy of compassion more than of anger, says the song. This compassion is not, however, without political content for it is the basis for "the complete independence for entire Tibet, the only goal that can satisfy the Tibetan people." The song continues with a request to Avalokiteshvara, the patron *bodhisattva* of Tibet, to "take care of those who will give up their bodies and will undergo hardships for this goal." It ends with an invocation to truth so that these prayers can be realised.

What is remarkable in this nationalist anthem is that it completely lacks the lingua usually associated with modern nationalism, the usual references to military prowess as in the French "Marseillaise" or to the natural beauties of the country as in the Swiss national anthem. Instead it focuses on typical Buddhist themes such as loving kindness, compassion, and the continuation of Buddhist teachings. Couched in the religious idiom, the song is often used as a religious prayer. Its religious character is also revealed by the concepts embedded in it. These concepts are by no means simple, as one might expect from a song intended for wide consumption. On the contrary, it uses sophisticated Buddhist philosophical concepts: "By the reality of the inter-dependence of appearance and emptiness, may our truthful prayers soon actualise without obstacles." Such concepts are certainly not the standard fare of national anthems. They are understandable only to a small minority of highly educated specialists who have spent the many years required to master them. And yet, they are used as focus of national awareness, the markers through which Tibetans imagine themselves as belonging to a single national community.

One may marvel at the high moral character of these songs and see them as reflections of Tibet's spiritual culture. This explanation is misleading, however, suggesting that Tibetans are some kind of extraordinary spiritual people different from the rest of humanity. I should make it clear that in stressing the role of Buddhist themes in the formation of Tibetan nationalism, I do not intend to participate in the mystification of Tibet as defined by some unique spiritual essence. Nor do I mean to argue that Tibetans in their national struggle are high-minded, though they often are. The peculiar religious focus of this form of nationalism must be explained in relation to the history of Tibet and the state of contemporary Tibetan society.

UNION OF THE RELIGIOUS AND THE TEMPORAL: OLD AND NEW

One way to understand Tibetan religious nationalism is to relate it to the ideological and practical organisation of Tibetan political life. The religious themes contained in the "Prayer of Truthful Words" reflect the arrangements of Tibetan political life over several centuries. During this time, one of the dominant features of Tibetan politics has been the political role of Buddhism and the monastic order. Such arrangements have been solidified in the ideology described as "the union of the religious and the political" (*chos srid zung 'brel*). Historically, this ideology is the result of a complex situation created by the fall of the empire, the inability of non-monastic groups to establish lasting kingdoms and the increasing political role of monastic groups. As is well known, this situation led to the establishment of the rule of the Dalai Lamas in the seventeenth and eighteenth centuries, a period during which the idea of the union between the religious and the political became enshrined as the official ideology of the Tibetan state. In the present situation the high spiritual and moral character of the Fourteenth Dalai Lama has made this Tibetan institution a world attraction. But such an institution is certainly more than the expression of Tibetan spirituality; it represents the practical and ideological arrangements of political life that Tibetans have developed over several centuries.[24]

---

[24] It would be a mistake, however, to believe that this political ideology is just the expression of the historical particularities of the Tibetan political situation. It reflects as well a deep motif within Buddhist traditions. In societies such as Tibet, Thailand, etc., where Buddhism has dominated and shaped the culture, one of the major problems that has to be addressed is that of the relation between Buddhism and the state. This relation is not just an ideological matter but a social one as well. The dominant paradigm within a Buddhist society is that of complementarity between monastic order and laity. Monks and nuns devote themselves to the practice of Buddhism, and laity supports their efforts, thereby gaining spiritual merit. This complementary relation is reflected at the political level by the complementarity between monastic groups and political authority. In Buddhist societies, the relation between the spiritual and the temporal has been problematic and unstable, and hence

This unification of the religious and the secular into one figure throws some light on the nationalist anthems we examined above. Their reference to loving kindness and other Buddhist principles now appears to be also the expression of the particular political arrangements and ideology characteristic of traditional Tibet. The "Prayer of Truthful Words" is a nationalist song that reflects what has been the dominant Tibetan political ideology for at least the last three centuries. Its reference to Buddhist concepts corresponds to the dual nature of the state in Tibetan politics. On the one hand the state plays its political role, which in a Buddhist society includes the support and protection of the monastic or quasi-monastic groups. On the other hand, the state in the person of the Dalai Lama also incarnates the religious ideals of the society and as such is in charge of leading the country religiously. This fusion of the two aspects is reflected in the "Prayer of Truthful Words," which is thus both a *bona fidae* nationalist song and a religious prayer.[25]

The nature of nationalism was further inflected by the experiences undergone by the Tibetan people both inside and outside Tibet after 1959. In particular, the experience of the exile and the encounter with Indian democracy were important in developing the commitment to human rights and democratic values expressed in the constitution promulgated by the Dalai Lama in 1963. This constitution in turn inspired activists within Tibet, particularly the young

---

constantly negotiated and renegotiated. Typically the state, while offering patronage, seeks to control and regulate the monasteries, which resist incorporation and subjugation. The king supports and protects the monastic order, which under the direction of prestigious religious teachers jealously maintains its prerogatives and relative autonomy. The political arrangements in Tibet after 1751 represent a particular solution to the tension inherent in the dual organisation of Buddhist societies. The Tibetan approach, to combine the spiritual and the temporal, collapses into one the two poles around which a Buddhist society is organised. In this Tibetan conception, the two functions are combined by the Dalai Lama. As the king, he is the leader of the polity and thus the patron of the monastic order. As the foremost religious teacher, he is also the head of the monastic organisation and has a special relation with its members.

[25] This is also reflected in the national flag adopted by the exiled community. At the centre of the flag is a snowy mountain surrounded by a pair of radiant snow lions. The mountain symbolises the geographical situation of the land often described as the Land of Snow (*gang can ljong*), the Realm Surrounded by Snowy Mountains (*gang ris bskor ba'i zhing khams*), etc. The snow lions, decorated with coloured manes and fangs, represent the union of the religious and the political, which we have examined. The graphic centrality of this motif illustrates the essential role played by this political ideology in the collective identity of modern Tibetans.

monks and nuns who demonstrated against Chinese rule in 1987–8. As Ron Schwartz (1994) has shown, these young people saw the Dalai Lama's stance as reflecting a progressive political position through his articulation of key traditional Buddhist concepts such as compassion, the prohibition of killing, etc. Against Chinese propaganda, these young activists argued that it is the Dalai Lama's constitution which represents a truly progressive regime, not the Chinese occupation, which was seen to fail miserably when measured against the criteria that it itself has set up.

These young activists based their democratic principles on Buddhism, which is depicted as a set of undogmatic religious and moral principles compatible with human rights and democracy. Buddhism commands non-violence, argue the young activists, who have been beaten up by Chinese military police for peacefully demonstrating around the Central Temple. It also commands respect for individual integrity. This principle of respect for people, which is mandated by Buddhism, accords with the general practice of the contemporary democratic world. Like the old Tibetan ideology, this one combines the spiritual and the secular. Now, however, this ideal has been reinterpreted according to modern democratic principles. Since the rule of the Dalai Lama is based on such principles and since he is recognised by international opinion as a foremost proponent of human rights, the old principle is now understood to imply a democratic regime.

In the situation in which these young monks and nuns find themselves the choice of human rights as a main issue is not surprising. In the contemporary climate in which human rights is a lively issue, its use against a regime that has deprived them of political rights is easy to understand. The influence from the outside world, which is real and moves through several channels, is also partly responsible for this development. Monks and nuns in Tibet are quite aware of the international political climate. By now, the broadcasting of daily news in Tibetan by the VOA has reinforced this global awareness. The prestige of the Western powers is great and the admiration for the UN-charter all the greater since it contradicts the present Chinese occupation.

The focus on democracy and human rights is not due, however, just to external factors. The arguments made by the young militants have a distinctively Buddhist flavour. Human rights are derived the right of people to pursue meaningful human lives understood according to Buddhist principles. Politically, this implies that Tibetans should have the right of self-determination. This in turn implies that people should have the right to be free from the different instances of human-made suffering such as beating, torture, mistreatment, abuse of power, etc. This conception of human rights is different from the formal view of Western democracies. It is substantive rather than formal. Human rights means the right to be free from certain concrete instances of suffering. Schwartz puts it quite well when he says:

> These are seen not so much as violations of certain specific, general and abstract rights, but rather as symptomatic and illustrative of a general condition in which the humanity of Tibetans goes unacknowledged. Quite simply, under Chinese rule Tibetans are not treated as human beings. (Schwartz, 1992:3-26)

The question of human rights is ultimately a matter of conditions for the pursuit of a meaningful human life. Here Buddhism provides the framework according to which such a life can be evaluated. Human rights are seen to have religious consequences in the larger sense of the word. To be free from undue interference means to be free to achieve what is valuable from a Buddhist standpoint. Thus, to practice human rights a political regime must provide favourable conditions for the practice of Buddhism.

Such a possibility is not provided by the present Chinese regime, which has no legitimacy and must be replaced by an independent Tibetan government. In this way, respect for human rights is based on Buddhist principles, which mandate Tibetan independence. Thus, there is a connection between Buddhism, democracy and the Tibetan cause. The connection between Buddhism and human rights made by the young Tibetan activists is not just a convenient gloss they lay over their actions or an opportunistic move to oppose the Chinese occupation by appealing to international opinion. Rather it reflects congruence between Buddhist and modern democratic worldviews that has not always been appreciated.

This congruence is not just political or moral but cultural as well. One of the reasons that young monks and nuns find human rights easy to associate with Buddhist values is that these ideas, which come from different horizons, seem to reflect a similar view of the person and the respect that such a person deserves. Buddhist ideas of karma and compassion view the person as an individual creator of his or her actions and bearer of the fruits of these actions. It is up to the individuals to decide about their own actions. Communities (traditional or modern) cannot override this responsibility and must respect the person's right to make his or her own decisions. Similarly, democratic values see the individual as being in charge of his or her decisions, which cannot be made by anybody else but the individual. Such an assertion of the right of individuals to make their own decision cannot but have a profound appeal to the young activists who face a situation in which they are denied precisely that right.

This is not to say that there are not other aspects of Tibetan Buddhist tradition that conflict with this individualistic view. Cultures are heterogeneous and contain conflicting views and practices that can co-exist even within a single individual. For example, Tibetans view the person as being not just bearer of his or her own karma but also as related to personal gods (*'go ba'i lha*) who are protective. The role of these gods goes further than mere protection, for in a certain way they constitute the person, who is said to contain these gods. A person, for example, contains the gods of his or her birthplace, family lineage, as well as some more personal god with whom that person may be associated. Such a person falls sick when these gods are offended or weakened. This view of the person as embedded in a community of beings (human and otherwise) is certainly not individualistic. It is worth noting that when young monks and nuns use traditional ideas, they do not turn to this view of the person and the millenarian practices that it entails. Rather they have recourse to more canonical Buddhist ideas, which they perceive to accord with modern democratic values.

The concordance between some Buddhist ideas and modern human rights should not, however, be mistaken for an identity. Tibetan views of the person are heterogeneous and the meeting between some Buddhist and some modern views is just a partial overlap. Moreover, the concordance between some Buddhist ideas and modern democratic values should not be idealised, for it does not guarantee that Tibetan religious nationalism does not contain its own dark side, as we will see shortly.

TIBETAN RELIGIOUS NATIONALISM AND THE DOMINANT MODEL

What the existence of religious nationalism among Tibetans shows is the degree to which the dominant model advocated by Gellner and

Anderson does not fit the Tibetan situation. In its incipience, the nationalism examined here owes very little to Western ideas and even less to orientalist fantasies. Rather it is traditional Buddhist ideas that have been pivotal in the emergence of Tibetan national awareness. The use by many Tibetans of religious motives to define themselves as a nation shows the degree to which the analysis of non-Western nationalisms as internalisations of Western orientalist discourse misses the mark. When Tibetans represented Tibet to themselves or to outsiders in the early 1960s, they did not lack the discursive means to represent Tibet as "unified, complete and coherent" (Lopez, 1998:200). They did not need and did not use "the pre- and post-diaspora fantasies of Tibet as a place unlike any other on the globe" (Lopez, 1998:205) about which Tibetans knew very little. Rather, they used their own traditional discourse to represent themselves as belonging to an independent country defined by its Buddhist values, its relation with Avalokiteshvara and its opposition to Chinese occupation.

Moreover when Tibetans borrowed Western ideas as they did increasingly after 1963, they used ideas of democracy and human rights, not the disempowering stereotypes that are the hallmark of orientalism. Thus, when the Dalai Lama or the young monks and nuns in Tibet articulated their vision of Tibet, they put forth a mixture of traditional Tibetan Buddhist ideas such as compassion, karma, and the unique relation between Tibetans and Avalokiteshvara, and Western ideas such as human rights and democratic values. The process that gave rise to this kind of nationalism involves a complex interaction between traditional Tibetan Buddhist culture, Western and Indian democratic ideas, and Chinese ideas and practices. To many contemporary Tibetan nationalists, democratic values are so convincing because they are seen as modern incarnations of traditional Buddhist ideals. This identification is certainly a new way for Tibetans to understand their political commitments, a way that is not, however, just an internalisation of alien values but an artful synthesis produced out of a complex heterological dialogue in which all the elements involved in the process interact with each other and change in the process.

Finally, the use by Tibetans of religious motifs in the formulation of their national identity also contradicts one of the other key assumptions of the dominant model, the necessarily secular nature of nationalism. According to this model, the rise of nationalism requires the transformation of the old social arrangements, which are based on local allegiances and involve complex and overlapping hierarchical relations, into a horizontal public space in which all participate equally. This development presupposes the emergence of a supra-local identity that allows people to function together as members of a single society. Such a supra-local identity is possible, however, only if there is a common culture that holds together anonymous, impersonal, and atomised social participants. In most cases, such a culture is fostered by powerful and authoritative public institutions (the state), which promote a standardised culture through education, telecommunication, etc. (Gellner, 1983:55, 77, 142). According to the dominant model, one of the necessary conditions for the emergence of such a common culture is the destruction of the traditional order, which is rooted in religion. Without the disappearance of the religious communities that constitute traditional societies, it will not be possible to develop the kind of common imagination necessary to the emergence of the nation (Anderson, 1984:12-36). Hence, the common culture necessary to the imagination of a nation presupposes a culture that has ceased to be dominated by religion and hence is secular.

The case of Tibetan nationalism challenges this dominant model, since it is not secular but imbued through and through by Buddhist ideas and values. Does this mean that the dominant model is simply wrong in its assumption that the development of nationalism requires the destruction of the religious world, and that nationalism can develop on the basis of a religious ideology? Or, does it mean that the dominant model is also wrong in its assumption that nationalism requires a common culture, as argued by Peter van der Veer (1994) in his analysis of Indian religious nationalism?

At first sight, the Tibetan case seems to suggest that the mistake with the dominant model is its assumption that religion cannot play the focal role that secular national culture has played in the emergence of nationalism in Europe. Would it not be possible to imagine a case in which religion would provide the commonality necessary to the imagination of a national community? The Tibetan case, as well as that of other countries such as Iran, seems to suggest such a scenario in which the traditional fragmented social space is being sublated into a more inclusive national sphere defined in relation to religious motifs. This has been the case for Tibetan nationalism particularly in its early stages, as reflected in the Prayer of Truthful

Words, which was written by the present Dalai Lama shortly after his 1959 flight into India.

Nevertheless, the place of religious nationalism in the Tibetan community has changed. Whereas in the 1950s and 1960s it rallied an overwhelming proportion of the community, things have changed. There are many Tibetan nationalists, both inside and outside of Tibet, who are markedly uncomfortable with religious nationalism. They argue that Buddhism should not have much of a role in Tibetan political institutions, and that the predicament of Tibet is due largely to Buddhism and its non-violent message, which they see as a possibly fatal liability for the future of Tibet. Such a stance has been expressed in several quarters. In the exile community, there are many Tibetans, who express dissatisfaction and frustration with the official view, which they hold to be ineffective. Strongly influenced by Western secular ideas, these people feel uncomfortable in the moral community reflected by the "Prayer of Truthful Words" or the National Anthem. They would rather have a secular democracy following Western norms. In recent years, some of these secularly minded Tibetan intellectuals have founded the Amnye Machen institute, which is devoted to the study of secular aspects of Tibetan culture and the translation of Western works, particularly political ones, in Tibetan.

Similarly, in the last two decades secular nationalism has emerged forcefully in Tibet, more particularly in A mdo literature. For example, in "The Heart-beat of a New Generation," a discussion of the works of Døn drub gyel (Don grub rgyal, 1953–85), a poet from A mdo who committed suicide, Pema Bum (cited in Schwartz, 1992:6) depicts the stance of his generation, the despair of his contemporaries who feel alienated from the two dominant cultures in contemporary Tibet, Chinese communism and Buddhism. The former has no credibility because it is the culture of the occupiers and has been enforced by "destruction, torture, poverty and famine." The other is perhaps more valuable and central to the Tibetan heritage, but it is unable to prevent the annihilation that threatens the Tibetan people. "Let alone save Tibet, Buddhism cannot even save itself" (cited in Schwartz, 1992).

This secularly minded nationalism is quite different from the religious nationalism I have examined here. It is important for the future of Tibet and I do not wish in any way to suggest that it is somehow less authentically Tibetan than the kind of religious nationalism I am analysing. The existence of such nationalism among Tibetans demonstrates, if there were any need to do so, that Tibet is not a unique culture defined by its essential spirituality. More importantly, such a secular nationalism reminds us that like any other nationalism, Tibetan nationalism is not a unified discourse but a site of contention where conflicting visions, religious and secular, compete for the allegiance of Tibetans. These competing visions often co-exist in the same community where people live together without necessarily agreeing on the definition of a common project. Sometimes, these visions clash. For example, in the mid-nineties a bitter debate took place in the exile community concerning the combination of the spiritual and the secular. The partisans of this ideology won by only a narrow margin, indicating that this is not the end of the story and illustrating the increasing audience of secular nationalism in the Tibetan community.

Still, as I have emphasised throughout this essay, it would be a mistake to think that secular nationalism will eliminate its religious competitors. It is even difficult to gauge the present opinion of Tibetans concerning this question. Are most of the exiled Tibetans committed to Buddhist nationalism? Or, are they just committed to the present Dalai Lama and will change their allegiance once he is gone? The opinions of the enormous majority of Tibetans, who are in Tibet, are even more difficult to gauge. The evolution of Tibetan nationalism does not reflect a teleological necessity. Contrary to what the dominant model asserts, there is no reason to assume that non-Western nationalisms will evolve like its Western counterparts, which emerged over the destruction of traditional society and its central institutions, including the church and dynastic rule. This scenario is certainly not necessarily appropriate for non-Western societies, which have followed different routes into modernity. For example, the development of nationalism in Thailand and Japan did not require the destruction of the dynastic order. On the contrary, the development of nationalism was fostered and greatly aided by the strength of the dynasties, which played pivotal roles in ushering these countries into modernity. Thus, the development of nationalism does not necessarily conform to any model. It has followed different paths in different societies. This is also true of the Tibetan situation where both secular and religious nationalism has played an important role.

BUDDHIST NATIONALISM AND ITS ILLIBERAL TENDENCIES

The debate between these contending national visions is important for the future of Tibetan political life, particularly for the religious national vision I have examined here. One of the great worries about religious nationalism is its propensity for intolerance. This danger is not surprising if we remember that religion is based on the idea of the sacred. How can one hold ideas, values and symbols that are sacred in any other way than absolutely? And if one does so, how can one avoid intolerance? The solution in most Western societies has been to establish a separation between the private and the public spheres and to limit religion as much as possible to the former. It is this fictional but useful separation that is compromised by religious nationalism, which threatens to introduce in the public realm the absoluteness that has come to be considered more appropriate to the private realm.

Given the sometimes devastating results brought about by the breakdown of the barriers between religious and secular domains and the violence perpetrated by proponents of religious nationalism, one cannot but wonder about Tibetan religious nationalism. Is it not threatened with similar illiberal propensities? This question may surprise given the nature of Buddhist ideas and their congruence with human rights in the Tibetan national struggle. Is it not the case that the Buddhist ideas of compassion and respect for karma guarantee, or at least augur well for, the future of Tibetan religious nationalism and allow us to hope that this religious nationalism will be able to avoid the illiberal tendencies mentioned above? The answer to such a question must be tentative since it concerns the future, a realm that notoriously escapes the grasp of scholars. Elements of an answer can be found, however, both inside and outside of the Tibet sphere, elements that cannot but invite caution.

First, outside of the Tibetan sphere, the record of Buddhist nationalisms in Asia is mixed. In certain respects, Buddhism, particularly Buddhist modernism, has provided an impetus for progressive and tolerant policies. In Sri Lanka, for example, Buddhist modernism has been the source of a commitment to socialist ideas that have played an important role in the orientation of the country. Similarly, Buddhist modernism has inspired a number of social movements such as Sarvodaya and the Ecology Monks throughout the Theravada world.[26] These movements have played a generally positive role and have worked toward tolerance. There is, however, a much darker side to Buddhist nationalism, which has resulted in the bloody confrontation with Tamils in Sri Lanka. As Tambiah (1992) and others have shown, the Buddhist nationalism that developed in Sri Lanka after World War II has been partly responsible for the increasing alienation of Tamils and has thus significantly contributed to the development of the bloody nightmare in which the island is still caught.[27]

Second, a cursory look at developments in the exile community cannot but suggest a similar cautionary note. In India, Tibetans have had the occasion to exercise democracy for four decades. There is no denying that during this time Tibetans have strengthened their democratic commitments. Nevertheless, there have been several instances in which the community has shown less than democratic behaviour. I know of several cases in which prominent Tibetan intellectuals (I am hesitant to mention names) were threatened because they had put forth ideas that were judged opposed to some of the more central Buddhist values. These cases are not limited to any particular period. Starting from the sixties, they have continued into the nineties. Often, these intellectuals were denounced, threatened and at time physically abused because they were perceived to oppose the Dalai Lama and the Buddhist values that he incarnates. In more recent times, it is what I have called 'the Shukden affair' that has unleashed a string of violent incidents including, but not limited to, the murder of three monks.

All these incidents show that Tibetan communities are not immune to intolerance and that their commitment to Buddhist values, far from being in itself sufficient to ward off illiberal tendencies, is not without its own dangers. There is no guarantee that even given the right opportunity Tibet would develop in a democratic direction. Buddhism may predispose Tibetans to adopt certain democratic principles, which they see as congruent with some of their religious commitments. This does not entail that these principles will neces-

---

[26] On the Sarvodaya movement, see the rather conflicting evaluations provided by Bond (1988:241-94) and Gombrich and Obeyesekere (1988:243-54). For the forest conservation monks movements, see Swearer (1995:124-8).

[27] For a scathing indictment of Buddhist nationalism, see Tambiah (1992). Bond (1990:75-129) provides a more moderate account that does not exempt, however, Buddhists.

sarily win the day. It does mean, however, that Tibetan religious nationalism is not an internalisation of alien values; it has little to do with Western orientalist fantasies about Tibet. Rather, it is a national vision around which many Tibetans have been able to rally. Whether they will be able to avoid the pitfalls of this vision is another question, which has yet to be put to the test.

56 GEORGES DREYFUS

BIBLIOGRAPHY

Anderson, B. 1983. *Imagined Communities*. New York: Verso.

Blondeau, A.M. 1984."Le Découvreur du *Maṇi bKa'-'bum* était-il Bon-po?" in Louis Ligeti (ed.), *Tibetan and Buddhist Studies Commemorating the 200ᵗʰ Anniversary of the Birth of Alexander Csoma de Kørøs*. Budapest: Akademiai Kiado, 77–123.

Bond. G. 1990. *The Buddhist Revival in Sri Lanka*, Columbia: University of South Carolina.

Brow, J. 1990. "Notes on Community, Hegemony, and the Uses of the Past," *Anthropological Quarterly* 63(1):1–6, and (2).

Chhodak, T. 1978. "The 1901 Proclamation H.H. Dalai-Lama XIII," *Tibet Journal* 3(1):30–33.

Dreyfus, G. 1994. "Proto-nationalism in Tibet," in P. Kvaerne (ed.), *Tibetan Studies*, Oslo: Insititute for Comparative Research.

Foster, R.J. 1991. "Making National Cultures in the Global Ecumene," *Annual Review of Anthropology*, 20:235–60.

Gellner, E. 1983. *Nations and Nationalism*. Ithaca: Cornell University Press.

Goldstein, M. 1989. *A History of Modern Tibet, 1913–1951*. Berkeley: University of California, 1989.

Gombrich, R. and G. Obeyesekere. 1988. *Buddhism Transformed*. Princeton: Princeton University.

Hobsbawm, E. 1990. *Nations and Nationalism since 1780*, Cambridge: Cambridge University Press, 46.

Hobsbawm, E. and T. Ranger (eds.). 1983. *The Invention of Tradition*, Cambridge: Cambridge University Press.

Klieger, P. Christiaan. 1992. *Tibetan Nationalism*, Meerut: Archana.

Lopez, D. 1998. *Prisoners of Shangri-La*, Chicago: University of Chicago, 1998.

Macdonald, Mme. 1969. "Histoire and Philologie Tibétaines," *Annuaire de l'Ecole des Hautes Etudes*, Paris: Sorbonne.

Shakya, Tsering. 1999. *The Dragon in the Land of Snows*, London: Pimlico.

Schwartz, Ronald. 1992. "Democracy, Tibetan Independence and Protest under Chinese Rule," *Tibet Journal*, 17(2): 3–26.

—— 1994. *Circle of Protest*, New York: Columbia University Press.

Swearer, D. 1995. *The Buddhist World of Southeast Asia*, Albany: SUNY

Tambiah, S. 1976. *World Conqueror and World Renouncer*, London: Cambridge University Press.

—— 1992. *Buddhism Betrayed?* Chicago: University of Chicago.

van der Veer, Peter. 1994. *Religious Nationalism*, Berkeley: University of California.

CHAPTER THREE

BIOGRAPHY BY INSTALLMENT:
TIBETAN LANGUAGE REPORTAGE ON
THE LIVES OF REINCARNATE LAMAS, 1995–99

KEVIN GARRATT (INDEPENDENT SCHOLAR)

INTRODUCTION

Tibetans have long laid considerable emphasis on recording biographical information about their spiritual teachers—or lamas[28]—in a
genre of sacred biography, which spans textual, iconographic and
oral traditions.[29] During the second half of the twentieth century
(C.E.[30]) those milieux increasingly came into contact with technologies and influences mostly unknown in traditional Tibet. This report
investigates how far the structure and content of the centuries-old
textual tradition has moved beyond the confines of a formal hagi-
ography into the sphere of contemporary Tibetan language print
media, through considering five periodicals over a sample five year
period—January 1995 to December 1999.

---

[28] The term 'lama' (*bla ma*) is usually applied by Tibetans to senior or well-
known figures within their Buddhist or Bon religious traditions, whereas most
Western and Chinese popular usage now renders it almost synonymous with
'Tibetan monk'.
[29] The textual tradition refers to traditional woodblock-printed hagiographies as
well as the wealth of material produced using more modern technologies.
Iconographic sources include painted scrolls, murals and frescoes adorning the
interiors of temples, shrines and caves; also stupas, rock paintings and other
adaptations of the natural landscape. Oral tradition takes in the tales of professional
itinerant storytellers, devotional songs (like those of Milarepa) and the social
comment of street and popular songs still heard today.
[30] Christian era.

SOURCES

Three newspapers are from Dharamsala,[31] India:

- *Dmangs gtso* ('Democracy'), a fortnightly broadsheet, was published independently by the Amnye Machen Institute between 1993 and 1996. Its masthead carried the legend "Independent reporting is a pillar of democracy" (*rang dbang gi gsar 'god ni dmangs gtso'i ka ba zhig yin*);
- *Shes bya* ('Knowledge') has appeared, mostly monthly, since 1968[32] and usually reflects the Dharamsala government's policy of the day. Summaries of some of its articles appear in an English language bimonthy *Tibetan Bulletin: the Official Journal of the Tibetan Administration of His Holiness the Dalai Lama*; and
- *Bod kyi dus bab* ("Tibet Times") is an independent fortnightly broadsheet launched in 1996 to fill the void left by *Mangtso*'s demise.

The other two publications come from Beijing, China (PRC):

- *Krung go'i bod ljongs* ("China's Tibet") is nominally a quarterly[33] magazine, focussing predominately on economic, social and cultural aspects of ethnic Tibetan life within the PRC; and
- *Mi dmangs brnyan par* ("People's Pictorial") is the monthly Tibetan language edition of *China Pictorial*,[34] which provides occasional glimpses of Tibetan religious activity within the PRC.

RELIGIOUS BIOGRAPHY

Most contemporary biographical material derives its inspiration from the standard sacred biography genre (*rnam thar* or "aspects of liberation [story]")[35] of classical Tibetan. Tibetan religious texts generally present their material in the form of a standard narrative account of the life and death of the deceased, usually couched in

---

[31] Seat of the Dalai Lama and headquarters of the Tibetan government-in-exile.

[32] Initially a private publication, it was handed over to the Central Tibetan Administation in 1971. For easier reference throughout the paper, *Shes bya* is abbreviated to "*Sheja*" and *dmangs gtso* to "*Mangtso*."

[33] Six issues appeared in 1999.

[34] The Tibetan language edition ceased publication at the end of 2000.

[35] Some newspaper obituaries prefer the honorific heading "Deeds" (*mdzad*).

elaborate, formal language and structured into clearly demarcated sections:

- that sequence often commences with a homage to objects of worship, normally a Buddha, tutelary deity or lineage of spiritual teachers;
- verses of praise and a general introduction to the deceased follow, including an outline of the text's component parts. They would normally cover sections on the deceased's birth, upbringing, studies, teachings received and given, travels, spiritual attainments and other religious or temporal accomplishments; and
- details on the circumstances of death come towards the end of the text, which concludes with auspicious verses and a colophon.

A *rnam thar* covers a single life of the reincarnate in question; the next 'instalment' dealing with the deceased's subsequent incarnation would not appear until after the passing of the successor. By contrast, modern newspaper reportage allows more or less contemporaneous coverage of events so the interested reader can follow a lama's career as it occurs, rather than life by life. Obviously, the exigencies of space prevent a newspaper format from ever attempting to maintain that traditional presentational approach. The necessary compression of information in order to meet broadsheet or magazine space constraints has brought about a considerable stylistic reappraisal of the structure and language of the *nam thar*. This is done in order to suit a journalistic medium, producing a format that amounts to a biographical sketch containing a pattern of certain recurrent themes.

CONTEMPORARY COVERAGE

Obituary notices cover the passing of leading Tibetan Buddhist and Bon luminaries. News items and features include reports on major Buddhist teachings and initiations given by high lamas both outside and within the PRC.[36] Discussion also covers a diverse range of related topics: constraints on their activities in the PRC, the progress of monastic building and education (mostly in India) and information

---

[36] Some degree of government control over subject matter cannot be overlooked. While limits on editorial freedom in Dharamsala may be relatively few, PRC material always complies with the dictates of Party and State.

on significant events in various lamas' lives. All of those areas remain of great importance to the Tibetan faithful, for whom articles often include a lengthy review of the subject's life. Matters do not rest there, of course, for Buddhist tenets on the cycle of lives enable reportage to proceed on into the lama's subsequent life. Thus the discovery of a reincarnation is followed by reports on a sequence of significant events, such as a new incumbent's enthronement and commencement of religious training. In this way, the newspapers become over time a valuable repository of biographical information on events from around the world, for which ready access in Tibetan is otherwise hard to find. That material falls under three generic headings:

- deaths of religious figures, ranging from detailed formal obituaries resembling those of the *rnam thar,* down to the briefest report in a few lines covering the subject's decease;
- return of reincarnations — their identification, recognition, enthronement and other formal steps; and
- the system of reincarnation itself.

DEATHS

Twelve reports appeared in the Dharamsala press, covering ten individuals,[37] and just one from Beijing (see Table 1). The length and content of any obituary have tended to depend on the publisher's perceived stature of the subject, which ranges from *Bod kyi dus bab*'s two pages for the resistance fighter and politician Lhamo Tsering (portrayed as a great Tibetan patriot) down to a few lines for Reting Rinpoche in *Krung go'i bod ljongs'* "News in Brief" column.[38]

---

[37] A death not covered in the Tibetan language press — that of Dungkar Rinpoche (1927–97), who had spent much of his life teaching in Beijing (steadfastly defending Tibetan culture and language) appeared in Dharamsala's English language press: "Leading Tibetan scholar dies at 70," (*Tibetan Bulletin*, May–June 1997:10).

[38] Unlike *Sheja*'s earlier years, when the most detailed obituaries usually were reserved for ordained figures, the longest now are of laity — especially those whose lives were devoted to the struggle for Tibet. Thus, while both the Ganden Throne Holder's obituaries covered less than a page of text, *Bod kyi dus bab* accorded Lhamo Tsering almost two closely printed pages.

TABLE 1

Death notices for Tibetan religious figures 1995–99

Issue	Name/Dates	Background
Sheja—6[39]		
95.6	Yeshe Dondrub (1910?–95)	99th Ganden Throne Holder
95.9	Lozang Nyima (1925–95)	Sharpa Chöjé
96.4	Dzeme Rinpoche (1927–96)	Noted Ganden scholar
97.2/3	Lozang Gyatso (19??–97)	Head of Bud. Dial. School
97.7	4th Andzin Rinpoche (1933–97)	Nyingma lama
97.12	Lungtog Gyaltsen, 2nd Rigyal Rime lama Rinpoche (1931–97)	
Mangtso—1		
95.5 31	Yeshe Dondrub (1910?–95)	The Ganden Ti
Bod kyi dus bab—5		
96.9 15	6th Tseten Zhabdrung (1915–85)	Noted grammarian
97.12 10	Lungtog Gyaltsen, 2nd Rigyal Rinpoche (1931–97)	
98.5 20	Lozang Tsondru (1939–98)	Abbot of Ngari Gacho mon
99.9 1	Kalzang Thabkhe (no dates)	former Drepung Gomang abbot
99.12 20	Tidu Rinpoche (19??–99)	Sakya lama and doctor
Krung go'i bod ljongs—1		
97.6	6th Reting Rinpoche	Successor of Regent of Tibet

Mi dmangs brnyan par—Nil

1 DHARAMSALA COVERAGE 1995–99

1.1 LANGUAGE, STRUCTURE AND BIOGRAPHICAL ELEMENTS

The formal terminology employed in these reports is that of the classical language of Tibetan Buddhist texts, refined over centuries. The contemporary title 'obituary notice' (*'das brda*) is never employed; instead the more formal and honorific 'saddening news' (*yid skyo'i gnas tshul*) generally serves as a heading, though higher levels of honorific terminology are utilised, as with the ninety-ninth

---

[39] In March 2000 both *Sheja* and *Krung go'i bod ljong* printed obituaries for Gungthang Rinpoche (died 1 March 2000), which, being of considerable relevance to this discussion, are considered below.

Ganden Ti's "sad news of passing" (*sku gshegs pa'i skyo gnas*). The use of honorific forms depends on the deceased's reputation and spiritual status within the Tibetan community. While lesser luminaries effect a "sudden passing away," the Ganden Ti and the Sharpa Choje "enact dissolution into the sphere of emptiness" (*chos dbyings su thim tshul bstan pa*). The sixth Reting Rinpoche passing (*Sheja*, January 2000:24) was described: his "mindstream departed with the aspiration that seeks others' welfare" (*dgongs pa gzhan don du gshegs*).[40]

Use of this often cryptic, technical vocabulary assumes a familiarity on the part of the reader with the philosophical concepts underpinning the religious canon, without which many reports cannot be readily understood. The high-flown phraseology of classical biography and the constant use of descriptive figures of speech are other key features of such material. This follows from the fact that many such notices are provided by a lama's household, so are likely to be the work of relatively well-educated monks or scholars. Though the stylised structure of these various elements still follows that of the *rnam thar,* its transfer into a newspaper medium has led to a steadily decreasing usage of the abstract and philosophical aspects of that genre.

Transfers of the *rnam thar* structure and some of its technical vocabulary are apparent from an examination of six biographical elements, readily identifiable as components of newspaper death notices. The six are: honorific titles, causes of death, the meditative absorption period *(thugs dam)*, signs and portents after death (including during the intermediate state [*bar do*]), a review of milestones and entreaties for a quick return.

1.2 HONORIFIC TITLES

The standard introduction comprises up to several lines of honorific appellations or courtesy and religious titles, in part reflecting the subject's standing in Tibetan society. The terminology's precise technical significance in the literature of *sutra* and *tantra* guides the informed reader through the deceased's spiritual credentials and

---

[40] Article title: *Rwa sgreng gi yang srid zer ba ngo 'dzin byas pa* ("Recognition of a So-called Reting Reincarnation").

attainments. For example, *Sheja*'s report on the Ganden Ti's passing commences with a sweeping praise:

> the ninety-ninth representative of Maitreya the Victorious One, the Drepung [monastery] Loseling [college] Lharampa [*geshe*], the venerable Yeshe Dondrub, the Supreme One. (*Sheja,* July 1995:18)[41]

1.3 CAUSES OF DEATH

Next follows details of the circumstances—usually illness—leading to death, with the majority of obituaries repeating stock phrases, which presumably simplifies the editorial work involved. The usual pattern is of the onset of a sudden illness for which Tibetan and Western, Indian or Chinese medicine (according to place of demise) proves of little or no assistance, as do religious rituals or the entreaties of the faithful. For the Ganden Ti, who was requested by the Dalai Lama to remain here longer, the following text appears:

> Although, in accordance with the general advice coming from the Precious One, the Dalai Lama, the Supreme Protector, on the need to be as careful as possible with medical treatment and health care, he had taken treatment including reliance on many renowned and skilled Tibetan physicians and many renowned doctors and hospitals in America. Furthermore, his monastery college and college house had strenuously performed rituals in accordance with the divination pronouncements of lamas and deities on rituals promoting his lifespan and had striven with methods of reversal, such as making many offerings and requests and entreaties and great assemblies of all the colleges at the three monastic universities and spiritual centres. That failed to effect a recovery, as if the Doctrine and humanity were in decline. (*Sheja*, September 1995:18)[42]

---

[41] *'Jam dgon rgyal ba'i rgyal tshab dga' ldan khri thog go dgu pa 'dras blo gling lha rams pa rje btzun ye shes don mchog.* Similarly with *Bod kyi dus bab*'s enconium for Tidu Rinpoche which extends to over two lines of text: "the incomparable Protector Tidu Rinpoche, Jamyang Lungtog Gyaltsen, the sole refuge of all sentient beings, including the gods."

[42] *Spyi nor gong sa skyabs mgon chen po mchog nas sman bcos 'phrod bsten gang gzab dgos pa'i bka' spyi bor phebs pa bzhin 'phags bod sman rjes mkhas pa grags can du ma dang/ a ri'i phyogs kyi sman khang dan sman pa grags can du ma zhig bsten gtugs sman bcos gnang ba dang/ gzhan yan grwa tshang dang khang tshan nas brtan bzhugs sku tshe tshe sgrub bla lha kag gi thugs dam bka' lung phyir phebs dgongs don zhabs rim 'bad sgrub dang/ gdan sa dang chos sde khag gi tshogs chen grwa tshang yongs la skyabs zhu bsnyen bskur mang 'gyed sogs zdog rim thabs shes 'bad sgrub ji ltar zhus kyang bstan 'gro'i gad chags lta bus bsdogs tu med par.*

The Sharpa Choje's obituary recorded the circumstances of his actual passing (*gshegs pa'i tshul*) in some detail, employing the standard phraseology of classical Tibetan texts:

> In the morning after washing and taking tea as usual, at 8:30, without [manifesting] any particular illness or additional pain at all, his mind dissolved into the sphere of emptiness, in order to exhort worldly-minded disciples to practice the Doctrine. (*Sheja*, September 1995:18-19)[43]

For the Ganden Ti, still more detail appeared:

> He performed his divination practice as usual and though a little bit unwell for some days there was no sign of serious illness and he had remained very comfortable. Just before 7 pm, when he normally performed the '60' ritual, he said "no need to do the 60 today, my time's up!" About two minutes past seven he looked reverentially towards the picture of the Dalai Lama on the altar in that small room he used for his divination, folded his hands together, breathed in and entered the clear light meditative equipoise in which he remained for seven days. (*Sheja*, October 1995:22-23)[44]

For senior lamas, the implication is always of a conscious decision on their part that their earthly presence has served its intended

---

[43] *Zhogs pa zhal khrus dang gsol chas 'char can ltar gnang rjes chu tshod 8 30 thog dmigs bsal bsnyun zug 'phar ma gang yang med par gdul bya rtag 'dzin can rnams chos la bskul phyir dgongs pa chos dbyings su thim par.*

[44] *Rnam kun bzhin thugs dam nyams bzhes mdzad cing\ zhag shas sngon nas sku khams cung Bde min bzhas nas yod kyang skur bsnyun zug sogs dza drag gang yang med par sku zhi ba'i ngang bzhugs mus nas de nyin phyi dro chu tshod 7 pa ma zin tzam la rnam kun drug cu ma 'bul gnang mdzad kyi yod kyang de nyin drug cu ma bzhengs mi dgos\ ngas bsdud tshar ba yin zhes bka' phebs cing\ de rjes chu tshod 7 dang skar cha 2 tzam la gzim chung mchod gshom steng du bzhugs pa'i thugs dam gyi rten gong sa skyabs mgon chen po'i sku par la thugs dad chen pos spyan gzigs te phyag gnyis thal mo sbyar ba'i stangs ka mdzad de bzhugs bzhin pa de ga'i mod la ljags dbugs bsdud te 'chi ba chos sku'i 'od gsal la snyoms par 'jug par mdzad de nyin mtshan bdun ring thugs dam la bzhugs, Zhi bar gshegs pa dga' ldan khri rin po che'i rnam par thar pa* ("Obituary of the Deceased Ganden Ti Rinpoche"). Three months earlier, *Sheja*'s brief death notice for him had included a short paragraph on the appointment of his successor: on 30 June 1995 Lozang Nyima, a Lharampa Geshe from Drepung Loseling monastery then holding the position of Jangtse Choje, was appointed by the Religious Affairs Department of the Dharamsala government (following approval by the Dalai Lama) to be the one hundredth Ganden Throneholder. See *Chos rig las khungs nas gnangs ba'i gnas tshul khag gsum* ("Three Matters Covered by the Religious Affairs Office"), (*Sheja*, July 1995:17–19).

purpose for that lifetime. In Buddhist terms theirs is the choice to leave a particular body and move on to another incarnation in order to best serve sentient beings. The act of passing away is always referred to as being the lama's final demonstration of the imperma- nence of conditioned phenomena and as stressing the need for spiritual practice. The standard phraseology–"in order to exhort worldly-minded disciples to practise the doctrine" (*gdul bya rtag 'dzin can rnams chos la bskul phyir*) appears time and again, as in the Ganden Ti and Sharpa Choje's obituaries. The ability to choose the time and place of death is well illustrated from *Bod kyi dus bab*'s brief report on Kalzang Thabkhay, a Drepung ex-abbot living in New Zealand who, at the end of June 1999, took a flight to China. Returning to his A mdo birthplace (Luchu Dzong), he "dwelt happily" in the local monastery for over a fortnight, then passed away (*Bod kyi dus bab*, 10 September 1999:4).[45]

Records of violent deaths are rare, though Lozang Gyatso's untimely death was a reminder of a darker side to Tibetan religious politics. *Sheja* viewed his murder at Dharamsala's Institute of Buddhist Dialectics on 4 February 1997 by a group of Shugden supporters in terms of his having "devoted his whole life to Tibetan religion, politics and the people," noting that he had been head of the dialectics school since its foundation in 1973 and in recent years an uncompromising critic of the Shugden protector practice. The report contained a brief biography but focussed more on the criminal dimensions of the events. It also covered the memorial rituals held two days later (attended by some 1,500 people) when his body had been brought back from Chandigarh hospital for cremation, con- cluding with what might be taken as his epitaph: "In short, his life was vast, his death was honourable too" (*mdor na khong gson pa ni rlabs chen yin la/ khong 'das pa'ang gzi brjid yin pa*) (*Sheja*, February–March 1997:31).[46] Eleven months later *Sheja* covered his death anniversary memorial service—held in the Dharamsala main temple and attended by about 1,000 people—at which his textual refutation of the Shugden practice 'A pure drop of truth' (*bden pa'i*

---

[45] *Yid skyo'i gnas tshul* ("Saddening News"). He died on 28 July 1999 at the monastery, Ganden Sherchin Chokhor Ling.

[46] Entitled *Yid shin tu skyo ba'i thabs sdug gnas tshul* ("Extremely Saddening, Shocking News").

tshang thig) was displayed (*Sheja*, January 1998:31).[47] In 1999 *Bod kyi dus bab* carried a call from his Institute for any material written by him for inclusion in a memorial volume.[48]

1.4 THE MEDITATIVE ABSORPTION PERIOD

Following what is conventionally regarded as the point of death, the lama's mindstream enters and remains in a state of meditative equipoise (*thugs dam*) or 'clear light meditative absorption' (*thugs dam 'od gsal*), often for a considerable period, without any deterioration in the state of the body taking place. The actual point of death then occurs at the end of that period. The number of days that a lama remains in such absorption, usually seated upright in meditational full lotus posture, is often mentioned as evidence of advanced spiritual attainment. Thus, *Sheja*'s obituary for the Ganden Ti noted that he "entered the death truth body clear light meditative absorption and remained [there] in a state of meditative equipoise for seven days and nights" (*Sheja*, October 1995:22-23).[49] *Bod kyi dus bab* (20 December 1999:20) attributed Rigyal Rinpoche's five-day period to his "pervasive excellent morality" (*tshul khrims dri bzang phyogs gang sar khyab pa byung ba*), recording that those who viewed him were struck by "a beautiful fragrance of morality and a radiance emitting from his *thug dam*."[50]

Departure from the *thugs dam* is referred to in terms of the "appearance of the nectar of the red and white mind of enlightenment" (*byang sems dkar dmar gyi bdud rtzi phebs*), which refers to a flow of blood and semen from the nose and genitals, respectively, marking the mindstream's departure and onset of deterioration of the corpse. The occurence of earth tremors or rainbows at that time is often recorded, with the implication of the lama possessing supermundane powers. *Bod kyi dus bab*'s obituary for Tidu Rinpoche (appearing as a paid advertisement, rather than a news report)

---

[47] *Lo mchod mchod 'bul* ("Anniversary Offering").

[48] *Gsung rtzom phyogs bsgrigs gsal bsgrags* ("Announcement on Publication of a Literary Work")(*Bod kyi dus bab*, 30 September 1999:6).

[49] *'Chi ba chos sku'i 'od gsal la snyoms par 'jug par mdzad de nyin mtshan bdun ring thugs dam la bzhugs, Zhi bar gshegs pa dga' ldan khri rin po che'i rnam par thar pa* ("Obituary of the Deceased Ganden Ti Rinpoche"),

[50] *Re zhig zhing khams gzhan du dgongs pa gtad pa* ("Mind Settled in Another Realm for a While").

described a rainbow appearing between two shrine buildings for about half an hour at the end of his three-day *thugs dam*. Also, a pillar shaped five-coloured rainbow emanating from the building housing his remains while a further rainbow rose from the crematorium into the sky, across which yet more rainbows spread. In support of these statements, the report emphasised that the many lay and ordained people present there had witnessed those phenomena.

Once the mindstream has left, disposal of the corpse can safely begin. Despite the lack of ready fuel on the Tibet plateau (and increasingly so in India), cremation is the usual means of disposal reserved for a lama's precious remains (*sku gdung rin po che*). That normally involves construction of a purpose-built enclosed (and often whitewashed) crematorium (*pur khang*), usually in the shape of a Buddhist reliquary stupa, with a chimney structure replacing the normal, elaborate finial.

1.5 SIGNS AND PORTENTS AT AND AFTER DEATH

Regarding the time of cremation, many reports record unusual optical or atmospheric effects, cloud formations, the direction of the smoke or the presence of particular birds circling, their number, colour and direction of flight. All such occurences are interpreted in relation to the lama's spiritual attainments or reincarnation prospects, given that Tibetans attach considerable significance to the appearance of paranormal phenomena in relation to a lama's birth, death or cremation. When Rigyal Rinpoche's pyre was lit, the report noted the sudden appearance above the crematorium of three white vultures, which then flew off to the west. That was taken as an indication of the direction in which the reincarnation would be found (*Bod kyi dus bab*, 10 December 1997:6).[51]

Reopening the sealed crematorium occurs on a day determined as propitious, usually by the lama in charge of the cremation. That could be days or weeks after the burning took place. Reports sometimes detail the metamorphosed relics (*ring bsrel*) found in the ashes, their number and size; Sharpa Choje's obituary noted that his "remains and relics casket" (*sku gdung ring bsrel za ma tog*) was

---

[51] *Yid skyo ba'i gnas tshul* ("Saddening News"). Similarly with Tidu Rinpoche's cremation, at which four white vultures were reported as appearing above the crematorium, circling anticlockwise; one then circled it three times in the opposite direction and left to the west (*Bod kyi dus bab*, 20 December 1999:20).

taken to his monastery and placed on his throne, before which cattas
were offered then devotional rituals performed (*Sheja*, September
1995:18).[52] The relics among Tidu Rinpoche's aquamarine-coloured
ashes formed a mandala pattern, among which "lay many marvels
beyond expression such as Sanskrit letters in the Lantsha script to
left and right" (*g-yas g-yon du lantsha'i yi ge gang byon sogs ngo
mtshar gyi lhag bsam brjod las 'das pa mang po zhig byung ba red*).
Sometimes body parts may remain untouched by the fire, which is
again ascribed to the power of the lama's spiritual practice. *Bod kyi
dus bab* noted that seven of Rigyal Rinpoche's joints were found
among the "many relics" in his ashes; on each of the 49 days of the
intermediate state (*bar do*), rituals were performed before them. The
report also listed the recipient of each joint.

1.6 REVIEWING MILESTONES

Next follows a chronological record of significant events in the
lama's life. References to birth may include the mother's significant
dreams. Regarding childhood, *Mangtso* viewed the Ganden Ti's
games—imitating religious pursuits such as making fire offerings,
ritual offering cakes (*gtor ma*) and giving teaching to playmates—as
evidence of his "not having any types of negative karmic predisposi-
tions [or] habits" (*las bag chags ngan goms kyi rigs gtan nas mi
mdzas*) (*Sheja*, October 1995:22).[53]

A wealth of detail usually follows: the monastery first entered,
dates of taking novice and fully ordained monk's vows and the
identity of the ordaining lamas. Particular prominence is given to any
contact with the thirteenth Dalai Lama, such as the receipt of vows
from him. Indeed, *Mangtso* marked the centenary of his accession to
secular and religious power in Tibet with a lead article on his life
(*Mangtso*, 15 October 1995:1).[54] Records of teacher/student relationships include *Sheja*'s coverage of the mutual exchange of roles
between the Dalai Lama and the previous Dilgo Khyentse Rinpoche.

---

[52] *Shar pa chos rje sku gshegs pa dang rnam thar snying bsdus* ("Death of the
Sharpa Choje and a Condensed Obituary").

[53] *Zhi bar gshegs pa dga' ldan khri rin po che'i rnam par thar pa* ("Obituary of
the Deceased Ganden Ti Rinpoche").

[54] *Dus dran gnyis 'dzoms srung brtzi zhus pa* ("Two Anniversaries Marked").
The second anniversary referred to was 125 years since the birth of Mahatma
Gandhi.

Thus these reports rapidly become a mine of biographical data. For exceptional individuals, the catalogue of accomplishments in all these areas can become truly breathtaking, including details of journeys to central Tibet and its monastic universities, sutra texts studied, the names of teachers, the level of Geshe Lharampa obtained,[55] retreats or pilgrimages completed,[56] oral transmissions of the entire Buddhist canon (the Kangyur and Tängyur texts) given and volumes of works composed.[57] The narrative then proceeds to tantric studies, usually detailing the rank attained in the Gelug hierarchy, from tantric chanting-master (*dbu mdzad*), disciplinarian (*dge skos*) up to abbot (*mkhan po*) and ex-abbot (*mkhan zur*). Thus Yeshe Dondrub, the Ganden Ti, spent six years as abbot of the Upper Tantric College then a further six as the Sharpa Choje, finally becoming the ninety-ninth holder of the throne of Ganden (*dga' ldan khri pa*) in Drepung monastery and thus head of the Gelug tradition of Tibetan Buddhism (*Mangtso*, 31 May 1995:5).[58]

---

[55] For Tibetan Gelug monks, the *dge bshad lha ram pa* degree is the zenith of non-tantric academic attainment. Yeshe Dondrub, the ninety-ninth Ganden Throne Holder, after passing his Geshe Lharampa examinations at age 45 in 1955, had been selected to participate in the traditional New Year debate on the five great treatises (*bka' pod lnga*), held before the Dalai Lama and a huge assembly of scholars during the 1956 Great Prayer Festival in Lhasa. There, he was awarded the pinnacle of Tibetan scholarly titles 'The First of the First Lharampa' (*lha rams ang dang po'i dang po*). See *Zhi bar gshegs pa dga' ldan khri rin po che'i rnam par thar pa* ("Obituary of the Deceased Ganden Ti Rinpoche") (*Sheja*, October 1995:22).

[56] Rigyal Rinpoche's *Bod kyi dus bab* biography (the first to appear as a paid advertisement, rather than as a news report) recorded that in Tibet he had offered many sets of full-length prostrations, including circumambulations of Mt Kailash, causing him to become known as 'Prostration Lama'. He had maintained that pitch of practice in India, reciting at least 700,000 *mani* mantras, offering hundreds of thousands of butter lamps at Bodh-Gaya and releasing 100,000 fish to remove obstacles to the Dalai Lama's longevity. See *Yid skyo'i gnas tshul khag gsum* ("Three Items of Saddening News") (*Sheja*, December 1997:30).

[57] Khewang Tsetan Zhabdrung's 'rough obituary' (*rnam thar rags tzam*) appeared in the "Introducing People" (*mi sna ngo sprod*) column of *Bod kyi dus bab*'s very first issue, see *Mkhas dbang tshe tan zhabs drung* ("Khewang Tseten Zhabdrung") (*Bod kyi dus bab*, 15 September 1996:6). Though he had in fact died eleven years earlier at Tashi Kyil monastery, he was still recalled within the exile Tibetan community as a grammarian, calligapher and lexicographer of great note, having taught at various institutions in western China.

[58] *Skyo gnas* ("Sad News"). A misconception common to many non-Tibetans is that the Dalai Lama, rather than the Ganden Ti, is head of the Gelug ('Virtuous Way') tradition. This may stem from the Gelug being numerically the largest of the four Buddhist traditions (Gelug, Kagyu, Sakya and Nyingma). Additional detail

The chronology inevitably covers activities in the diaspora, including visits to Tibet for rebuilding monasteries or educational initiatives. Dzeme Rinpoche, a noted educator and grammarian, established the first Tibetan secondary school in Lhasa, as well as a teachers college in India and publication of Tibetan language textbooks (*Sheja*, April 1996:26).[59] Lozang Tsondru was noted for having spent 28 years in Tibet and south India "teaching the path of religion to the people" (*mi dmangs la chos kyi lam ston mdze*) (*Bod kyi dus bab*, 20 May 1998:3).[60] Though much of Andzin Rinpoche's page and a half obituary (*Sheja*, July 1997:17).[61] comprised a history of his three predecessors and his many teachers, it did mention his establishment of a Tibetan settlement in Orissa, the building of monasteries and stupas, performance of retreats and pilgrimages in Bhutan and his status as a *terton*.[62] The Tibetan medicine text he located had, when opened, emitted a rainbow.

1.7 ENTREATIES FOR A QUICK RETURN

Nearly all entries conclude with a customary entreaty for the "speedy return of a 'supreme emanation' reincarnation" (*mchog gi sprul sku'i yang srid myur du byon pa*) of the lama (*Krung go'i bod ljongs*, 2000(3):2–5).[63] That can extend to publication of a prayer for recitation by the faithful. The Dalai Lama's recognition of Gendhun Chokyi Nyima as the eleventh Panchen Lama in 1995, included composition of a long life prayer for the boy, published in *Sheja*

---

provided on Yeshe Dondrub included his performance of a five-year retreat between the ages of 25 and 30. In his late fifties he took the great Yamantaka retreat. In 1964 (aged 53) he had taken part in a tantric retreat with the Dalai Lama, his two tutors and debating partners (in all over 30 senior lamas, at the Dalai Lama's Old Palace, above McLeod Ganj), at which he was awarded the supreme accolade of 'Tantric Master First Class' (*sngags rams ang dang po*).

[59] *Yid skyo'i gnas tshul* ("Saddening News").

[60] *Mnga' ris dga' chos dgon pas btang ba'i skyo gnas* ("Sad News Sent From Ngari Gacho Gonpa").

[61] *Zhi bar gshegs pa snga 'gyur rnying ma'i spyi zur a 'dzin rin po che'i rnam thar* ("Obituary of the Deceased Former Assembly Member for the Unreformed Nyingma, Andzin Rinpoche").

[62] A finder or revealer of hidden religious treasures (*Gter ma*).

[63] It included material on this aspect—for the very first time—in its 2000 obituary for Gungthang Rinpoche, *Gung thang rin po che sku phreng drug pa'i rjes dran du phul ba* ("Offered in Memory of the Sixth Gungthang Rinpoche").

(May 1995:7).[64] Worldly formalities are not overlooked—official messages of condolence sometimes appear as well as mention of the closure of Tibetan government offices and shops for a half day or more as a mark of respect for the deceased, as on the day after the Ganden Ti's death (*Mangtso*, 31 May 1995:5).[65]

1.8 SECULAR FIGURES

Naturally, the subjects of these obituaries extend well beyond the religious sphere, with over twice as many entries covering Tibetan politicians and government officials of both pre-1959 Tibet and the refugee era. No obituaries of women appeared. The longest entries were from the independent press, providing detailed information on individuals perceived as outstanding Tibetan patriots, notably Phuntsog Tashi Taklha (1923–99) (*Bod kyi dus bab*, 20 June 1999:4; *Sheja*, June 1999:17)[66] and Lhamo Tsering (1924–99) (*Bod kyi dus bab*, 20 January 1999:3; *Sheja*, January 1999:19).[67]

Takhla had maintained a high profile for over half a century: He was married to the Dalai Lama's elder sister in 1937, was a China scholar in Nanking under the Kuomintang, translator at the 1951 signing of the Seventeen-Point Agreement, Security Minister in Dharamsala and a member of the first Tibetan fact-finding delegation to Tibet in 1979. *Sheja* noted that the Chinese always remarked on his Mandarin skills. His later research work covered the history of Tibet's relationship with the Mongols then, in 1997, a three-volume autobiography; six days before his death, the Dalai Lama had come to visit him at his home in Dharamsala. The longest obituary over the whole period was *Bod kyi dus bab*'s finely-crafted two pages on

---

[64] *Zhabs brtan gsol 'debs bzhed don lhun 'grub ces bya ba bzhugs so* ("Spontaneous Fulfillment of Aspirations and Entreaties for a Long Life"). It followed a traditional structure and metre: twelve verses, each containing four nine-syllable lines.

[65] *Skyo gnas* ("Saddening News").

[66] *Bka' zur stag lha phun tshogs bkra shis mchog sku tshe'i 'phen pa rdzogs pa* ("Completion of Lifespan for Former Minister Taklha Phuntsok Tashi"), and *Yid skyo'i gnas tshul* ("Saddening News"), respectively.

[67] *Bde srung bka' blon zur pa lha mo tshe ring mchog sku tshe ma brtan pa* ("End of an Enduring Life for Former Security Minister Lhamo Tsering"), and *yid skyo'i gnas tshul* ("Saddening News"). After 1959 Lhamo Tsering had managed both the entire CIA operation at the Mustang guerilla base in Nepal as well as all clandestine activities in Tibet until 1973. He was Security Minister in the Dharamsala government in the mid-nineties.

Lhamo Tsering (composed by the historian Tashi Tsering), which portrayed him as someone intimately involved in the cause of Tibetan independence, who had never put personal advancement ahead of the common goal of the struggle for Tibet. *Sheja*'s shorter offering completely ignored his guerilla days, focussing instead on his subsequent literary output. It was a history-cum-memoirs (*lo rgyus snying bsdus*) of modern Tibet as part of a projected ten volume series "Aggression and National Salvation" (*btzan rgol rgyal skyob*), which he had begun in 1987. The Dalai Lama twice visited him in hospital in Delhi and his cremation drew some 1,500 people as well as closure of Tibetan offices and shops.

Other freedom fighters received considerable attention too. Apha Alo (Lozang Tsewang), born in Litang in 1903 and who died in a hospital in Lanzhou in 1997, bore witness to life in eastern Tibet under the Manchus, Christian warlords, Kuomintang and Communists (*Sheja*, October 1997:20, 28).[68] As elder brother of the reincarnation of the great lama, Jamyang Shaypa, he had lived at Tashi Kyil monastery meeting both the Dalai and Panchen Lamas on their return journey from Peking in 1955. Imprisoned for ten years during the Cultural Revolution he too was lauded as a great patriot who had strongly upheld Tibetan culture and values throughout his life. On a wider canvas, reportage of non-Tibetan figures covered prominent Indians (possibly to bolster Indo-Tibetan relations), world leaders and those involved with Tibet, such as Moraji Desai, former prime minister of India *Sheja*, October 1997:20, 28; *Mangtso*, 15 April 1995:6),[69] Mother Teresa (*Sheja*, September 1997:17; *Bod kyi dus bab*, 10 September 1997:6),[70] Francois Mitterand (*Sheja*, January 1996:19),[71] and the assassinated Yitzhak Rabin (*Sheja*, November 1995:22).[72] *Sheja* avoided any obituary for Deng Xiaoping (see

---

[68] *Yid skyo'i gnas tshul* ("Saddening News").

[69] *Srid zur mora ji rde saye sku gshega par bod gzhung mang nas mya ngan zhus pa* ("Condolences Offered by the Tibetan Government and People on the Death of Former Prime Minister, Moraji Desai"), and *Rgya gar gyi srid blon zur pa mo ra ji dhe sa'e mchog dgongs pa rdzogs pa* ("Former Indian Prime Minister Moraji Desai Dead"),

[70] *Gzhan phan snying rjes'i bdag nyid ma rdar kre ri sa mchog dgongs pa rdzogs pa* ("Death of the Supreme Mother Teresa, the Embodiment of Compassion Benefitting Others"), and *Ye shu'i btzun ma mah dhar te re sa sku grongs pa* ("The Christian Nun, Mother Teresa, Dead"),

[71] *Pha ran si'i srid zur sku gshegs pa* ("Former French President Passes Away").

Tibetan Bulletin, March–April 1997:12).[73] The death from cancer of Michael Aris, renowned scholar of Tibet and Himalayan cultures and husband of Burmese Nobel Laureate, Aung San Suu Kyi, received a small entry in 1999 (*Bod kyi dus bab*, 10 April 1999:4).[74]

Untimely deaths, such as suicides or assassinations (though little sensationalised) seem to fascinate the Tibetan press. Saturation coverage was given to Thubten Ngodup's April 1998 self-immolation in New Delhi for the cause of Tibet; *Bod kyi dus bab*'s banner headline quoted his final cry of "Long Life to the Dalai Lama! Victory to Tibet!" (10 April 1999:4).[75] His obituary appeared as part of a frontpage news report. The suicide of the (unnamed) caretaker of the ninth Panchen Lama's stupa at Tashilhunpo appeared in *Mangtso*'s front page 'News from Tibet' column; he had refused to denounce Gendhun Chokyi Nyima as the true Panchen Lama reincarnation (*Mangtso*, 15 August 1995, 1).[76] A brief entry in *Bod kyi dus bab* covered Tenzin Sonam, a Tibetan volunteer in the Indian army, killed in action in 1999 at Kargil fighting Muslim irregulars from Pakistan (30 September 1999:2).[77]

---

[72] *Ai si ral gyi srid blon bkrongs pa'i skyo gnas* ("Sad News of Israeli PM Death").

[73] An article on his passing did appear in the *Tibetan Bulletin*, drawn from the Dalai Lama's 20 February 1997 condolence message to Beijing: "Deng's Death, China's Loss."

[74] *Bod rig pa'i mkhas dbang zhig 'das grong* ("A Tibet Scholar Dead").

[75] *Bod mi zhig gis rang lus la me sbar nas sku srog btang ba* ("A Tibetan Sacrifices his Life Through Self-immolation"). The report also provided brief biographical details: born in 1934, he was a monk in Tashilhunpo monastery until fleeing to India as a refugee, then a roadworker in the Himalayas. After 23 years in Tibetan settlements in south India, he entered political activism (from the mid-nineties), participating in peace marches and volunteering for fasts untill death. *Sheja*'s obituary (May 1998:3) noted that in his final days after the self-immolation, the Dalai Lama visited him in hospital urging him to be calm, not angry, and that he would offer prayers for Ngodup to gain a precious human birth in his next life. *Sku gshegs dpa' bor mya ngan rjes dran zhu* ("Memorial to the Passing of an Heroic Being").

[76] *Rang srog bcad pa* ("Committed Suicide").

[77] *Bod kyi dang slob dmag mi zhig 'das grongs* ("A Tibetan Volunteer Soldier Killed").

2 BEIJING COVERAGE 1995–99

Beijing's sole report was a modest eight lines, at the end of a 1997 "Tibet News in Brief" (*bod khul gyi gsar 'gyur gnad bsdus*) section, on the passing (*dgong pa chos dbyings su thims*) in Lhasa of Tenzin Jigme, the sixth Reting Rinpoche, aged 50 (*Krung go'i bod ljongs*, 1997(2):47).[78] He was described as "the great patriotic and spiritual lama who was very well known in Tibetan Buddhism;" the only other information given was his official political and religious positions in the PRC and Tibet Autonomous Region (TAR) hierarchies.[79] Reting remains significant in Tibetan religious politics as one of the few lamas who traditionally can have a critical say in the succession of a new Dalai Lama and act as regent during his absence or minority. Given the blatantly political controversy over the Panchen sucession since 1995, Reting's passing assumed far greater significance when Beijing announced, on 16 January 2000, its unilateral recognition of two-year old Sonam Phuntsok as his reincarnation.[80] It remains a matter of conjecture whether the timing of the recognition was a direct reaction to the defection of the seventeenth Karmapa to India some two weeks earlier or simply mere coincidence. *Sheja* denounced the recognition as a meaningless political appointment (January 2000:24).[81]

---

[78] *Rwa sgreng bstan 'dzin 'jigs med mchog mya ngan las 'das pa* ("Death of the Supreme Reting Tenzin Jigme").

[79] Four were listed: permanent member of the Chinese Buddhist Association standing member; member of the TAR Assembly; Vice-chairman of the Tibet branch office of the China Buddhist Association and head of the Buddhist Association in Lhasa city.

[80] The sixth Reting had died on 13 February 1997; Sonam Phuntsok's birth (given as 13 July that year) was only six months later. On the time period required for reappearance of a reincarnation, see the "Gendhun Chokyi Nyima" section, below.

[81] *Rwa sgreng gi yang srid zer ba ngo 'dzin byas pa* ("Recognition of a So-called Reting Reincarnation"). It noted that although the haircutting ceremony was conducted in Lhasa's main temple, no recognition document for a successor had been issued by the Dalai Lama (who had done so for the sixth Reting, born in 1948). Thus the child would never be accepted by the Tibetan government or people; the Chinese had merely found out that he might have been reborn, so had seized on that for their own political ends. The report also noted that the Dalai Lama's 3 December 1999 divination had indicated the situation regarding return of a true reincarnation remained unclear. He had recommended recitation of the names of Manjushri

That minimalist treatment of Reting's death is in stark contrast to *Krung go'i Bod ljongs* glowing six-page account (with four colour photographs) of Sonam Phuntsok's recognition as the seventh Reting Rinpoche, that appeared in March 2000—far removed, in content, format and style, from the previous cursory treatment of Tenzin Jigme. This time a whole column was devoted to the sixth Reting's life, though in line with Beijing's standard reportage, it focussed simply on his religious titles, political posts held, meetings with Chinese leaders and involvement in establishing a 'new' Tibet.

RETURNS

1 SIGNIFICANT EVENTS CONCERNING A REINCARNATION

Tibetan Buddhist belief in a cycle of lives accepts that reaching certain levels of mental development enables a person's stream of consciousness to exert varying degrees of control over the time and place of subsequent rebirth. That ability is usually ascribed, in part at least, to a reincarnate's motivation of seeking to serve all other sentient beings, as opposed to mere propulsion into another rebirth through the force of previously accumulated karmic dispositions. Tibetans tend to perceive their reincarnate lamas (*yang srid*) as manifestations of that ideal; newspaper reportage of the processes involved in their return and recognition covers a number of steps:

- ritual offering practices (*zhabs rten*), carried out after the predecessor's death, to avert hindrances and obstacles to the *yang srid*'s return, success and longevity;
- the search (*btzal 'tshol*) stage, in which names of likely candidates are gathered, considered by specially convened search committees and submitted to a senior lama for a decision, often requiring divination;
- formal recognition is followed by the offering of a full set of monk's robes to the child and its family. The passage from a secular to a monastic life is marked by the naming (*mtshan gsol*) and haircutting (*gtzug phud*) ceremonies;

400,000 times to assist with the identification process and had also composed a prayer for Reting's speedy return.

- enthronement, or the 'entering the doctrine ceremony' (*chos zhugs mdzad sgo*),[82] covers the reincarnate's formal entry into a monastery, usually the one most closely associated with the predecessor. It also denotes commencement of religious studies and involves appointment of one or more tutors; and
- the *rig chung* (small reasoning) ceremony marks the start of the child's training in debate.

Correct identification of a reincarnate may occur within a framework of competing claimants and so is a serious and significant undertaking in Tibetan society, sometimes attracting considerable community attention and thus receiving corresponding column space in the Tibetan press. Interest inevitably focusses on those lamas whose attainments or stature were exceptional in their immediately preceding life, so the finding of a true incarnation and his recognition by the Tibetan establishment are crucial events not just in religious terms but in a political and social dimension too. Indeed, considerable political influence can extend well beyond Tibetan society over a constituency of the faithful, as has occurred in recent years with both the Panchen Lama and Karmapa lineages. In a sense, that reportage, in aggregate, comes close to being a sacred directory covering Tibetan religious culture. Publication of such material ensures Tibetans can participate in their collective memory and thus assist in maintaining a national identity.

1.1 RECOGNITION OF REINCARNATIONS

Reports on the recognition of reincarnations covered just five individuals (Table 2), though the quantity of material on the Panchen Lama far exceeded that for the others combined. There were no reports of female reincarnates, possibly reflecting the relatively limited opportunities for Tibetan women, particularly nuns, to study and practise their religion.

---

[82] *Krung go'i bod ljongs* also referred to a "lineage continuity ceremony" (*mtshan gnas rgyun 'dzin*) in the case of the seventh Reting Rinpoche.

TABLE 2

Announcements of the recognition of reincarnations

Issue	Name	Previous Incarnation
Sheja		
95.5	Panchen Lama	
	Gendhun Chokyi Nyima	2nd highest lama
96.1	Dilgo Khyentse Rinpoche	Head of Nyingma tradition
98.10	Changkya Tulku	Gelugpa, d. in Taiwan 1958
99.2.25	Rato Chuwar Rinpoche	Senior Gelugpa lama
Mangtso		
95. 5 15	Panchen Lama	
	Gendhun Chokyi Nyima	
Bod kyi dus bab		
98.?	Ninth Zhabdrung Karpo	Bon master
98.10	Changkya Tulku	
Krung go'i bod ljongs		
96.1	Panchen Lama	
	Gyansten Norbu	
Mi dmangs brnyan par		
96.4	Panchen Lama	
	Gyansten Norbu	

2 THE ELEVENTH PANCHEN LAMA

The political, religious and social importance to Tibetan society of the Panchen Lama's reincarnation guaranteed a massive reportage on both the Dalai Lama's recognition of Gendun Chokyi Nyima and China's recognition of Gyantsen Norbu. Qualitatively, however, that material is biographically elusive as the primary focus remained on the political sphere; the usual biographical details became secondary, even minor, considerations. Still, this was the only coverage by both camps of the same reincarnation,[83] thus providing an opportunity to contrast their respective approaches, which are easiest followed chronologically.

---

[83] Coverage of Reting Rinpoche's reincarnation occured just after the period under discussion (see *Sheja*, January 2000, and *Krung go'i bod ljongs*, March 2000).

2.1 GENDUN CHOKYI NYIMA

The Dalai Lama's recognition of Gendun Chokyi Nyima was
momentous news for all Dharamsala papers, which portrayed the
event as reimbuing Tibetan Buddhism with a political stance that
could not be ignored. *Mangtso*'s 15 May 1995 banner headline
proclaimed "Confirmation of the true reincarnation of the Omniscient Panchen Rinpoche", above a photograph of the child.[84]
Along with a separate article reproducing the full Tibetan text of the
Dalai Lama's 14 May recognition statement (*ngos 'dzin gsal bsgrags
bka shog*), *Mangsto* also touched on the Dalai Lama's account of the
selection and divination process he had employed in reaching that
outcome. This was taken from his address at the Dharamsala main
temple announcing the recognition. *Mangtso* opined that the PRC
might well recognise the child, given Beijing's need to demonstrate
some accomodation with the Tibetan people and their religion,
reasoning (wrongly, as it turned out) that since no Tibetan would
recognise a rival Panchen installed by the Chinese, it was in Beijing's interests to accept the Dalai Lama's choice. The article's
conclusion briefly summarised the tenth Panchen Lama's achievements, stressing his unceasing efforts for the nation and people of
Tibet, which had yielded "not insignificant results too" (*'bras bu
yang mi nyung ba song yod*).

The *Tibetan Bulletin* noted that the boy had been born a mere
three months after the passing of his predecessor, who had stated in a
taped address made a couple of days before his death, that from a
Tibetan Buddhist perspective there was no need for up to a year to
pass before the birth of a successor. The tenth Panchen had cited the
case of the seventh Dalai Lama, born a year before the passing of his
predecessor, thus affirming that a realised being could manifest in
many forms simultaneously (*Tibetan Bulletin*, May–June 1995:9).[85]
In the same month *Sheja* presented a withering six-page indictment
of *Krung go'i bod ljongs*, condemning it as a "black propaganda
publication" (*dril bsgrags yig cha nag po*) containing mainly
"fabrications and distortions incompatible with the reality of events"

---

[84] *Kun gzigs pan chen rin po che'i yang srid 'khrul bral nges rnyed byung pa*
("Confirmation of the True Reincarnation of the Omniscient Panchen Rinpoche").

[85] "The seventh Reting Rinpoche (installed by China) was born only five months
after the death of the predecessor.

(*dngos yod gnas tshul dang mi mthun pa'i rdzun gtam 'khyog bshad*; *Sheja*, May 1995:12–18).[86]

2.2 DIVINATION PROCESS USED BY THE DALAI LAMA

Sheja's verbatim report of the Dalai Lama's 14 May address was of particular biographical interest, through providing valuable detail on the discovery process itself (*Sheja*, May 1995:4–6).[87] He noted that after the tenth Panchen's passing, ritual offerings had been made for his speedy return[88] and consultations held with the PRC about a Dharamsala search committee's visit to the tenth's Tashilhunpo stupa and Lhamo Lhatso (*lha mo'i bla mtsho*), the lake principally used for obtaining visions of the whereabouts of reincarnations. Beijing's strictly political focus meant those feelers were rebuffed, instead Tibetans in India took the initiative, with the exile Tashi-lhunpo monastery managing to check the Dharamsala area and central and outlying areas of Tibet and Ladakh. That drew a blank until the beginning of 1995. From biodata of the most promising candidates (20–30 histories, most with accompaying photographs) the Dalai Lama culled those lacking the appropriate marks and signs (*rtags dang mtshan ma*) of a reincarnate, though he did not mention what those were.

His "final choice process" (*mtha' ma'i thag gcod byed stangs*) involved a number of sets of divination. The first was to settle whether any of the remaining candidates could be the true reincarnation, followed by dice to identify the most promising children. He repeated that procedure three times (in accordance with his own practice), all of which consistently gave the same result. Not wishing

---

[86] *Rgya'i rtsom yig la dpyad pa'i gtam btsan 'dzul par mdun lam med pa* ("Lack of Perspective in Aggressive Analytical Rhetoric in Chinese Publication").

[87] *Spyi nor gong sa skyabs mgon chen po mchog nas/ kun gzigs ye shes kyi nyi ma pan chen thams cad mkhyen pa'i yang srid mchog sprul rin po che sku tshe mdzad 'phrin rgyas pa'i chos phyogs kyi mchod 'bul thugs smon rgya che mdzad pa* ("Extensive Prayers and Religious Offerings made by His Holiness the Dalai Lama, the Supreme Great Protector, for the Longevity and Expansive Deeds of the Precious Supreme Emanation Reincarnation of the Omnisicient Sun of Wisdom, the All-Knowing Panchen"). The speech was given at the main temple in Dharamsala on the day of the third lunar full moon, auspicious as the anniversary of the Buddha giving the Kalachakra root *tantra* as well as the anniversary, in the Hinayana tradition, of the Buddha's birthday.

[88] These would also have involved tantric practices to avert obstacles and hindrances to the life and success of the reincarnation.

to rely on dice alone, he turned to the tsampa ball technique (*zan brtags sgril*),[89] which also produced an identical result: "Thinking 'this one's it for sure!', I made my decision" (*'di rang tan tan re 'dug bsams pa'i thog nas thag bcad pa yin*).

Regarding the child's whereabouts, he worked from the available biodata but combined that with the ninth Panchen Lama's approach used in identifying the Thirteenth Dalai Lama (no details given).[90] All these procedures pointed towards the Tsongkha area of A mdo (in northeast Tibet)—the same region where the tenth Panchen had been born and to which he had returned a number of times prior to his death. For the Dalai Lama, that suggested a close link between that region and the Panchen's enlightened activities (*mdzad pa 'phrin las*), carried out over successive lifetimes. Taking into account the Panchen's "extremely great responsibilities" as well as the pressing need for resolution of the succession, he made a final decision that Gendhun Chokyi Nyima was the correct child.

Thereafter, the Dharamsala press watched developments closely, with *Sheja* expressing concern only a month later about his well-being as his whereabouts were already unknown (June 1995:27).[91] The report noted China's justification to the UN for taking him into detention—a parental request to the government to protect him from "the risk of possible abduction by splittists" (*kha drel bas btzan khrid bya rgyu'i nyen kha*). Five months later, when the PRC had coerced even sick lamas and tulkus in Beijing into accepting China's own candidate, *Mangtso* admitted that China would never accept the Dalai's choice (15 November 1995:1).[92]

2.3 GYANTSEN NORBU

With Tibetan Buddhism seen as a rallying point for Tibetan nationalism, any element of religious biography in the Beijing press

---

[89] This method of divination involves rolling up slips of paper (a candidate's name written on each one) in small balls of tsampa. On reciting the name, the ball containing the name of the true reincarnation is supposed to move.

[90] No details were given of Thubten Chokyi Nyima's method, which, the Dalai Lama stated, had been passed on to him orally by his own tutors.

[91] *Pan chen dge 'dun chos kyi nyi ma bkag nyar byas pa rgya nag gis khas blangs pa* ("China Accepts Panchen Gendhun Chokyi Nyima Detained").

[92] *Rgya gzhung nas pan chen yang srid gsar pa bsko 'char* ("The Chinese Government Selects a New Panchen Reincarnation"). Reportedly, Gungthang Rinpoche strongly expressed support for the correctness of the Dalai Lama's choice.

featured only to the extent of serving Beijing's policy agenda on Tibet. The noticeable increase in *Krung go'i bod ljongs'* reportage, mostly translations of material from Chinese,[93] was presumably another facet of China's strategy of seeking to ensure control over the next Panchen—in readiness for the crucial role he might play in the recognition of a fifteenth Dalai Lama. To help legitimise its approach, Beijing did facilitate a formal, though rushed, recognition process—in an attempt to satisfy Tibetan Buddhist traditions. Fortuitously, that led to the unprecedented publication of valuable biographical material concerning this illustrious line of reincarnates. Further, the many references in that material to aspects of the tenth Panchen's life shed further light on his often controversial religious and political status.

The Beijing press, like its Dharamsala counterpart, sought to extract maximum propaganda mileage through its publications. Thus *Krung go'i bod ljongs'* first 1996 cover showed Gyantsen Norbu—clad in yellow silk robe and cap—enthroned after the 29 November 1995 golden urn selection ceremony; inside was a full colour centrefold of those events, including Drogmi Rinpoche, his future tutor, carrying out the haircutting ceremony.[94] Ideological support for the Chinese position came in the form of a four-page translation of State Councillor Li Ruihan's speech from the 13 November 1995 edition of *Renmin Ribao* (*Krung go'i bod ljongs*, 1996(1):2–5).[95] It bluntly stated that Dharamsala's selection was:

- contrary to Chinese law;
- the political work of the Dalai Lama's splittist clique who sought to make trouble in Tibet; and
- split China by reversing the well-settled system and history of patriotic and religious order in the Panchen succession.

---

[93] Their vocabulary mostly shuns transliterated Chinese loan words with syntax and grammar maintaining a Tibetan pedigree, albeit distinct from non-PRC writings.

[94] The centrespread's headline read thus: *Pan chen sku phreng bcu pa'i yang srid gser bum dkrugs te ngos 'dzin gnang ba dang gser khrir mnga' gsol gyi mdzad sgo chen po* ("Recognition of the Tenth Panchen Reincarnation through Shaking the Golden Urn and the Great Ceremony of Ascending the Golden Throne").

[95] *Pan chen rin po che'i yang srid btzal 'tshol 'go khrid tshogs chung gi tshogs 'du thengs gsum pa'i thog gi gtam bshad* ("Speech at the Third Sub-committee Meeting by the Leadership Searching for the Reincarnation of the Panchen Rinpoche").

A further six reasons supporting use of the golden urn ritual[96] all related to identification of the correct successor necessitating that process. In the same issue, "Tibet regional news in brief" (*bod khul gyi gsar 'gyur gnad bsdus*) castigated the Dalai's lack of integrity, as "breaching the rules and laws of dharma." By contrast, it portrayed the TAR's selection process (agreed to by Beijing) as striving for national unity and accomplishing the great aims of Buddhism through fulfilling the wishes of the faithful (*Krung go'i bod ljongs*, 1996(1):42).[97] The second 1996 issue maintained that approach, with a six-page article on Gyantsen Norbu's selection and recognition including the text of the Chinese government's official announcement on the issue. Yet, the article provided only scant information on the identification process itself, simply noting its commencement in June 1989, visits to the sacred lakes for visions, appropriate rituals performed and three meetings of the official search committee over the years (*Krung go'i bod ljongs*, 1996(2):2–6).[98] Throughout, the emphasis was on Chinese involvement in the recognition process; indeed, many of the accompanying photographs focussed more on prominent Chinese officials, at the expense of Gyantsen Norbu. In the same issue, a five-page article on his enthronement ceremony (held on 8 December 1995 at Tashilhunpo monastery) credited Drogmi Rinpoche with the statement:

---

[96] The six reasons were: its use since 1792 to identify the correct candidate; its according with religious custom; being carried out by a qualified tulku endorsed by the Chinese government; the ritual process requiring government supervision; identification of a tulku needing government approval; the Chinese government's need to supervise the ensuing enthronement ritual.

[97] *Kun gzigs pan chen rin po che'i yang srid btzal 'tshol 'go khrid tshogs chung gis gros tshogs 'tshogs pa* ("Meeting of the Sub-committee Leadership Searching for the Reincarnation of the Omniscient Panchen Rinpoche").

[98] *Kun gyi mig lam sdud pa'i cho ga dan/ lo brgyar 'phrad rgyu dkon pa'i mdzad chen bstod* ("The Ritual Convened Before the Eyes of All and Praise of a Great Event which is Rarely Met in a Hundred Years"). The search committee had met in 1991, 1993 and 1995. In November 1995 Beijing organised its own ritual to choose a boy as Panchen and issued an extraordinary document describing mysterious events and signs surrounding his birth and infancy that were taken as proof of his being the true reincarnation.

Now I am happy from the depths of my heart that the great goal of enthroning the reincarnation has been easily accomplished, through the kindness of the Buddha's teachings and the Chinese government. (*Krung go'i bod ljongs*, 1996(2):7–11)[99]

This blaze of publicity was replicated in *Mi mang brnyan par*. Its April 1996 'Special Feature' (*deb 'di'i ched rtzom*) was entitled "The magnificent Snowy Land Buddhist Doctrine—steps in deciding the eleventh Panchen" (*gangs ljongs bstan pa'i gzi dpal—pan chen sku phreng bcu gcig pa thugs thag chod rim*). Pride of place among the shots of the Lhasa selection ceremony was reserved for one subsequently taken in Beijing: Jiang Zemin receiving a *khatag* from Gyantsen Norbu, with a beaming Li Ruihan looking on; again the Chinese dominate the composition, in what appears to be a symbolic statement of Tibetan Buddhism's subservience to the paramount interests of the Chinese state (*Mi dmangs brnyan par*, April 1996:6–11).[100] Six months later the magazine ran a follow-up 'Special Feature' entitled "The eleventh Panchen takes the novice vows" (*pan chen sku phreng bcu gcig pas dge tshul gyi sdom pa mnos pa*). It included six panoramas of that event, held at Tashilhunpo monastery on 1 June 1996 (*Mi dmangs brnyan par*, October 1996:38).

2.4 DHARAMSALA ON THE 'FALSE PANCHEN'

Dharamsala's stance necessitated a forthright response to these events, with *Sheja*'s initial riposte entitled "Tibetans cannot accept a Panchen reincarnation who was chosen by coercion (November 1995:17).[101] Published shortly before the golden urn ceremony took place, it noted that the 75 lamas, tulkus and TAR Communist Party members, including a hospital patient, brought together in a Beijing hotel to endorse the PRC's approach had been held there under

---

[99] *Yang srid gser khrid mnga' gsol ba'i don chen 'di Bde blag ngang legs grub byung ba de'ang sangs rgyas brtan pa dang krung dbyang srid bzhung rang gi bka' drin yin pas kho bo'i sems gting nas dga' po byung* in *Pan chen sku phreng bcu gcig pa gser khrir mnga' gsol gyi mdzad sgo chen po* ("The Great Ceremony of Enthroning the Eleventh Panchen").

[100] President Jiang Zemin instructed him to "uphold the leadership of the Party, have a deep love for the nation, for the people and for socialism." The boy reportedly replied, "I thank the Party's Central Committee and President Jiang. I will certainly study hard and become a patriotic and religious Living Buddha."

[101] *dbang shed kyis gtan 'bebs byas pa'i pan chen gyi yang srid bod mis khas len byed mi thub.*

duress and were pressured to denounce the Dalai's choice. *Sheja* saw the importance of the issue to the Chinese leadership reflected in visits to the hotel by leading members of the Chinese establishment—Jiang Zemin, Li Peng and Li Ruihan—whose uniform message had been to seek destruction of the Dalai clique and its policies. For *Sheja*, calling the drawing of lots from a golden urn 'definitive' was simply political theatre, in which no one could place any confidence. Sheja reiterated Dharamsala's stance that over 95% of Tibetans, even TAR cadres and officials, believed in the Dalai Lama's choice.

Following Gyantsen Norbu's selection, *Sheja*'s tone grew harsher. A report entitled "Nauseating theatre of settling the false Panchen reincarnation" (*pan chen gyi yang srid rdzun ma gtan 'bebs byed pa'i skyug bro ba'i zdos gar*) (December 1995: 7–9), tersely outlined the golden urn ceremony,[102] referring to him as the "child who poses as the reincarnation" (*yang srid du rdzus pa'i bu*). *Mangtso*'s equally condemnatory "'Panchen reincarnation' selected by the Red Chinese government" (30 November 1995:3)[103] insisted that no Tibetan doubted the Dalai Lama's choice, whereas Beijing's coercive approach ran counter to legal usage and history. It asserted that Drogmi Rinpoche, whose only public appearance in Lhasa had been to actually draw the lot from the urn, had been taken there from Beijing two weeks earlier and kept in what amounted to a comfortable prison, with no outside communication. Mangtso's next issue took a similar line under the heading of "Special protest announcement at the Red Chinese government's coercive creation of a false Panchen Rinpoche reincarnation" (15 December 1995:4).[104] The *Tibetan Bulletin* summed up Dharamsala's position: Beijing had

---

[102] The report provided an outline of the proceedings: the urn contained slips of paper on each of which was one of three candidates' names (in Chinese); the contents were stirred by Lama Tsering, head of the Tashilhunpo Democratic Management Committee; a slip was chosen by the Ganden geshe Drogmi Rinpoche and handed to the TAR government leader, Gyantsen Norbu, who announced that the child Gyantsen Norbu was the new Panchen Rinpoche. The child then ascended the throne and Drogmi Rinpoche conducted the hair cutting ceremony, giving him the name Lozang Jampa Lhundrup Chokyi Gyalpo. Celebrations were then held at his (not identified) abode in Lhasa, rather than in the Jhokhang.

[103] *Rgya dmar gzhung nas "pan chen yang srid" bsko bzhag.*

[104] *Rgya dmar gzhung nas dbang shed kyis pan chen rin po che'i yang srid rdzun ma bzos par rgol gtam ched bsgrags.*

simply invoked an obsolete lottery system as a useful weapon in its continuing war with Tibetan Buddhism. It also carried the Dalai Lama's statement about China's announcement of a rival Panchen: "the search and recognition of the Panchen Rinpoche's reincarnation is a religious matter" for which he had diligently conducted all the necessary religious steps, thus "my recognition of the Panchen Rinpoche's reincarnation cannot be changed" (*Tibetan Bulletin*, September–December 1995:2, 4). *Sheja* sought additional support from overseas Chinese sources, running a six-page feature in April 1996 from *The Nineties*, a Hong Kong periodical, which viewed China's continuing control of the Panchen as Beijing's tool for ensuring control over the choice of a fifteenth Dalai Lama (*Sheja*, April 1996:16–22)[105]

Meanwhile *Krung go'i bod ljongs'* Panchen coverage continued unabated. The cover of the third 1996 issue showed Gyansten Norbu at a Tashilhunpo ceremony unveiling a plaque, its four golden Chinese characters (penned by President Jiang Zemin) reading "Protect the nation, benefit the people" (*rgyal srung dmangs phan*); pictures inside that issue showed the child participating in rituals there. The final 1996 issue provided brief profiles and pictures of the two unsuccessful candidates in the golden urn ritual, Ngawang Namdrol and Kunzang Wangdu (*Krung go'i bod ljongs*, 1996, 4:8–10).[106] At the same time, the first anniversary of the false Panchen's enthronement, *Sheja* reaffirmed Dharamsala's disgust with China's approach, asserting that Tibetans participating in the golden urn ritual had had no choice but to present a false outward appearance, whereas in their hearts they accepted the Dalai Lama's choice. It vigorously asserted that, both in Tibet and internationally, Gyaltsen Norbu had no cachet at all, the first anniversary ceremonies in Beijing being just another charade from a desperate Chinese government (*Sheja*, December 1996:19–20).[107]

---

[105] Zhao Ming and Tan Li. *Pan chen yang srid gser bum dkrugs skabs kyi phyi mis mi shes pa'i nang gyi gnas tshul* ("The Inside Story, not Known by Outsiders, of when the Golden Urn was Drawn [for] the Panchen Reincarnation").

[106] *Dad pa'i stobs kyis bstan pa 'dzin la spro* ("Joy at Holding the Teachings through the Strenght of Faith").

[107] *Rgya mi'i pan cen gyi lo 'khor dus dran dang gang can bla ma* ("Marking the Anniversary of the Chinese Panchen—and Gangcen Lama"). The article disparaged Ganchen Lama, the first ordained Tibetan from outside China to publicly accept the false Panchen (through offering him a catta at a public audience). It noted that he

Over the next two years the Panchen issue took a lower profile. Beijing offered piecemeal information on Gyantsen Norbu's activities, such as his meeting with Premier Li Peng in the Great Hall of People (*Krung go'i bod ljongs*, 1997(1):43),[108] initiations from Tashikyil's Akhu Lama into the Yamantaka, Guhyasamaja and Heruka tantras (*Krung go'i bod ljongs*, 1998(5):2)[109] and his large donation for those affected by Yangzi river flooding (*Krung go'i bod ljongs*, 1999(1):43).[110] Photo essays on his life in Beijing included a 1997 centrespread, dealing with a ceremony at the Yonghegong temple on the first anniversary of his enthronement (*Krung go'i bod ljongs*, 1997(1): centrespread)[111] and receiving a long life initiation at the Western Yellow *gonpa* in 1998 (*Krung go'i bod ljongs*, 1998(4):front endpaper).[112] Dharamsala went quiet too, with only *Bod kyi dus bab*'s brief mention in August 1998 of "False Panchen propaganda", which noted that photo shops in Tibetan areas of the PRC were now obliged to display and sell pictures of "the boy from Lhari Dzong, Gyaltsen Norbu." It also noted that Chinese government offices in eastern Tibet were displaying his picture, with Labrang monastery's offices forced to do likewise (*Bod kyi dus bab*, 31 August 1998:3).[113]

2.5 THE TENTH PANCHEN LAMA

The 1999 tenth anniversary of the tenth Panchen Lama's death sparked a resurgence in press interest. *Bod kyi dus bab*'s regular "Comment" (*bsam tshul*) page covered the "Confidential situation

---

resided at a Tibetan Buddhist centre in Italy, implying that he was not representative of the mainstream Tibetan exile community.

[108] *Pan chen sku phreng bcu gcig pas cungli li pheng mjal bar phebs pa* ("The Eleventh Panchen Comes to Meet Premier Li Peng").

[109] *Pan chen er te ni sku phreng bcu gcig pa mchog gis gsang dbang mnos pa* ("The Supreme Eleventh Panchen Erdeni Receives Tantric Initiations").

[110] *Pan chen bcu gcig pa mchog gis gnos skyon thebs khul la zhal 'debs gnang ba* ("The Supreme Eleventh Panchen Makes a Donation to Disaster Areas").

[111] *Dga' ldan byin chags gling nas pan chen sku phreng bcu gcig pa gser khrir mnga' gsol gyi lo 'khor mdzad sgo gzab rgyas spel ba* ("The Extensive Ceremony at Ganden Yinchag Ling on the Anniversary of the Enthronement of the Eleventh Panchen").

[112] *Pan chen er ti ni sku phreng bcu gcig pa mchog gis nub kyi dgon pa ser por gsang dbang zhus pa* ("The Supreme Eleventh Panchen Erdeni Attends a Secret Initiation at the Western Yellow Monastery").

[113] *Pan chen rdzun ma khyab bsgrags* ("False Panchen Propaganda").

regarding the sudden death of the supreme Omniscient One" (31 January 1999:2).[114] It offered no fresh insights—rather it simply queryied his sudden death, given his perfect health in the period beforehand. *Sheja* reviewed the Dalai Lama's 25 January tenth anniversary speech at the Dharamsala Tibetan Children's Village, which provided some anecdotal material of biographical interest on their meetings and travels in Tibet, China and India (February 1999:4–12).[115] Recalling his letter to the Panchen about possible outcomes of the March 1959 events in Lhasa—written from Lhoka Kyishong during his escape to India—he somewhat ruefully recalled that he had never been able to find out whether it ever reached its destination. He characterised the tenth Panchen as "a peerless holy being" who had selflessly worked for Tibetan Buddhism and for the teachings of Maitreya Buddha—a hero who had risked his own life for the Tibetan people's culture and freedom, as demonstrated by his famous 70,000 character petition to the Chinese government.

Meanwhile, three successive editions of *Krung go'i bod ljongs* continued to chart Gyantsen Norbu's upbringing and development:

- his first large public audience in Shigatse on 28 June, with attendee Dekyi Tsering volunteering, through tears of joy, that:

  > The Party's religious policy is very good. I am praying that this policy will not change. My meeting the supreme Panchen Rinpoche is completely the result of the Party's good policy! (*Krung go'i bod ljongs*, 1999(4):44)[116]

- conducting various religious rites in Lhasa and Shigatse:
  1) Pictured arriving at Tashilhunpo in his yellow limousine, strewn with *khatag* and a stupa finial on its roof, he gave a long life initiation reciting over 10,000 mantras in two hours. His "small speech" extolled the faithful to love the Party and China's socialist system, strengthen national unity through guarding the principle of one China and quoted him as "loving the religion of the faithful, I con-

---

[114] *Kun gzigs mchog glo bur dgongs pa rdzogs pa'i gsang ba'i gnas bab.*

[115] *Kun gzigs pan chen sku phreng bcu pa chen po zhi bar gshegs nas lo bcu 'khor bar rjes dran gzab rgyas zhus pa* ("Elaborate Commemoration on the Tenth Anniversary of the Passing of the Omniscient Great Tenth Panchen").

[116] *Pan chen sku phreng bcu gcig pas mjal kha gnang ba'i byed sgo chen po thengs dang po mdzad pa* ("The Eleventh Panchen Conducts his First Great Public Audience Ceremony").

tinue to spread the fine patriotic and spiritual system of the tenth Panchen" (*nang mi dad pa'i chos lugs la dga' zhen sgos pan chen sku phreng bcu pa'i rgyal gces chos gces kyi srol bzang mu mthud s?dus spel*). (*Krung go'i bod ljongs*, 1999(5):3–9)[117]

2) Some personal details appeared at the end of the article: Now almost ten years old, he rose daily at 6 30 to study for five or six hours; had mastered 290 rituals and 480 Chinese characters; loved running, football, ping-pong and bike riding; indoors he had toys, a camera and a television. The centrespread pictures included a meeting with the young Karmapa, but they are seen touching heads, as if equals, rather than the latter prostrating to Gyantsen Norbu, as if his junior in the religious hierarchy.

- the sixth issue covered Drogmi Rinpoche's justification of his golden urn role, with statements like "the choice I made for sure was not mistaken and I'm happy and comfortable with my decision" and "I didn't rebel in 1959 or flee abroad" (*Krung go'i bod ljongs*, 1999(6):2–5).[118] At least it did provide two pages of information on his 82 years: birth in a poor nomad household, recognition at age eight as the first Drogmi Tulku and gaining his Geshe Lharampa degree in 1958[119] in the same group as the Dalai Lama. Inevitably, there was a swipe at the Dalai who "was just a nominal first-class Lharampa" (*tah la'i bla ma ni ming thog gi ang dang po yin*) whereas others in that group "were the real thing" (*don dngos thog gi ang dang po yin*). The chronology jumped the period 1959–73, resuming with his resignation as abbot of Lhasa's Shol gonpa in order to take up a succession of political appointments, including running a tulku training school.

In sum, the Panchen material shows that this important biographical strand still has far to run, with controversy over the succcession and its likely impact on a possible Dalai Lama reincarnation far from resolved. However, eliciting accurate information from any of these

---

[117] *Dad pa'i mchi ma ngang gis 'dzum* ("Smiles Through Tears of Joy").

[118] *Ngas bdams pa'i lam 'di dngo gnas nor mi 'dug* ("The Path I Chose is Definitely not Mistaken").

[119] Editorial error for 1959.

sources and its accomodation within a biographical framework continues to require circumspection, given the selectivity of material presented by both camps to suit their wider political and propaganda agendas.

3 OTHER REINCARNATES — DHARAMSALA

3.1 RECOGNITION

Coverage of the four other recognitions reported in the Dharamsala press ranged from a frontpage headline to just a few lines hidden away in a backpage "Dharamsala" (*dha sa*) column.

- For Dilgo Khyentse Rinpoche, *Sheja* detailed the circumstances relating to his discovery, including a long and detailed list of the Nyingma lamas who had been involved in the search. Though providing the date of the Dalai Lama's certificate of recognition (15 December 1995), no date of birth was given (*Sheja*, April 1996:4).[120]

- The circumstances leading to discovery of the eighth Changkya Tulku at the relatively late age of 18 were sufficiently unusual to warrant headline treatment in *Bod kyi dus bab* (20 October 1998:1).[121] Unlike *Sheja*'s presentation, it provided considerable detail on the steps in the discovery process,[122] as well as featuring a separate paid article on the Changkya lineage (*Bod kyi dus bab*, 20 October 1998:3)[123] Both reports agreed on the predecessor's death in Taiwan in 1958, with no successor found. The Dalai Lama's 1996 divination had suggested a rebirth in Tibet,

---

[120] *Skyabs rje dil mgo mkhyen brtze rin po che'i yang srid 'khrul bral nges rnyed byung ba* ("Recognition of the Genuine Reincarnation of the Protector Dilgo Khyentse Rinpoche").

[121] *Cang skya sku phreng bdun pa'i yang srid ngos 'dzin gnang ba* ("Recognition of the Seventh Changkya Tulku Reincarnation"). See also *Gong sa mchog nas lcang skya sprul sku ngos 'dzin dang mtshan gsol mdzad pa* ("The Dalai Lama Recognises and Names Changkya Tulku"), (*Sheja*, August 1998:16).

[122] The Dalai Lama had first been consulted in 1983 but his list of 23 names for further investigation could not be followed up in Tibet. A condensed list, presented to him in 1997, elicited no response; when offered again in 1998, he asked for a shortlist concerning the three great monasteries in south India. From some 35 names, he focussed on 20 recent arrivals from A mdo, all living in the Gomang college of Drepung monastery. Eventually he narrowed the field to Donyo Gyatso.

[123] *Lcang skya rin po che'i sku phreng rim byon gyi ngo sprod rags bsdus* ("Condensed Introduction to the Successive Incarnations of Changkya Rinpoche").

with the child by then a sixteen-year old monk in the Tsongkha region. So it was. He had returned in 1980, been ordained at an early age, came to India as a refugee in 1998, dwelling in Drepung monastery in south India. He was formally recognised by the Dalai Lama on 11 August 1998.

- For the reincarnation of the eighth Zhabdrung Karpo, a Bon master and great *mo*[124] thrower who had died in 1991, *Bod kyi dus bab* drew on a 19 January 1998 Xinhua report which had covered the recognition in Qinghai Province of six-year old Yanggyal Bum (31 January 1998: 1).[125] According to the provincial government's search committee head, its work had been done secretly through the agency of Kumbum monastery and in accordance with Tibetan religious practice. Kumbum's then-abbot, Akya Rinpoche,[126] had been consulted, with related divination conducted by the predecessor's tutor.

- In the case of the ninth Rato Chuwar Rinpoche a small back page item in *Bod kyi dus bab* recorded the 17 February 1999 recognition of Tsering Donden as his reincarnation (25 February 1999:4).[127] It touched on the Dalai Lama's divination, which had indicated a return in Dharamsala, where the ninth had lived. The robe offering and enthronement ceremonies were stated to be taking place "soon," although they were never reported. *Sheja*, which had covered his predecessor's passing in detail in September 1992, gave no coverage at all.

3.2 OFFERING THE ROBES

The next rite of passage, the offering and donning of an ordainee's robes (*na bza' sgron 'bul*), can involve considerable ceremonial, as described in *Sheja*'s report for the very young Dilgo Khyentse Rinpoche. Fourteen days after recognition by the Dalai Lama, an elaborate robing ceremony was held at the Maratika cave in Nepal, a

---

[124] Divination using dice.

[125] *Zhabs drung dkarpo sku phreng brgyad pa'i yang srid gtan 'bebs byas yod zer* ("Reincarnation of the Eighth Zhabdrung Karpo Reportedly Settled").

[126] Later the same year Akya Tulku fled from Tibet, rather than have to formally accept Gyaltsen Norbu as the real Panchen Lama. See *A kyah sprul sku skyabs bcol du yong ba* ("Akya Tulku Comes as a Refugee") (*Bod kyi dus bab*, 10 November 1998:6).

[127] *Rwa stod chu dbar yang srid ngos 'dzin* ("Rato Chuwar Reincarnation Recognised").

pilgrimage site closely associated with the Dilgo Khyentse lineage. It was attended by representatives of all Tibetan Buddhist traditions as well as by those from the Dharamsala and Bhutanese governments. The report listed all their offerings, as well as details of the long life ritual performed for him the next day; it concluded with the Dalai Lama's statement that he would perform the hair cutting ceremony "soon", thus indicating the stature of this particular reincarnation (*Sheja*, January 1996:4).[128]

3.3 HAIRCUTTING CEREMONIES

This ceremony, involving removal of a final tuft of hair (usually by a senior lama) from the reincarnate's almost shaved pate, signifies departure from a worldly into a religious life. Three such reports appeared in *Sheja*, which devoted a column to the one for Dilgo Khyentse Rinpoche, conducted by the Dalai Lama in his palace in February 1996 (March 1996:17),[129] describing related *khatag*, mandala and prayer rituals. Three months later *Sheja* briefly noted a 2 May ceremony for Tenzin Jamyang Rinpoche, reincarnation of the Sakya abbot, Sanggyay Tenzin (June 1996:24).[130] In the case of the "Chinese Panchen" (*rgya mi pan chen*), *Sheja* simply noted in passing that after his selection by Drogmi Rinpoche, the latter quickly carried out the haircutting ceremony (December 1995: 7–9).[131]

---

[128] *Skyabs rje dil mgo mkhyen brtze rin po che yang srid 'khrul bral nges rnyed byung ba* ("Recognition of the Genuine Reincarnation of the Protector Dilgo Khyentse Rinpoche").

[129] *Gong sa mchog nas dil mkhyen mchog sprul rin po che'i dbu skra gtzug phud 'bul bzhes mdzad pa* ("The Dalai Lama Carries out the Haircutting Ceremony for the Dilkhyen Supreme Emanation Rinpoche"). See also *Tibetan Bulletin* (March–April 1996:32).

[130] *Chos rig las khung nas gnang 'byor* ("Report from the Religious Affairs Office"). It stated that be would enter the Guru Sakya monastery at Ghoom, above Darjeeling, "in due course."

[131] *Pan chen gyi yang srid rdzun ma gtan 'bebs byed pa'i skyug bro ba'i zdos gar* ("Nauseating Theatre of Settling the False Panchen Reincarnation"). *Krung go'i Bod ljongs* also referred to the ceremony, see "The path I chose is definitely not mistaken" (1999(6):2–5). The Chinese, though not wishing to elevate religious ceremonial, politically had to accept some ritual in order to validate their chosen child (in the eyes of Tibetans and outsiders).

3.4 ENTHRONEMENT

Dharamsala's only other report on this stage covered the Drigung
Chennga Dragpa Jungnay reincarnation, in a ceremony carried out in
India by the head of the Drigung Kagyu tradition, Chetsang Rinpoche, on 15 March 1999. Curiously, no details of the actual event
appeared, instead just an outline of the origins of the lama's title and
lineage (a fusion of the unreformed Nyingma and Drigung Kagyu
lines), which stretched back to the time of the fifth Dalai Lama
(*Sheja*, April 1999:28).[132]

4 OTHER REINCARNATES — BEIJING

Beijing's remaining articles covered the present reincarnations of
four notable reincarnations, the Karmapa, Gungthang Rinpoche,
Dorje Phagmo, and Reting Rinpoche, as well as three lesser figures.

4.1 THE SEVENTEENTH KARMAPA

Through the 1990s Beijing had pinned its hopes of controlling
religious affairs in Tibet on Urgyen Trinley, the seventeenth
Karmapa,[133] who was being groomed as a patriotic figure loyal to the
CCP and expected to make statements expressing approval of
Chinese policies. With his enormous spiritual authority within and
outside Tibet and a lineage far older than those of the Dalai or
Panchen Lamas,[134] he was a unique figure recognised by both Beijing
and the Dalai Lama in 1992 when seven years old as the true seventeenth reincarnation. Coverage of his activities was low-key
throughout this period and always tailored to the PRC's policy

---

[132] *'Bri gung spyan sna grags pa 'byung gnas kyi yang srid khri 'don zhus pa*
("The Drigung Chennga Dragpa Jungnay Reincarnation Enthroned").

[133] A rival seventeenth Karmapa, Trinley Thaye Dorje, had been enthroned in
New Delhi in 1994 at the behest of the Sharmapa, one of the four regents governing
the Karma Kagyu school after the Sixteenth Karmapa's passing in 1981.
Historically, the Sharmapa was empowered to identify and recognise Karmapas, the
present incumbent having been confirmed by the sixteenth Karmapa as second in
rank within the Karma Kagyu tradition. Thus, controversy now dogs that tradition in
terms of which of the two recognised Karmapas can validly claim the ultimate
symbol of Kagyu authority — the sixteenth's famous Black Hat — which is due to
occur on the (correct) seventeenth's twenty-first birthday.

[134] The first recorded instance of recognition of a Tibetan reincarnation was that
of the Karmapa in 1284 C.E.

position on Tibetan Buddhism. Nonetheless, the following items do contribute towards a biographical thread:

- 'News in Brief' in 1995 noted his completion of the basic level of religious textual studies (*dma' rim gyi chos dpe slob sbyong*), which was marked by the traditional *rig chung* ceremony held at his Tsurphu seat (*Krung go'i bod ljongs*, 1995(3):43).[135]
- A 1999 article on his second tour of China's eastern provinces (*Krung go'i bod ljongs*, 1999(3):2–10)[136] detailed his visit to Beijing's Yonghegong and his cordial meeting with State Councillor Li Ruihan in the Great Hall of the People. But as with *Krung go'i bod ljongs'* 1995 report of his first visit east (in September–October 1994), this article's eight pages were more a vehicle for fanfaring China's economic advances, with him pictured in Shanghai inspecting a Pudong city development model and also television sets.
- The next 1999 issue again focussed on the meeting with Li Ruihan, who urged him to "work patriotically and for dharma, for economic progress, social development and a happy life for the community of peoples." Given the Karmapa's defection to India just a year later, the content of his response is noteworthy:

Now, my tour of China's interior complete and definitely taking Chairmen Jiang Zemin's and Li Ruihan's advice as a basis, I will study well and offer prayers for peace in our nation, maintenance of the people's happiness, good fortune for increasing [our] nationalities' unity and expansion of a patriotic and spiritual Tibet. (*Krung go'i Bod ljongs*, 1999(2):45).[137]

---

[135] *Karma pa sprul skus dma' rim gyis chos dpe slob sbyong gnanag tshar ba* ("The Karmapa Tulku has Finished the Basic Level of Religious Textual Studies").

[136] *Sprul sku karma pa mchog gis mes rgyal nang sar zhabs sor bkod pa* ("The Supreme Karmapa Tulku Comes to China's Heartland").

[137] *Da res nang sar gzigs skor du phebs rjes ngas nges par du kru'u zhi cang tze rmin dang kru'u zhi li ru'i hon gyi bka' slob gzhir bzung slob sbyong yag po byed pa dang rgyal gces chos gces kyis bod kyi dar rgyas dang/ mi rigs mthun sgril dang gong 'phel 'gro phyir legs skyes 'bul rgyu dang nga tsho'i rgyal khab zhi Bde dang mi dmangs Bde sdod yong ba'i smon 'dun zhu rgyu yin* in *Li ru'i hon gyis karma pa sku phreng bcu bdun par mjal 'phrad gnang ba* ("Li Ruihan Meets with the Seventeenth Karmapa"). Anecdotal information suggests that the Karmapa refused to make statements supporting the Chinese-appointed Panchen or prostrate to him at their 4 July 1999 meeting.

4.2 GUNGTHANG RINPOCHE

Jigme Tenpai Wangchuk, the sixth Gungthang Rinpoche (1926–
2000), also exerted tremendous spiritual authority in Tibet.
Rehabilitated by China after the Cultural Revolution, he was
consistently portrayed by *Krung go'i bod ljongs* as a shining example
of religious freedom in Tibet, though no mention was made of his
unswerving support for both the Dalai Lama and Tibetan
nationalism. Considerable biographical information appeared in a
six-page 1995 article covering the tenth Kalachakra initiation he had
given, this time at Tashi Kyil monastery to some 200,000 people
(*Krung go'i bod ljongs*, 1995(2):13–18).[138] It included a one-page
review of his life up to the 1950s, covering somewhat random
milestones such as his recognition, studies, *geshe* degree obtained at
the prodigously early age of 19 and other Kalachakras he had given.
No mention was made of his 21 years in Chinese prisons—the
chronology simply carrying on from the 1980s to cover three more
Kalachakras and a visit to America. The report was phrased to suit
the Party line, thus he simply "worked for others," rather than "for
the Tibetan people," as his *Sheja* obituary subsequently put it. Not
unexpectedly, *Krung go'i bod ljongs* emphasised his advice to
Tibetans to respect the Party leadership, be involved in political
campaigns and support the one-China policy.

Considerably more detail on his life appeared in a March 2000
four-page full colour obituary, "An offering in memory of the sixth
Gungthang Rinpoche" (*gung thang rin po che sku phreng drug pa'i
rjes dran du phul ba*)(*Krung go'i bod ljongs*, 2000(3):2–5.).[139]
Though it sought to portray his support for "Tibet's democratic
reform" and "the Chinese government's policy of religious freedom," it also took in his social welfare activities for the cause of
Tibetan education. His prison years were euphemistically glossed
over: "Ddue to various political circumstances, he was otherwise
engaged away from his monastery for 21 years" (*Krung go'i bod
ljongs*, 2000(3):3).[140] Most unusually for atheist Beijing, the report

---

[138] *A lags gung thang tshang gis dus 'khor gyi dbang thengs bcu pa gnang ba*
("Ala Gungthangtsang Gives his Tenth Kalachakra Initiation").

[139] *Gung thang rin po che sku phreng drug pa'i rjes dran du phul ba* ("An
Offering in Memory of the Sixth Gungthang Rinpoche").

[140] *Chab srid kyi don rkyen sna tshogs kyi rkyen gyis khong rang dgon pa dang
kha brel nas sna gzhug lo ngo nyer gcig phyin.*

ventured into his death ceremonies, going so far as to mention the "many metamorphosed relic pills" (ring bsrel ril bu mang po) found in his ashes. Indeed, the article even concluded with an entreaty for his speedy return—the presentation of these aspects coming much closer to the traditional obituary style employed by the Dharamsala press. As with the magazine's January 2000 article on Reting Rinpoche, this apparently sympathetic presentation may indicate some refinement in China's policy towards Tibetan Buddhist affairs. Certainly, these lavish articles are clear evidence of Beijing's growing involvement in (and manipulation of) the traditional Tibetan religious framework—seemingly as a tool in the quest for control over important reincarnations.

The final 1999 issue covered "Conversations between the sixth Gungthang and the tenth Panchen Rinpoche" (Krung go'i bod ljongs, 1999(6):15–20),[141] which comprised a number of anecdotes of their meetings and travels together over the forty years from 1949. The rather ponderous article provided little of biographical significance, save perhaps a record of their last conversation two days before the Panchen's sudden demise. Following the latter's consecration of a stupa at Tashilhunpo, after which he had held audience for 10,000 people, Gungthang had advised him that "in order to spread the Buddhadharma, it's now most important you take care of yourself well!" (sangs rgyas kyi bstan pa spel phyir/ da lta khyed kyis sku gzugs la thugs cag yag po gnang rgyu de ches gal che ba red).[142] Not unexpectedly, the article made no mention of Gungthang's subequent refusal to recognise Gyantsen Norbu.

4.3 DORJE PHAGMO

Tibet's most celebrated female reincarnation, the twelfth Dorje Phagmo (then aged 53) of Samding monastery, was the subject of a

---

[141] Gung thang sku phreng drug pa dang pan chen rin po che sku phreng bcu pa'i bar gyi gtam rgyud ("Conversations Between the Sixth Gungthang and the Tenth Panchen Rinpoche").

[142] A different perspective appeared in Sheja's March 2000 obituary for him. It recorded that he held firm to the Dalai Lama's choice of Gendhun Chokyi Nyima as the eleventh Panchen, never accepting the Chinese-appointed Panchen and stating publicly that he was not afraid of returning to prison for that stand. Two days after his 1 March 2000 death, the Dalai Lama had attended public rites in Dharamsala for his passing; Drepung Gomang, his monastery in south India, held a week of memorial rituals, Yid skyo gnas tshul ("Saddening News") (Sheja, March 2000:24).

four-page article in 1995 (*Krung go'i Bod ljongs*, 1995(3):25–28).[143]
Besides descriptive material on the history of her lineage, biographical details for the period up to 1960 (all with a strong pro-China
slant) covered her recognition at age five, installation at Samding,
her baseless fear of the PLA's arrival in 1951 (despite splittists
warnings of "the Red Chinese plan to murder lamas and tulkus"
(*gung khran tang gis bla sprul dmat gsod gtong rtzis yod*)), and her
forced removal to India in 1959 by "counter-revolutionary bandits"
(*ngo log jag rkun tsho*). There, it informed, she thought only of
returning home. Contact with the Chinese consulate in Kalimpong
had yielded a flight to New Delhi, thence through Pakistan, Afghani-
stan, and Moscow to Beijing where both the Party and the people had
applauded her patriotic action. From Lhasa in 1960, the account
abruptly jumped to 1995, mentioning just her political appointment
as Vice-Chair of the TAR People's Assembly.

4.4 RETING AND OTHER TULKUS

A seven-page article covered recognition of the seventh Reting
Rinpoche. Both its length and lavish use of colour headlines and
photos suggested a Chinese push to build up the child's credentials.
Further support came in the form of considerable detail on the line of
Reting reincarnations, which stressed their pro-Chinese stance
(*Krung go'i bod ljongs*, 2000(2):2–7).[144] It also dealt with the search
process for the sixth's successor, various recognition ceremonies
performed in Lhasa's Jhokhang for Sonam Phuntsok, his ceremonial
first entry to Reting monastery as well as his family background. It
concluded with a statement that his enthronement would take place
at "an auspicious time" during the Iron Dragon year (the 2000–01
lunar year); that event, held at Reting on 14 July, was later covered
in a single page colour photo essay (*Krung go'i bod ljongs*, 2000(5):
rear endpaper).[145]

Finally, a 1995 article by Lhalu Tsewang Dorje entitled "On
events surrounding the recognition of my three boys as reincarnates"
displayed a reporting pattern very close to that of the Dorje Phagmo

---

[143] *Bsam sdings Rdo rje phag mos bdud rtzi ril bu bsgrubs pa'i skor gleng ba*
("Report on Receiving Nectar Pills From Samding Dorje Phagmo").
[144] *Bstan pa'i mdzad chen* ("Important Doctrinal Ceremony").
[145] *Rwa sgreng sku phreng bdun pa mchog gi khrir gsol mdzad sgo gzab rgyas
'tshogs pa* ("The Supreme Seventh Reting's Elaborate Enthronement Ceremony").

article (*Krung go'i Bod ljongs*, 1995(2):30–4).[146] For each son, reference to recognition in the 1950s was followed by a sudden jump to 1995 and the political position each then held. Once again, potentially useful biographical strands are tempered by the paramouncy of political correctness:

- the second son, Jigme Choying, Vice Chairman of the Shigatse Buddhist Association, had been recognised by the sixteenth Karmapa in 1951 as the reincarnation of the ninth Tagna Tulku. His robe offering ceremony took place in Lhasa in 1952;
- the third son, a member of the Tibet Religious Association, had been recognised in 1954 (following divination by the Dalai Lama) as the reincarnation of the Sera lama Phurcog Rinpoche and had commenced religious studies in 1958; and
- the fourth son, Vice-Chairman of the Tibetan Peoples Religious Affairs Office, had been recognised and enthroned in 1955 as the reincarnation of the ChA mdo lama, Chagra Tulku (again following similar divination).

THE SYSTEM OF REINCARNATION

Arguably, the role of the tulku system transcends religion's usual universal function as an explanation of suffering and a template for salvation; it can be viewed more as a symbol of Tibet's identity and civilisation, through going well beyond just ensuring a renewal of Tibet's past in simple religious terms. However, the reincarnation of important political figures, the Dalai and Panchen Lamas, the Karmapa and Reting Rinpoche, is far from being a purely religious phenomenon. The political and economic dimensions of the tulku system ensure its close, if not crucial, linkage with the struggle over the future of Tibet. In that respect, the Panchen Lama controversy exemplifies Beijing's growing interest in influencing the selection of important reincarnate Tibetans. Now seeming to regard Tibetan Buddhism itself as a potential threat to Chinese rule in Tibet, Beijing has embarked on a strategy designed to exercise control over the reincarnations of leading lamas, a policy also likely to further exacerbate the splits over religion and ideology prevalent in the Tibetan diaspora. Dharamsala's anxiety over these issues was

---

[146] *Ngos kyi bu gsum sprul skur ngos 'dzin byas pa'i gnas tshul skor.*

reflected in a spate of articles pondering the system's implications for Tibet's future, particularly the Dalai Lama succession.

The newspaper *Mangtso*'s 31 May 1995 editorial (3), entitled "Reincarnate controversy" (*yang srid rtzod rnyog*) looked at the issue generally, starting with the adverse effect on Tibetans of *New York Times* and *Newsweek* reports covering problems facing the Spanish ten-year old reincarnation of Lama Thubten Yeshe. Asking "How could that possibly be Tibetan Buddhism?" (*bod kyi nang chos ni de bas kyang ga la yin*),[147] it castigated the Tushita Tibetan Buddhist organisation run by the child's Western disciples, alleging that they had put out a lot of false publicity and rumour at the time of his recognition. That misinformation had been seized on by some Western media and subsequently fed into the Indian press, thus eroding Tibetans' standing in India. The editorial also sought to stress the importance of reincarnates not seeking wealth and fame. It cited the paper's 15 April edition that year, which had reported the discovery of four tulkus in comfortable circumstances in Taiwan as well as the "unusual" (*ngo mtshar ba*) case of a lama in America recognising a laywoman as a tulku,[148] who had then moved on from Tibetan Buddhism to found a music society. The editorial saw birth into poor circumstances as a more appropriate indicator for tulku recognition, citing the cases of the present 'true' Panchen and the Karmapa, both of whom had come from poor nomad backgrounds.

1 A FIFTEENTH DALAI LAMA

Increasing concern amongst Tibetans in 1997 over recognition of a future Dalai Lama led the Dharamsala press to publish a number of his speeches, that set out his own views on the subject. *Bod kyi dus bab* quoted at length from a June address:

> Should I die whilst here in exile and if it's the wish of the vast majority of the Tibetan people that my reincarnation is needed, then I can say with certainty that it would only occur somewhere in the world outside [China]; I would not come into the hands of the Chinese. Why so? The purpose of a reincarnation returning is that where something has been started in a previous life and the outcome remains incom-

---

[147] For the editor, those divisive circumstances exemplified the antithesis of all that for which the tulku system supposedly stood.

[148] Catherine Burroughs, a Brooklyn (New York) hairdresser, was recognised as the reincarnation of Jetzunma Akhon Lama, a female Tibetan adept.

plete, a successor is required; otherwise, by not staying to see it through, you couldn't know whether what had been started in a former life would be ruined in the present one. But though it's uncertain if I'll die whilst we remain in exile, who knows whether my reincarnation would possess my own stream of consciousness. Anyway there's plenty of potential left in the present fourteenth incarnation! Best of all, if the Tibetan people want it, in all likelihood it would certainly happen at a place outside [China]—never into the hands of the Chinese. I can say that with certainty. Understood? (*Bod kyi dus bab*, 10 June 1997:1)[149]

He took a similar line that year in a 29 July address to the "Dharamsala people long life ritual preparation committee" (*dha sa mi mang rtan bzhugs gra sgrig tshogs chung gi tshogs mi rnams*)—then in the process of organising a ritual for his longevity (*Bod kyi dus bab*, 10 August 1997:3, 5)[150] This time he drew on examples from Tibetan history of an incumbent tulku identifying his own successor, though saw no reason why he should leave a will or testament to cover the

---

[149] *Ngas kyang tshur phyogs 'dir gal srid nga btzan byol la yod pa'i ring shi ba dang/ ci ste bod rgya che'i mi dmangs kyi 'dod pa la nga'i wang sprul cig dgos kyi yod pa yin na/ de ni nges par du rgya mi'i lag par med pa'i 'dzam gling phyi logs la yong gi re ma gtogs/ rgya mi'i lag 'og tu yong gi ma re ces ngas thag bcad nas shod gyi yod/ ga re yin zer na/ yang srid yong ba'i dgos don btzugs nas da lta 'dras bu yongs su ma smin par lhag bsdad pa de'i mjug skyel mkhan zhig yong dgos pa re ma gtogs/ tshe gong ma des mgo btzugs pa da lta mtha' bskyel rgyu lus bsdad pa der gtor bzhig gtong bar yong shes kyi ma red/ de 'dra yin dus/ ci ste nges med nga tsho btzan byol du sdod pa'i ring nga shi ba yin na/ nga'i skye ba nga rang gi rnam shes ngo ma de yin min gang shes te/ gang ltar da lta'i sku phreng bcu bzhi pa las 'byon thang che ba zhig dang/ legs pa shig bod mi dmangs kyi 'dod par yod na tan tan yong mdog kha po re/ de yong sa yang phyi logs la yong gi ma red ma gtogs/ rgya mi'i lag par rtza ba nas yong gi ma red/ de ngas thag bcad nas bshad thub kyi re/ shes song ngam/* in *Bod kyi bla na med pa'i dbu khrid gong sa mchog gis bod rang btzan dang sku'i yang sprul skor la bka' slob bka' drin btzal ba* ("Tibet's Incomparable Leader the Dalai Lama has Kindly Given an Address on Tibetan Independence and His Reincarnation"). Arguably, the disappearance of Gendhun Chokyi Nyima and the subsequent designation of a Beijing-appointed Panchen were a dress rehearsal for what may occur after the present Dalai Lama's death. The mere fact that he has said also that his successor, if there is one, would not be born in Tibet and would be unlikely to stop Beijing authorities from 'discovering' its own Dalai Lama. Indeed, Beijing's interest and involvement in 'reincarnation politics' now extends to announcements that even searches for reincarnations by Tibetan monks must have Chinese approval, likewise with the recognition of authentic reincarnations.

[150] *Gong sa mchog gis bod don dang sku'i yang srid skor la bstzal ba'i bka' slob* ("The Dalai Lama's Address Given on the Tibet Question and His Reincarnation").

contingency of his own sudden death in exile. *Sheja*'s longer coverage of that address (August 1997:4–10) noted his views that the question of recognition was one for Tibetan society generally, rather than just being a matter for a particular lama's household, and that the manner in which the present reincarnation system functioned depended on the type of karma previously accumulated by all concerned. In conclusion, he sought to reassure his audience about his determination to carry on working for Tibetans:

> The body's healthy, mind's happy, I sleep well and have got a good appetite; so no need for you to be anxious even after you've offered the long life ritual. Rest easy![151]

2 OTHER MATERIAL

Related items in the Dharamsala press consistently stressed the underlying religious nature and purpose of the tulku system and sought to defuse China's overtly political approach to the Dalai Lama succession:

- In 1998, *Bod kyi dus bab*'s article on "Tulkus and Tibetan Custom" (28 February 1998:4)[152] looked at China's attitude to

---

[151] *Gzugs po ni Bde thag chod dang/ sems ni skyid thag chod yod/ gnyid ni skyid po khug gi 'dug/ lto chas la ni bro ba chen po 'dug khyed rang tshos brtan bzhugs phul nas dngangs skrags byed dgos don rtza ba nas med/ blo dbe po byas te sdod.*

[152] Lhag sam, *Sprul sku dang bod mi'i goms gshis* ("Tulkus and Tibetan Custom"). The article's long and plodding general introduction to the system of reincarnation covered Tibetan Buddhist theory with which most of its readership would surely be well versed. In essence, it stated that Buddhists believe in past and future lives, the basis of which is the mind; from beginningless time a mental continuum has attached to every individual as they circle endlessly from life to life in the three worlds. Liberation from that cycle is possible through attaining Buddhahood; those close to achieving that result, known as Bodhisattvas, find the suffering of other sentient beings unbearable so take rebirths as spiritual teachers to guide others towards liberation. Following an explanation of the history of Tibet's special relationship with Chenrezig, the Bodhisattva of Compassion (who manifests as the Dalai Lama), the article went on to note that the first recorded instance of recognition of a reincarnation was that of the Karmapa in 1284, though the oral tradition relating to the lineage of Kadampa *geshes* going back to Pandit Atisha's death in Tibet in 1042 suggested similar instances in that period. The first certain recognition in the Gelug tradition was in the line of Dalai Lamas, when Panchen Lungrig Gyatso recognised the three-year old second Dalai Lama, Gendun Gyatso as the reincarnation of Gendun Drub, posthumously recognised as the first Dalai Lama. With the relationship between Chenrezig and the Bodhisattva Amitābha (who manifests as the Panchen Lama) "like the sun and moon in space" (*nam la nyi zla*

the issue, asserting that reincarnation was part of the virtuous activity of Buddhas and Bodhisattvas, who take rebirth in accordance with the degree of receptivity of disciples. Thus, their recognition could never be resolved willy-nilly by kings or political dictates, as was China's approach to Tibet;

- Later that year *Sheja* discussed fake letters of recognition for reincarnations (September 1998:28).[153] This arose from a Drepung Gomang monk's fabrication of a Dalai Lama certificate, purportedly recognising him as a Nyingma lama. The article warned readers to be wary of such deception, but queried the monk's motive as his forgery was obvious, containing mixed Tibetan scripts and a photocopied seal and signature;[154] and

- *Sheja*'s July 1999 editorial debated the reincarnation question (July 1999:3–5),[155] once again placing it solely within the religious domain. China's statement that a fifteenth Dalai could not be recognised unless born in China was viewed as just another political trick to gain control of him. *Sheja* pointed out that any successor nominated by Beijing would still require Tibetans' approval. The 'theatre' of the golden urn and enthronement ceremonies for Gyantsen Norbu was dismissed as but a means of clearing the way for China's political future in Tibet. The reality remained that the purpose of reincarnation is to complete work not finished in a previous life; thus *Sheja* urged its readers to consider whether they desired a fifteenth reincarnation.

---

gnyis), thus developed the historical relationship between the two principal reincarnates in Tibet.

[153] *Sprul sku ngos 'dzin gyi bka' yig rdzun ma bzos pa* ("False Letters of Tulku Recognition Fabricated").

[154] The issue surfaced again in *Sheja*'s January 2000 issue, which warned of Lama Lozang Yeshe's activities in South India. Allegedly trying to pass himself off as the reincarnation of Kundeling Tatsag Rinpoche, he had written to the Bangalore authorities informing them of his status and built his own Kundeling monastery in the Mysore hills. *Sheja* saw such brazen conduct as harming both the religious and secular dimensions of the Ganden Phodrang government (the Government-in-exile in Dharamsala), especially as it brought into doubt the recognition of tulkus by the Dalai Lama. See *'Bras sgo mang sgrwa tshang gi rgol gleng khag gnyis* ("Two Controversies in Drepung Gomang College") (*Sheja*, January 2000:27).

[155] *Bla ma'i yang srid ni chos phyogs dang 'brel ba'i gnas tshul zhig yin pas/ chos med dmar por the byus byed dbang med* ("As the Reincarnation of a Lama is an Issue Relating to Religion, the Atheist Chinese Strategy has no Authority").

The Beijing press maintained complete silence on such issues. *Krung go'i bod ljongs'* sole contribution was from the innocuous angle of a book review entitled "Lamas and tulkus passage of lives" (*bla sprul skye 'pho*) (1995 (4):48).[156] Even then, the very brief review simply enumerated the book's contents: identification, religious training and studies, monastery life, death processes, treatment of remains, relics and memorials. It offered no critique of that material at all.

CONCLUSIONS

The discussion reveals that the textual biographical tradition of Tibetan Buddhism has now spread into the realm of contemporary Tibetan language newspapers and magazines:

• They provide a valuable, multifaceted picture of Buddhist and Bon masters, interweaving information on past and present lives.

A sharp divergence in content between the Dharamsala and Beijing presentations remains.

• Beijing, from its apparent position of strength in the Tibet equation, can afford to be selective in tailoring Tibetan material to suit its current political policies;

• Dharamsala seeks to cover all aspects of Tibet-related issues from around the world in order to bolster the position of Tibetans in and outside Tibet, as well as discredit Beijing wherever possible.

Beijing's coverage of religious figures and events remains limited.

• Subject-matter exemplifies a piecemeal approach, emphasising the activities of leading religious figures for whom potentially biographical material is presented primarily to justify Chinese political claims concerning religious freedoms;

---

[156] Chai Titun and Hong Haoyin. *Bla sprul skye 'pho* ("Lamas and Tulkus Passage of Lives"). Publication by the Chinese Social Science Publishing House perhaps suggests that the book approached the subject from a social science perspective.

- The tenor of PRC reports suggests that political, not religious, dictates remain the overriding concern; the appearance of a biographical strand is a coincidental but fortuitous outcome.

Dharamsala's broad coverage maintains a traditionally Tibetan emphasis on the spiritual dimension, linking documentary detail with social purpose and providing a strong sense of the Tibetan biographical tradition concerning reincarnate lamas.

- Reports combine traditional and modern Tibetan perspectives, using news reports, obituaries and condensed biographies, thus providing a valuable picture of these individuals;
- These occasional instalments become a distinct and useful historical and biographical record that charts the life and lives of both celebrated and lesser-known lineages.

The tulku system continues to claim agency as a challenge to Chinese hegemony. To some extent it is able to reclaim Tibetan historical and geographical identity through religious events.

- These reports convey respect for a tradition that has produced unique individuals, suggesting a firm intention on part of the respective camps to maintain Tibetan religious values—albeit for vastly different purposes;
- Both strive to utilise this medium as a means of instilling the consciousness of national identity, Tibetan or Chinese, for their respective political ends;
- Controversy over leading tulkus is indicative of Beijing's growing interest in using the politics of reincarnation as a means to contain Tibetan nationalism.

The serial nature of this specialised subject matter is sufficient to form a sound basis from which the readership can, over time, construct a biographical framework.

- These developments respond to a need in Tibetan society as a whole for information on a social group which remains of fundamental importance to the survival of a unique culture;
- The continuing evolution of this emerging tradition of biography by instalment is a valuable addition to a body of scarce Tibetan literature.

CHAPTER FOUR

POLYANDRY IN DHARAMSALA: PLURAL-HUSBAND MARRIAGE IN A TIBETAN REFUGEE COMMUNITY IN NORTHWEST INDIA

NELLIE GRENT (UNIVERSITY OF AMSTERDAM)

The custom of one woman marrying two or more men is both a rare and characteristic feature of Tibetan culture in Tibet and in Tibetan exile communities. My contention is that polyandry in the Tibetan refugee community of Dharamsala is based on a specific combination of material considerations, i.e. on economic and practical aspects on the one hand, and immaterial considerations, i.e. derived from a collective religious-political ideology and individual, psychological aspects on the other hand. These considerations are molded by historical and personal life events and are closely related to the presentation of Self to insiders and outsiders, as part of Tibetan ethnic and national identity.

In this paper I will discuss theories on polyandry, and relate them to my fieldwork data on polyandry, ethnicity and nationalism in Dharamsala, and summarise the results in my conclusion.

Throughout history polyandry has been practiced in several cultures around the world[157], traditional Tibetan society being one of

---

[157] Cases are reported from *ancient Greece* (Perenditis, 1997); *pre-Islamic Arabia* (Henneman, 1954); the *Marquesans* (Otterbein, 1968); some *North American Indian tribes* (Park, 1937, and Stewart, 1937). Most frequently polyandry was/is practised in *Asia* by several populations in *Sri Lanka* (Hiatt, 1985, and Tambiah, 1966), *India* (cf. Berreman, 1980, 1987a & 1987b; Bhatt, 1980 & 1987; Chandra, 1987; Crook, 1987; Crook and Crook, 1988; Das-Gupta, 1921; Gough, 1968; Kapadia, 1990; Leach, 1955; Majumdar, 1960; Mandelbaum, 1938; Parmar, 1975; Saksena, 1954; Singh, Sharma & Sankhyan, 1996; Singh, 1988; and Walker, 1986), *Nepal* (Aziz, 1978; Corlin, 1975; Dunham, 1991; Dunham, Chozam and Head, 1993; Fisher, 1987; Fürer-Haimendorf, 1975; Goldstein, 1976, 1987a & 1987b; Goody, 1990; Levine, 1980a & 1988; and Schuler, 1983 & 1987), and amongst *Tibetans in Tibet and in exile* (Beall and Goldstein, 1981; Bell, 1928; Dargyay, 1982; Das, 1893; French, 1995; Goldstein, 1971c; Goldstein & Beall, 1982; Gombo, 1985; Herbert, 1997; Hermanns, 1953; Klieger, this volume; Korn,

them. Presently polyandry is prevalent in only 0.5 to 1% of all societies and it is on the decline, supposedly involving about 40 million people (Murdock in Trevithick, 1997:155).

Since the Chinese invasion of Tibet in 1949, thousands of Tibetans have fled into exile in India, Nepal and several other countries (Shakabpa, 1988, and Shakya, 1999). At the moment the Tibetan refugee community consists of 122,078 exiles. Out of this population 85,147 Tibetans live in India (Planning Council, 2000:7).

In the winter of 1992/1993 and in the spring of 2000 I did research on polyandry in Dharamsala, a Tibetan refugee community in northwest India. I came to choose this topic after having met a girl whose two uncles had married one wife and having been introduced to them in 1990. This polyandrous marriage form is unknown in Western society and I, a Westerner, became even more interested when I found how little profound or recent scientific information was available on polyandry among Tibetan exiles. In addition, according to the Tibetan government-in-exile in Dharamsala, and in other exile communities, polyandry is rarely practiced (personal correspondence 1992; Planning Council, 2000:202–14,1071–491).[158] But I had met the people, so what was going on? So when I returned to Dharamsala in 1992 the only thing I knew for sure there was at least one polyandrous family.

This family would be the starting point for my research and from there on I wanted to explore my research questions. First, on a general level: how many plural-husband marriages actually do occur in Dharamsala? Then: where and in which circumstances do the polyandrous spouses and their family members live? Furthermore, while researching the separate cases, are the husbands related to each other? What were the reasons for forming a polyandrous union? How is paternity over the children established?

In 2000 I elaborated on these questions and added a few more, focusing especially on ethnic and nationalistic matters. This boiled down to one main issue: In what way is polyandry in exile related to

---

2000; Macartney, 1994; Palakshappa, 1978; Peter, 1963; Smith, 1998; Stein, 1972; Stephens, 1988; Taring, 1978; Trevithick, 1997; and Vajda, 1985). Less frequently it is found among some populations in *Africa* (Levine and Sangree, 1980; Muller, 1980; and Vangeenberghe, 1957).

[158] In the questionaire of their demographic survey no detailed questions on types of marriages are asked.

the nationalistic issue of 'preservation of traditional Tibetan culture'? Can polyandry be seen as a marker of Tibetan ethnic identity? And, with regard to the future, is polyandry a traditional custom that needs to be preserved as well, or do other factors come into play?

RESEARCH METHODS AND RESEARCH QUESTIONS

The results of my research on polyandry in Dharamsala have come about by means of participant observation, interviews and informal talks. In 1993 I[159] had 21 formal interviews, in the course of which I used a standardised questionnaire. Furthermore I had 66 unstructured interviews, based on a list of key points regarding marriage, poly-andry and related topics. In between I had at least 100 informal talks, at which the topic polyandry popped up.

In 2000, I managed to do 8 formal, standardised interviews and 25 unstructured interviews, added by at least 30 informal talks.

My initial intention was to record the interviews, and I did so a few times. But since people were even more reluctant to talk about polyandry in the presence of a recorder, I switched over to writing down my talks, interviews and observations either during or as soon as possible after the event.

Languages used were Tibetan, English and Dutch. My command of the Tibetan language is minimal, so on several occasions I was assisted by a translator.

Informants were predominantly living in Dharamsala, were from all ranges of Tibetan society, and had different nationalities and ethnic backgrounds.

The extensive terrain of Dharamsala, the segmented population, and the reluctance to talk about polyandry had repercussions for my research. Besides the fact that most polyandrous people do not easily present themselves as being polyandrous, non-polyandrous people were sometimes willing to indicate plural-husband families but none of them was acquainted with all the cases in Dharamsala. They knew or suspected only some of their relatives, colleagues, or neighbors to be involved in polyandry, though names and background details could not always be given. Therefore the search for the polyandrous

---

[159] Even though I use the term 'I', I could not have collected my fieldwork data without the help of countless people whom I owe many thanks.

individuals and families in itself took up a major part of my research; just finding them posed quite a challenge.

THEORIES

Over the years anthropologists such as Gough (1968:49), Leach (1955), and Peter (1956, 1957 & 1963) have been proposing detailed definitions of polyandry, but in my view it is most clearly described by Sangree and Levine (1980:iii):

> ... truly polyandrous [are] only those formally recognised marital unions where the wife's husbands all not only have legitimate access to her, but also have the opportunity of being recognised as the pater (either differentially or jointly) of the children she bears.

But what makes a relationship a 'marital union'? Again theories are abundant (cf. Bossen, 1988; Dillingham, 1975; Dumont, 1968; Kurian, 1979; Quale, 1988; Reynolds & Kellett, 1991; and Westermarck, 1903). However, I think Kloos (1991:58) states accurately that only the combination of both an economic, sexual, and reproductive relationship between people makes it a marriage bond. Marriage itself is contracted in order to legitimise the kinship ties and inheritance rights between the spouses and their offspring.

In case of a formal marriage a legal contract and a wedding are involved, but when looking at polyandry these two elements are not always clearly distinct. Therefore I emphasise the importance of informal marriage, when people are regarded married by society after they start living together, sometimes after a small ceremony. At the same time, in attempts to define polyandrous marriage, complications turn up. A woman sharing a house with several brothers does not have to be married to all of them, and polyandrous spouses do not always live in the same house. Since law in India and in other countries forbids polyandry (Crook & Shakya, 1988:729 and Skolnick, 1973:22), people may formally register themselves as (one) husband and wife, but there may be another husband involved. Which is hard to discover because, as said earlier, generally Tibetan exiles do not identify themselves as being polyandrous married.[160] For example, a woman says: "This is my husband and this is his

---

[160] Palakshappa (1978:70) observed this already over two decades ago in Mundgot, South India.

brother." In most cases remarks of outsiders lead me to the polyandrous families and at further inquiry they turned out to be polyandrous or not. I argue the viewpoint of the polyandrous individuals
holds the decisive opinion, no matter what outsiders may say about
them.

Polyandry has over time been explained in different ways.
Scholars in the 19th and 20th centuries, mainly Westerners, believed
polyandry to be the unnatural remainder of an earlier, polyandrous
stage of human civilisation (Cassidy and Lee, 1989:1–11; Fielding,
1942; and Fischer, 1942 & 1952). In my opinion this reflects a rather
limited ethnocentric point of view, assuming non-Western people to
be less developed.

Another surprising theory I do not agree with was postulated by
Prince Peter (1963), who concluded from his extensive fieldwork
among polyandrous populations in South Asia that polyandry could
be looked upon as a near-incest relationship.

Present day scientists such as Crook & Crook (1988) and
Reynolds & Kellett (1991) are inspired by behavioural and ecological studies of polyandry in both human and animal populations, but
this topic lies beyond the scope of my paper.

MATERIAL CONSIDERATIONS

By and large anthropologists regard polyandry amongst Tibetans as
both a production and a reproduction strategy, intertwined with
demographic, gender, political, ideological and psychological issues.
A few scientists (Herbert, 1997:77; Klieger, this volume;
Palakshappa, 1978:69; and Saklani, 1984:107) mention polyandry
among Tibetans in exile. Polyandry in long-term existing societies
either in traditional[161] Tibet or in Tibetan culture areas in the
Himalayas (see note 1) has been described more elaborately instead.

---

[161] In present day Tibet polyandry is forbidden by Chinese law, but it is resurgent
(Macartney, 1994) and demands further research (cf. Goldstein, 1989, and Goldstein
& Beall, 1990).

PRODUCTION STRATEGY

In explanations for polyandry usually is referred to the very difficult economic and ecological circumstances in which the people live(d). Aziz (1978), Goldstein (1971a, 1971b, 1971c, 1973 & 1987b:200–9), Goody (1990:137–53), and Levine (1988) state polyandry in traditional Tibet was mostly found in families who had inheritable tenant rights to land. In exchange these tenants were obliged to pay taxes to the landowner and to render certain duties. Both arable farmland and labour were scarce[162] and in order to prevent fragmentation of family property in a patrilineal, direct vertical inheritance system, brothers[163] formed polyandrous unions. With their joint wife the husbands established a new joint family, but did not necessarily form a household whose members shared a house. Most often the wife stayed at the farm with one husband and her in-laws, while the other husband(s) traveled long distances to the pastures with the animals, went to places for business, and/or to render army services. By implementing this strategy[164] land, labour and different sources of income (farming, trading, and animal husbandry) were pooled. Korn (2000:359–61) complements this explanation by emphasising that the combination of available technology, the individual skills of the people to operate this technology and the soil condition of the land in use were important as well.

Furthermore, by applying the mono-marital principle a *stem family* would be created whose aim was to keep the family property together[165]. In each family generation only one marriage for all brothers was allowed, who would inherit the family property, usually land, either in ownership or as a tenant.

---

[162] Uncertain is the matter of the scarcity of arable land and labour. Bell (1928: 193) argues arable land became in disuse because of a decreasing population. Ekvall (1972) and Goldstein (1981) discuss this matter in detail.

[163] Husbands are usually brothers, sometimes father-son or unrelated polyandry occurs as well.

[164] Trevithick (1997:166) refers to this strategy as a 'last resort strategy', but since these families did not belong to the poorest of society his term is highly debatable (cf. Goldstein, 1993:5).

[165] Other ways of creating a stem family are through the patrilineal parallel-cousin marriage in the Middle East, the primogeniture inheritance of one son in twelfth century Japan, and in South France of the Middle Ages one son would inherit most of the familyproperty and the others smaller parts (Quale, 1988:132–38,149).

Tibetan polyandry is not necessarily equal to impartible inheritance, as demonstrated by Aziz (1974:23–39), Goody (1990), and Levine and Sangree (1980:391) in their criticism on the patricentric viewpoint of theorists. Traditionally Tibetans were believed to inherit patrilineally and to live patrilocally. However, the Tibetan inheritance and kinship system can better be termed 'bilineal', for both patrilineal and matrilineal kinship ties are considered important at life events such as marriage. Goody (1990:2f.) shows in particular in his theory on diverging devolution how in Eurasian societies both sons and daughters inherit family property. In traditional Tibetan society brothers not joining in polyandry would be entitled to a small share of the family property in the form of cash or goods. They could leave the family estate to start their own family, either neolocally, or marry matrilocally as a *magpa* into another family that had only daughters. Or these brothers could take up monastic vows[166], and their rights to the family property could be reclaimed at a later stage if abandoning religious life. Sisters of polyandrous brothers could be compensated by the donation of movable property (clothes, jewelry) at their wedding. Unmarried sisters could remain at the family estate (French, 1995:38-9,172-3.).

But how does this theory on production strategy relate to the present situation in Dharamsala?

DHARAMSALA

Dharamsala is a former British hill station in district Kangra, located in the predominantly Hindu state Himachal Pradesh in northwest India (Singh, Sharma and Sankhyan, 1996:11). Its population is rather diverse and migration and refugeehood characterise the history of Dharamsala. In the past the British came, and after the 1908 earthquake most of them left again. In 1947, following India's independence, the Muslim inhabitants of Dharamsala went to Pakistan and the Hindu refugees from Pakistan came to live in Dharamsala. When in 1959 the Dalai Lama and several thousand

---

[166] Not all four Buddhist schools follow celibacy; some allow marriage. How this relates exactly to polyandry needs to be examined in future research.

other Tibetans were forced to flee Tibet, Dharamsala[167] was offered as their new, temporary home. In the years that followed more Tibetan refugees settled until the present number of almost 9.000 inhabitants (Planning Council, 2000:63, and Russell, 2000:13). Over time the town became more prosperous, main sources of income are being generated from tourism, retail business, handicrafts, sponsorships, medical services, military services, Tibetan government jobs, and working for Tibetan organisations.

The town itself consists of different parts, stretching out over a hill with about 10 kilometers distance between the bottom and the top. At the bottom of the hill is *Lower Dharamsala* where mostly Pahari, an Indian ethnic population of 20.000 inhabitants, live. Up the hill is *Gangchen Kyishong*, with many of the offices and staff quarters of the Tibetan government-in-exile, the Library, the Medical Institute, etc. Halfway up the hill is the densely populated Tibetan refugee village of *McLeod Ganj*, where the residence of the Dalai Lama, several other Tibetan organisations and a wide variety of tourist hotels and shops are located. Above McLeod Ganj, is *Upper Dharamsala* with amongst others the Tibetan Children's Village (DIIR, 1999; Fürer-Haimendorf, 1990:59–71).

Dharamsala is a community in motion, people are constantly coming and going. Added up to the 9.000 permanent[168] inhabitants one can count a huge, but varying number of temporary residents and visitors.[169] In a nutshell[170] one could say Tibetans come to India to stay,[171] return to Tibet, or move on to the West.[172]

---

[167] Dharamsala is also known as the 'Capital-in-exile' because the Dalai Lama, the Government-in-exile, and several important Tibetan institutions reside there. Another name for it is 'Little Lhasa in India' (cf. Anand, this volume, and DIIR, 1999).

[168] Registered as living in Dharamsala.

[169] Ranging from recently arrived Tibetans from Tibet, Tibetan exiles visiting family or friends, Tibetans contracting business, and non-Tibetan researchers, journalists, Tibet-affiliated sponsors and supporters, students of Buddhism and Tibetan language, volunteers working for a Tibetan organisation, and tourists, of all kind of nationalities.

[170] Reasons for the departure of the newcomers from Tibet vary. Several Tibetans had to escape in fear of repercussions due to (presumed) prior political activities. Of the newcomers some came as pilgrims to see the Dalai Lama and/or to bring a child to receive Tibetan education in India. After a while these Tibetans return to Tibet. Others stay longer, seeking religious or secular education and therefore are forwarded to Tibetan monasteries and schools in other places in India. Quite a few come to join family or friends. Also, economic opportunities and freedom of speech, religion and education in general draw Tibetans to India, and more and more often,

The permanent Tibetan inhabitants of Dharamsala can roughly be divided into two types of refugees. The first group, which local Tibetans in personal communications refer to as 'long-timers', fled in or shortly after 1959. Almost all originate in the Central-Tibetan province U-Tsang and therefore speak Lhasa-dialect. Quite a number were from rich families, even though they could bring only moveable property.[173] Land, houses and cattle had to stay behind in Tibet. The second group, known as 'newcomers', arrived in the eighties and nineties after the loosening of Chinese control in Tibet. A large number of the latter group comes from the Eastern-Tibetan provinces Kham and A mdo. As a result of the Chinese occupation they generally speak Chinese, if they speak Tibetan it is in their local dialect. They dress and behave quite differently from the long-timers who described them in 1993 (Dolma, personal communication) as "rough, uneducated, dirty, not modern." Last year, only seven years later, mutual understanding and cooperation seemed to have improved a lot.

By the year 2000 three generations of long-timers had settled in Dharamsala and in 31 cases polyandry was still practiced. Also four cases of polyandry among newcomers were reported, adding up to 35 polyandrous families or 108 spouses from three different generations.

Of two families of longtimers their age was unspecified, as well as from the polyandrous newcomers. The first generation consists of elderly Tibetans (60 +) who were born, raised and married in Tibet. Of the longtimers, 9 families had married polyandrously, but in 5 cases the wife was younger than her husbands and therefore of the second generation.

The second generation comprises Tibetan families in the ages between about 41 (=born in 1959, the last ones born in a relatively free Tibet) and 60, who came as a child or youngster to India around 1959. In this generation in 1993 the longtimers represented the largest number of polyandrous marriages: 19 cases, out of which in 2

---

to the West. Statistical data can be found in the Tibetan Demographic Survey (Planning Council, 2000).

[171] With the ideal to return to a free Tibet some day.

[172] A friend of mine put it like this: "India has become a stop-over to the West" (Ögen, personal communication, 1993).

[173] Mainly jewels, clothes, religious objects, household utensils.

cases the wife was much younger and therefore from the third generation.

In the third generation, which consists roughly of Tibetans in their reproductive years (roughly between the ages 15 and 40–45), among the longtimers only one case of polyandry was reported. I met one brother who had married the same wife as his brother. They were in their middle twenties at the time of the wedding in 1997, which was celebrated extensively. The brothers, their wife and their two children live most of the time in Dharamsala, unless they leave for retail business in places like Delhi or go to their families in the refugee settlement nearby where they were born. I was told repeatedly that I would find more cases in the more traditional structured Tibetan refugee communities in South India. In future research these communities could be examined as well.

The newcomers also married polyandrously. In two cases the ages were completely unknown, in one case the spouses were in their thirties (i.e. third generation) and in the last case, involving father and son, they are clearly from different generations but also their exact ages remain to be researched for this time my focus was on the impact of long-term residence on polyandry.

Most long-timer polyandrous individuals themselves or their family originate from the Central Tibetan province U-Tsang, speak Lhasa-dialect and had escaped Tibet either as an adult or as a child. The polyandrous families lived all over Dharamsala, except for Lower Dharamsala. Palakshappa (1978:67) states that because the houses are much smaller than in Tibet, in exile the nuclear family replaces the extended family and polyandry is more difficult to practice. I have seen no evidence of such a phenomenon in the polyandrous families in Dharamsala, but it may discourage people to start an extended family. Their houses generally were small, with only one room, but some families owned large houses with several rooms. Depending on the economic and family situation other household members were servants, children, parents of the spouses, and other family members.

Tibetan refugees in India found several economic niches in Indian economy: farming new types of crop, sweater business, handicrafts, and tourism.[174] With regard to the theory on polyandry as a produc-

---

[174] Supplemented sometimes by international sponsorships and financial support from family members in Western countries.

tion strategy, one would expect farmland and livestock if there were polyandry around. Which is true for Tibetan communities in South India, but not for Dharamsala. Since other sources of income predominate there, how can polyandry then be accounted for?

Before exploring this matter, it has to be kept in mind that fraternal polyandry is only one of the several choices in the flexible marriage system of the Tibetans, both in Tibet and in exile. In general non-marriage, i.e. divorcees, widow(er)s, and celibates (monks, nuns), was quite common. Monogamy was the most often practiced marriage form but polygamous marriages were contracted as well, both in polygyny[175] and polyandry. Individuals may engage in different types of marital alignments during their life cycle. They may also be involved in different types of polygamous marriages, largely determined by factors such as age, death, birth, economic needs and personal wishes (Bell, 1928:192; French, 1995:38-9; Goldstein, 1971c; Goody, 1990:137; Kawaguchi, 1903:352; and Tucci, 1967:159), as illustrated in the next Dharamsala case.

> One man named Dawa[176] first married monogamously one wife in 1969 and they got one son. One year after their wedding he got an *affair* with her sister. When she conceived a son[177] of him as well, she was considered his second wife and thus a polygynous marriage was constructed. The first marriage was arranged by their parents, both families came from Pari in U-Tsang and since the wife only had sisters Dawa went to live with her family as a *magpa*. This marriage was celebrated with an official ceremony and a big wedding party; the second marriage was validated by mutual agreement of the parties involved and public recognition. A few years later his first wife died and instead of becoming a widower Dawa once again became a monogamous husband, married to his second wife of course. They got one more son. Then, some years later, his brother joined them, without official ceremony, and he became the father of their only daughter.

Altogether I found 41 polyandry-related cases, out of which 35 cases were truly polyandrous. Six cases could not be identified as polyandrous because in two cases a single man refused to join in poly-

---

[175] Sisters, mother-daughter or unrelated women might join in marriage.

[176] Dawa is not his real name. In order to protect the privacy of the people in this paper I sometimes use pseudonyms.

[177] Remarkable fact was that the two children of the two sisters were always referred to as 'the twins', even though they only had the same father. At the same time it reflects the principle of the stem family.

andry, in two other cases the parents of a single man were polyandrous and living outside Dharamsala, in one case it was *pseudo-
polyandry* and in the last case it was *unaware-polyandry*.

The latter terms I constructed in order to label types of polyandry
not previously discussed in literature. In Dharamsala one case of
pseudo-polyandry[178] was reported. A woman had married one
husband, while his two brothers lived in the same house. People in
Dharamsala said this family formed a polyandrous union, but the
family members explained it was actually monogamy and in-living
brothers. The exile situation has also given rise to the new phenomena of unaware polyandry, when spouses get spatially separated.
In Dharamsala I was told one such case. A woman was forced to
leave her first husband in Tibet, did not receive news from him for
years while she was in India and presumed he was dead. She married
another husband and then, after some time the first one showed up in
Dharamsala too. Since she was still married[179] to the first one, she
was not aware she actually contracted polyandry by marrying the
second husband.

Among the 35 cases of real polyandry some subtypes of polyandry were present, involving both long-timers and newcomers. To
my knowledge, there are no cases of 'mixed' polyandrous marriage,
involving both long-timers and newcomers. As before in traditional
Tibet *fraternal polyandry* was the most frequent type of polyandry in
Dharamsala, being prevalent in 26 cases. Out of which among the
long-timers 23 cases turned out to be *bi-fraternal* (involving two
brothers), one case was *tri-fraternal* (three brothers) and one case
was *quadri-fraternal* (four brothers). Of the newcomers it was said
one family was involved in bi-fraternal polyandry.

Even though fraternal polyandry was the most prominent form of
related polyandry in Tibet, the more rare cases of *intergenerational
polyandry* were reported as well. Father and son[180] would share one
wife,[181] at the wedding only the son would be present and paternity
over the children would be accredited only to the son. Usually this

---

[178] It differs from *quasi-polyandry*, a term Aziz (1978:153) uses for a woman and
her lovers.

[179] This can be debated, since spatial separation can be regarded as divorce as
well. It depends on the viewpoint of the spouses.

[180] I also heard about a man and his uncle sharing one wife.

[181] The second wife is not the son's mother.

type of polyandry was constructed when the mother of the son had died or left. If the father had remarried separately, any children born from this marriage would threaten the inheritance of the son (French, 1995:38, and Goldstein, 1971c:69). In Dharamsala however in one case a father married a (second) wife[182] first, and when his son (also newcomer) joined him from Tibet he was told[183] he was included in the marriage as well. It is unknown whether the son accepted and how paternity would be settled over any children born from this marriage.

The Tibetan government-in-exile managed to establish agricultural settlements all over India (Mahmoudi, 1996:54). Economic activities in Dharamsala are not based on agriculture, so why still polyandry? When looking at the separate polyandrous cases it turned out that in two cases there was a link with agriculture however: one husband was living in Dharamsala, while the other husband and their wife lived in agricultural communities in South India. Also the polyandrous household arrangements gave opportunity to pool labour and income, just like before in Tibet. In 18 cases the construction was the same: previously husbands would be gone for long periods of time to take care of the cattle, to go on business or perform army duties, nowadays in Dharamsala polyandrous spouses[184] left home for a long time in order to engage themselves in sweater business, join the army or perform other kinds of jobs outside the community.

Unrelated men joining in polyandry occurred also in traditional Tibet, this very rare construction usually developed out of friendship or as a business alliance and would be found among people with no or very limited access to land. Now and then a woman might marry a second husband if she liked him too or if she was dissatisfied with her first husband. In unrelated polyandrous marriages there might be one or two weddings, sometimes years apart. The husbands normally lived in separate houses and it was known which children they had fathered (Bell, 1928:192; French, 1995:38f.; Goldstein 1971c;

---

[182] It is unknown what has happened to the first wife.

[183] In a way for the son it is also unaware polyandry.

[184] The economic role of Tibetan women has grown substantially. Wives no longer stay at home all the time, they also travel to big cities all over India to sell sweaters or do other kinds of business. Cf. Levine and Sangree (1980:8), who state polyandry was installed because of Ḍ "the combination of a harsh environment with a limited productive role for women."

Goody, 1990:137; Kawaguchi, 1903:352; Levine, 1988; Stephens, 1988; and Tucci, 1967:159). In Dharamsala among the long-timers six cases of unrelated polyandry were reported. In some of these cases the husbands lived in separate houses, sometimes with one or more children. The wife would come and visit them at their respective houses. Several reasons were given for unrelated polyandry. Husbands had become friends in the army and joined in marriage. Or the wife had fallen in love with another man and her husband accepted him as the second husband. In one case it was said a woman had seduced her second husband into marriage because he was very rich, therefore an informant labeled this marriage as based on 'money love' (Tsering, personal communication, 2000). Of the two cases of unrelated polyandrous newscomers only few details could be given, insufficient to present as accurate data.

To what extent both related and unrelated polyandry are also practiced for reproductive reasons has been discussed at length by several scholars.

REPRODUCTION STRATEGY

In traditional Tibet families practicing related polyandry limited their offspring to one set of children who in the long-term inherited most of the family property as an inseparable unit. These children belonged to their paternal family-group, irrespective of which husband was their biological father. Usually the eldest brother would be addressed as father, and the other brother-husbands as uncles (Levine, 1980). In the short-term polyandry served as a reproduction strategy: the household would not be faced with having too many small children who had to be fed but were too young to help at the farm. Another disadvantage of too many children was that pregnant women produced less, while their labour was of vital importance (Korn, 2000:360). Also it was presumed paternity over the children was secured for it was believed the wife would not easily be tempted to infidelity during a husband's absence as another husband would still be around (Hiatt, 1980).

In Dharamsala however there is no such need to limit family size through polyandry. In the first place because economic-ecological circumstances are much better than in Tibet, so bigger families can be raised. In the second place, if families want to put a stop on their number of children,[185] access to modern birth control provides a more direct means. In relation to their situation as refugees an informant even claimed polyandry should be abandoned in favour of producing more children through monogamy:

> Tibetans should try to have as many children as possible, we are already a small population and these children would make up for the Tibetans who have been killed by the Chinese. (Norbu, personal communication, 2000)

And as explanation for unrelated men marrying one wife Stephens (1988:356) states "[unrelated] polyandry would appear a viable female reproductive strategy ... and a viable male reproductive strategy in situations of cultural overlap with differential access to resources and women." Even though she refers to unrelated men from different cultural backgrounds, this theory might also be applied to the people in former Tibet who had limited or no access to economic resources derived from land or cattle. Whether this applies also to Dharamsala, has not been confirmed.

With regard to a woman's infidelity in Dharamsala, this seems difficult to realise because there are so many people around and the houses are small and built closely together. Still, in one case a woman left her three husbands for her lover.

In contrast with traditional Tibet, where the eldest brother would marry first, in Dharamsala sometimes a younger brother married a woman and fathered her children first. Later on an elder brother joined in polyandry and fathered other children. The children addressed their fathers in different ways: either as father and uncle, or all as father—regardless of whether a child knew a man to be its biological father or not.

Another demographic element of polyandry is the presumed imbalance in the male-female ratio,[186] therefore 'forcing' men to marry polyandrously (cf. Pakrasi, 1987). In traditional Tibet supposedly more women than men died at an earlier age, due to the harsh living conditions and in childbirth. Since no statistical research has been done in those days, it is hard to prove. And although there are

---

[185] Whether this is influenced by the promotion of small families of the Indian government needs yet to be examined.

[186] See the demographic discussion by Ekvall (1972), Goldstein (1976 & 1981) and Goldstein, Tsarong and Beall (1983).

some reports of female infanticide among other polyandrous populations (Goldstein, 1981:725), this did not seem to be case among the Tibetans. A different phenomenon however did occur when Tibetans started to escape from Tibet after the Chinese occupation. Goldstein (1981:728) is told by Tibetan refugees in Nepal that many women with small children stayed behind in Tibet, therefore causing "a disproportionate number of nulliparous and low-fertility females."

Statistics of the Tibetan government-in-exile do not give these kinds of details. It does demonstrate however that in the different age groups generally there are more Tibetan men than women in India, except for the two age groups between 40 and 49. Regarding their marital status, data show 12,212 Tibetan men in India to be husbands in relation to 12,623 married women. But when looking at the different age groups, all the way up to the age of 55 more women than men are married, from 55 till 90 more men are married. This may indicate that after their flight to India there were less marriageable women available, but whether this has lead to polyandry in Dharamsala has not been confirmed in my research.

As for Dharamsala, the demographic details show 4.711 male inhabitants of whom 1.759 individuals live in institutions (monastery, TCV) and 2.952 non-institutional males. I presume the latter figure incorporates the (potential) husbands. The lower number of 3.983 female inhabitants consists of 1.379 women in institutions compared to 2.604 non-institutional women (Planning Council, 2000:63,87,203). In relation to marriage these details may not be very significant since potential spouses are found all over the Tibetan diaspora community and not just in one place.

A related matter is the occurrence of polygyny in the upper strata of traditional Tibetan society: rich men marrying several wives of lower strata. For the poorer men there would not be enough wives left, so they had to join in polyandrous marriage. I doubt about the huge number of women involved, because the aristocrats formed only a small percentage of the population. The other way around makes more sense: many women remained unmarried because many men were involved in polyandry or became celibate monks (cf. Schuler, 1987). In Dharamsala I found two cases of polygyny, but they were from poor families. Such a small number cannot have had that much of an impact on the decision of other people to marry in polyandry.

Now that I am discussing men-women relations, from a gender point of view in traditional Tibet a woman might improve her economic and social prospects by entering a multi-husband marriage that was looked upon with high esteem by the Tibetans.[187] And, being the only wife in one family generation, she did not have to compete with any prospective wives of her husband's brothers (cf. Bhatt and Jain, 1987; Chandra, 1984; Jain, 1980:83–90; Levine, 1981a; Nandi, 1987:422–34; and Schuler, 1978). She would only have to deal with her female in-laws. The other side of the story is that the wife has to keep several husbands satisfied, not an easy task I think, as is also noted by Levine (1981b:113). In Dharamsala both household and job arrangements do not confine the wife mainly to the house anymore (cf. Nowak, 1980). Husbands and wife all take part in the household chores, a domain that previously was reserved to women only. Both women and men have paid jobs these days and take care of the children. In one polyandrous family I witnessed how the two husbands were doing the cooking, while their wife was still out on the street selling sweaters and came home when dinner was ready. And in another case one much older husband took care of their small children.

In that respect a divorced woman once jokingly said she would like to have six 'army husbands'. She said they should take turns in their annual two months leave from the army and come home to her to do all kinds of chores in the house, while at the same time handing in their salary (Tsering, personal communication, 2000).

NON-MATERIAL CONSIDERATIONS

In anthropological theories on polyandry immaterial factors, especially the collective ones derived from the religious-political ideology and the individual ones based on personal, psychological elements, are considered less important than the economical and practical considerations. To begin with, eventhough some religious rituals are performed prior to the wedding, Tibetan marriage is not

---

[187] Polyandry among the Pahari is looked at less positive and only fraternal polyandry is to be found. Pahari women do not obtain a higher status as polyandry is viewed from a different perspective. Berreman even suggests to call it a different type of polyandry, even though the outside charasteristics are the same (cf. Berreman, 1987a, and Goldstein, 1987b).

considered to be a religious matter (French, 1995:38). And, the main religion of Tibet is Buddhism and only Buddhist Tibetans practice polyandry: Muslim and Christian minorities forbid this marriage custom. Therefore: what is the relationship between religion and polyandry? In what way does Tibetan Buddhist ideology justify a woman having more than one husband? Which thought makes this custom morally acceptable? After all, as Levine and Sangree (1980:392) state, populations living in the same harsh circumstances as the Tibetans do not practice polyandry. As opposed to this phenomenon, people in Nigeria whose habitat is completely different from the Tibetan environment, do practice polyandry. How can these differences and similarities then be accounted for? Levine and Sangree (ibid.) conclude, and I concur with them, that populations have different opinions regarding the regulation of sexual relations. In societies where a man asserts exclusive rights on a woman polyandry is unacceptable. In Tibetan polyandry the husbands share these rights, but how about the 'psyche' and feelings of the poly-androus individuals? After all, polyandry is one of the several marriage options. What makes individuals choose polyandry? In Western society marriage has a romantic notion (cf. Fisher, 1992), but in what way do personal feelings of individuals come into play in an arranged Tibetan plural-husband marriage? Smith (1998:244) refers to the psychological domain, but again there is no real expla-nation:

> ... polyandry is an expression of one or more psychological mecha-nisms that allow humans to track local environmental conditions and vary mating and kin-affiliation strategies according to fitness-correlated payoffs ... the exact nature of such mechanisms is unknown ...

One explanation that is often heard refers to the high status of polyandry in itself, since it abides to the ideal of promoting the union of the family through solidarity of the brother-husbands. This ideal is justified in Buddhism, which stresses the importance of putting others above self in the quest for enlightenment (cf. Lopez, 1997, and Thurman, 1995). All Tibetans want is to be reborn in a better world, which can be realised by the ascetic practice of non-attachment. However, this ideal clashes with practical circumstances and human feelings and a concession has to be made. "Self-restraint, sexual fidelity and fulfillment of one's duties ... are advocated ... within the bounds of marriage" (Levine, 1981b:111,113).

Thus, by not posing exclusive rights on one wife, group survival might be enhanced. In order for the group to survive, persons cannot live according to their individual wishes. In spite of this, to make especially a polyandrous marriage successful, personal feelings are crucial because:

> a wife must inspire the affections of her husbands to secure her position in a new household, and her husbands must try to make her circumstances as pleasant as possible. (ibid.:120).

She can enlarge this security by linking strongly with one husband — even though this is against the ideal of not favouring any husbands in a polyandrous marriage. Nakamura (1964:304) even argues "Tibetans ... are not strongly conscious of any personal bond between man and woman," but how can they link without having personal feelings for each other? I believe their intimate relationship transcends the sexual bond between them (cf. Cabezón, 1992, and Stevens, 1994) and also their psychological bond consolidates a marriage into a success. Mukerji (1950:56–65) even argues that jealousy originating from this close bond might lead to crime (cf. Aiyappan, 1937). I agree there are tensions deriving from jealousy in polyandrous marriages, just like in any other type of marriage. In Dharamsala one of the before mentioned three husbands who were left by their joint wife for her lover, threatened to kill her unless she returned to her husbands. It was a big scene and ultimately she did come back. But whether in Dharamsala in general polyandrous families are faced with more marital problems than monogamous or polygynous marriages cannot be asserted at this time.

An informant (Norbu, personal communication, April 2000) postulated also that polyandrous husbands who do not want full family responsibility (as in monogamy) "still obtain marital status and offspring, are taken care of by the wife in times of sickness and at the same time enjoy freedom to go their own way, while the other husband stays with their wife and children."

Another reason for choosing to marry polyandrously may be found in the occupational specialisation of the polyandrous spouses in Dharamsala. In most cases one or more spouses were working for the Tibetan government-in-exile or for Tibetan institutions, therefore providing the family with relatively low income but high status jobs that enlarge the social standing of the family. The remaining family members generated other sources of income, so in this way status and income were more effectively combined.

A number of informants explained their marriage option of one woman marrying two or more husbands by simply stating: "It is our tradition." But now all kinds of reasons have been summed up explaining why polyandry is prevalent in Dharamsala, it still leaves open the question why the third generation hardly practices this tradition anymore (cf. Levine, 1994, 1997). Many of the young people I talked to distanced themselves from it, with the motto "We are modern now." One young man even became furious, screamed: "No! No! We don't do that anymore!" and refused to talk about it. My impression was that polyandry has become associated with shame, and therefore it is no longer the ideal form of marriage. But why shame about a custom that has been practiced for ages in Tibet? Isn't it the policy of the Tibetan government-in-exile to preserve traditional Tibetan customs? Answers on these questions lay in the complicated, segmented ethnic identity of Tibetans in exile.

IS POLYANDRY A MARKER OF TIBETAN ETHNIC IDENTITY?

Traditional Tibet was not a homogenous society: people were divided according to religious sect, socio-economic strata, region, gender, and age, which lead to multiple identities (Korom, 1997b:2). Besides being part of both a family and a household, they felt affiliated to their estate and district, not to the country of Tibet as a nation (Kolas, 1996:53; Korom, 1997b:1–8; Levine and Geleg, 1990:56–65; Samuel, 1993:42-3; and Smith, 1997:17).

Goldstein (1978b:403), Klieger (1992), and Nowak (1984) argue the Tibetans in India have well adapted to Indian society, referring to the development of a standard intercultural interaction, adaptation to the Indian democratic laws and institutions, and a limited Indo-Tibetan interaction. The central aim of the Tibetan exile government is to preserve Tibetan culture, with the ultimate goal of returning to a free Tibet. In this policy the veneration of the Dalai Lama is a strong binding force. The longer the Tibetans live in India, the more acculturated they have become into Indian society, familiarised themselves with the language, songs, customs, rules and regulations. Depending on the degree of acculturation additional ethnic identities have been developed: long-timer/newcomer and refugee/pilgrim/ visitor, all in certain age categories and overlapped by a pan-Tibetan national identity.

Several scholars (cf. Corlin, 1975; deVoe, 1981a & 1981b; Diehl, 1997; Gombo, 1985; Kolas, 1996; Korom, 1997a & 1997b; Kvaerne and Thargyal, 1993; Nowak, 1984; and Subba, 1990) have been writing about ethnicity, nationalism and refugeehood, but not in conjunction with polyandry. Often polyandry has been mentioned as one of the most characteristic features of pre-occupied Tibet (e.g., Bell, 1928:29, and Stein, 1972:97), but is this still the case in exile? After the occupation Tibetan refugees have come from their isolated homeland to the plural society of India where they were also drawn in modern, multicultural global society. When looking at polyandry among the Tibetan exiles, the issue of identity markers is a prominent matter. Outside markers are clothes, food, language and the body, which are easily notified and which Alba (1990:xiii) names 'symbolic ethnicity'. Inside markers are intangible aspects: active compassion derived from Buddhism and, in my view, including marriage customs. In exile marriageable individuals do not only have to deal with their inner group, the family, but also with their outer group, the nation. In the political-historical context of the Tibetan exiles a Tibetan marrying a Tibetan can be seen as an ethnic issue, as well as marital status and marital type: to be unmarried (as a child, celibate, widow(er), bachelor/spinster) or married (monogamous, polygamous in polygyny or polyandry). Indicative is also how Tibetans "present themselves to other Tibetans ...," to others, and how they are "categorised by others" (cf. Yeh, this volume) as Tibetans, as Khampas, as refugees, and so on.

With regard to the presentation of self to other Tibetans regional and district affiliation is very strong. Towards outsiders a pan-Tibetan ethnic identity dominates, symbolised by Tibetan culture in general and Tibetan Buddhism in particular, personalised in the Dalai Lama. Tibetans identifying themselves as 'refugees' specifically stress the importance of the Dalai Lama, and the nationalistic symbol of *rang zen* (independence) (deVoe, 1981a, and Nowak, 1978).

Education plays an important role in the transfer of these symbols and identity markers, especially in formal education at Tibetan schools (Pathak, 1997). But what kind of messages and information on polyandry are consciously and unconsciously transferred at schools, at home, in the streets, in the media, on the Internet, and so on? And to which non-Tibetan information are they more receptive? The global orientation of the Tibetans is more directed towards Western culture than towards Indian culture, both for political and humanitarian support for their cause,[188] and for personal material and cultural attractions. Political and legal authorities of Western countries however have carefully built up a national marriage system that is aimed at perpetuating

> ... a *particular* marriage model: lifelong, faithful monogamy, ... bearing the impress of the Christian religion and the English common law ... (Cott, 2000:3)

In this ideology all sorts of polygamy, including polyandry, are regarded as unusual, strange or even repulsive customs. In their view it is degrading for women and comes close to adultery. First the national minorities of these Western countries were molded into this model, and now that the world is becoming a global village non-Western societies are faced with cultural values and attitudes opposing their own. With regard to the Tibetan exiles this means they are being drawn into two directions, especially the younger generations. On the one hand they are pushed towards the material temptations of Western society and start copying Western customs. On the other hand they are pulled back into Tibetan traditions, which causes role conflicts in ideal behaviour and actual behaviour (cf. Levine, 1994 & 1997, and Subba, 1990:55f.).

Two polyandrous families in which one husband got the opportunity to go to America expressed this conflict in different ways on the application form. Knowing their family construction would be regarded as illegal bigamy, one husband filled in he was unmarried while the other one registered as being married.

With regard to marriage Tibetans in Dharamsala in general select their potential spouse on the basis of a range of criteria, ethnic identity taking up a major part. Problem nowadays is that these criteria cannot always be checked, in this diaspora community not everybody knows anybody anymore and references cannot always be made. Love marriage seems to replace arranged marriage, and also then only a few criteria are checked. Marriage with Westerners has

---

[188] The struggle for a free Tibet.

become an exile phenomenon, but only in monogamy. Preference is still given to marrying a Tibetan, preferably of the same region in Tibet, and until a decade ago, of the same socio-economic stratum in endogamy. Exogamy is still practiced, spouses should not be related for seven generations and their family should have a good reputation. Tibetans raised in India also prefer a well-educated and decently employed spouse, providing a good income and high job status. Also the ability to speak the 'proper' Tibetan language, i.e. Lhasa dialect, which in exile has become the 'national' language, is valued very much.

As for the marriage type, as discussed before older people used to marry in polyandry but young people prefer to have one spouse in monogamy. They say they are modern now and therefore renounce polyandry, which may as well be seen as an adaptation to Western values. As for maintaining this marriage custom, Tenzin (personal communication, 1993) said: "Polyandry should not be continued because it is a traditional custom, but because it is according to people's situations."

So in marriage selective ethnicity is applied, i.e. only those customs are transferred that are accepted by outsiders whose support is needed. In my view polyandry is a traditional cultural phenomenon, which does not fit in the presentation of Tibetans as modern global citizens. This leads to a confused ethnic identity, which in relation to polyandry was expressed by Tashi (personal communication, 1993): "one-one is better for the cause, two-one is my preference, but it is their [his children's] choice."

With regard to the wedding rituals in Dharamsala these have also become a mix of modern and traditional (cf. Buffetrille, 1987; Das, 1893; Diehl, 1996:102–5; Dunham and Baker, 1993:58–64; Herbert, 1997; Shastri, 1993; and Tucci, 1967). As for the polyandrous marriages that were established in the first decades after arrival in India, most of the Tibetans were poor and did not have money to celebrate a big wedding or even consult an astrologer or lama. Sometimes a small ceremony was held, or none at all. Likewise, little exchange of goods in marital transactions took place.

Now that people are becoming more affluent old marriage customs are revived and new ones are blend in, while still marking their ethnic identity. For example, nowadays the invitation card is written both in Tibetan and English[189], traditional music and dance is alternated with disco, and while the bridal couple weares traditional clothes[190] their guests wear both traditional *chupa* and jeans. The wedding gifts are modern utensils and money in a 'Free Tibet'-envelope, all wrapped in a *khata* and accordingly given during the traditional *khata*-ceremony. Traditional Tibetan foods and drinks such as butter tea, *chang*, *thukpa*, and meat are still being served, sometimes in combination with Indian and Western food and beverages.

Traditionally at polyandrous weddings either one husband would be present and the others were automatically included, or all husbands attended the ceremony. In the before mentioned case of a young polyandrous family in Dharamsala both husbands were present at the wedding, which was celebrated elaborately. Whether this was the last polyandrous marriage in Dharamsala remains to be seen.

CONCLUSION

Summarising, I think profound theories on polyandry have been developed but still many questions remain to be answered. Often the scope of the theories is too limited or insufficient information is provided on polyandry in Tibetan refugee communities. The circumstances in exile are very different from the situation in traditional Tibet, but still ethical contradictions and practical temptations determined by situational factors mark polyandrous marriage and morals. In my view, polyandry is an individual response to specific circumstances. Faced with certain ecological, economical, political, social, and psychological conditions an individual decides, in consultation with other individuals and families involved whether or not to engage in a polyandrous union. In this decision different types of Tibetan ethnic identity, either inherited, ascribed, or constructed in exile, are examined closely.

In Dharamsala, predominantly among the older generations, plural-husband arrangements have been set up and the new types,

---

[189] It would be interesting to research any other languages being used.

[190] Cf. Seng and Wass (1995) on the nationalistic meaning of the wedding dress in Palestina.

pseudo polyandry and unaware polyandry, have appeared. Younger generations prefer to marry monogamously, rarely establishing polyandrous unions, and celebrate their weddings with a mixed style of modern and traditional elements. Despite ideology playing an important role in polyandry, it also is a reason for its decline. Influences of modern, multi-ethnic society are bringing about big alterations in the ways of thinking and behaviour of Tibetans in Dharamsala. People had become reluctant to talk about polyandry, but at the same time this reluctance is representative of the demise of polyandry. The changing points of view are brought about by frequent contacts with Indian and Western ideologies and life styles, which do not know or accept polyandry. Through direct personal interaction and through better education, easier travel, satellite television, movies, and the Internet, the entire world is unfolding and this is having an impact on traditional Tibetan norms, values, and customs.

I conclude that although material motives definitely are an important explanation for polyandry, immaterial aspects form the ground for both its presence and its decline. Tibetans in exile do put much effort in preserving traditional Tibetan culture and upholding Tibetan ethnic identity. In spite of this centuries-old tradition, polyandry may not be continued for much longer and a characteristic marker of Tibetan identity will have vanished.

BIBLIOGRAPHY

Aiyappan, A. 1937. "Polyandry and sexual jealousy," *Man* 37:104.
Alba, Richard D. 1990. *Ethnic Identity: The Transformation of White America*. New Haven: Yale University Press.
Anand, Dibyesh. 2002. "A Guide to Little Lhasa in India: the role of symbolic geography of Dharamsala in constituting Tibetan diasporic identity," in P. Christiaan Klieger (ed.), this volume.
Aziz, B. N. 1974. "Some notions about descent and residence in Tibetan society," in C. von Fürer-Haimendorf (ed.), *Contributions to the Anthropology of Nepal*. Warminster: Aris and Phillips, 23–39.
—— 1978. *Tibetan Frontier Families: Reflections of Three Generations from D'ing-ri*. New Delhi: Vikas Publishing House.
Beall, C.M. and M. Goldstein. 1981. "Tibetan polyandry: a test of socio-biological theory," *American Anthropologist*, 83:5–13.
Bell, C. 1928. *The People of Tibet*. Oxford: The Clarendon Press.
Berreman, G.D. 1980. "Polyandry: Exotic custom vs. analytic concept," *Journal of Comparative Family Studies*, XI(3):377–83.
—— 1987a. "Pahari polyandry: a comparison," in M.K. Raha and P.C. Coomar (eds.), *Polyandry in India*. Delhi: Gian Publishing House, 155–78.
—— 1987b. "Himalayan polyandry and the domestic cycle," in M.K. Raha and P.C. Coomar (eds.), *Polyandry in India*. Delhi: Gian Publishing House, 179–97.
Bhatt, G.S. 1980. "Constraints of being polyandrous-tribal: the case of Jaunsar Bawar," in S.M. Dubey, P.K. Bordoloi, and B.N. Borthakur (eds.), *Family, Marriage and Social Change on the Indian Fringe*. New Delhi: Cosmo Publications, 59–83.
Bhatt, G.S. and S.D. Jain. 1987. "Woman's role in a polyandrous Cis-Himalayan society: an overview," in M.K. Raha and P.C. Coomar (eds.), *Polyandry in India*. Delhi: Gian Publishing House, 405–21.
Bossen, Laurel. 1988. "Toward a theory of marriage: the economic anthropology of marriage transactions," *Ethnology* 27:127–44.
Buffetrille, K. 1987. "Un rituel de mariage tibétain", *L'Ethnographie*, Numero 100 & 101:35–63.
Cabézon, J.I. (ed.). 1992. *Buddhism, Sexuality and Gender*. Delhi: Sri Satguru Publications.
Cassidy, Margaret L. and Gary R. Lee. 1989. "The study of polyandry: A critique and a synthesis," *Journal of Comparative Family Studies*, XX(1):1–11.
Chandra, R. 1984. "Sex role arrangement to achieve economic security in north Himalayas," in C. von Fürer-Haimendorf (ed.), *Asian Highland Societies*. New Delhi: Sterling, 203–13.

—— 1987. "Polyandry in the northwestern Himalayas: some changing trends," in M.K. Raha and P.C. Coomar (eds.), *Polyandry in India*. Delhi: Gian Publishing House, 130–54.

Corlin, C. 1975. *The Nation in Your Mind: Continuity and Change among Tibetan Refugees in Nepal*. Ph.D. dissertation, University of Göteborg.

Cott, Nancy F. 2000. *Public Vows: a History of Marriage and the Nation*. Cambridge (USA): Harvard University Press.

Crook, J.H. 1980. "Social change in Indian Tibet," *Social Sciences Information*, 19(1):139–66.

—— 1987, "Polyandry in Ladakh," in M.K. Raha and P.C. Coomar (eds.), *Polyandry in India*. Delhi: Gian Publishing House, 23–53.

Crook, John and Stamati Crook. 1988. "Explaining Tibetan Polyandry: socio-cultural, demographic and biological perspectives," in John Crook and Henry Osmaton (eds.), *Himalayan Buddhist Villages*. Bristol: University of Bristol, 735–86.

Crook, John and Tsering Shakya.1988. "Six families from Leh," in John Crook and Henry Osmaton (eds.), *Himalayan Buddhist Villages*. Bristol: University of Bristol. 701–34.

Dargyay, E.K. 1982. *Tibetan Village Communities: Structure and Change*. Warminster: Aris & Phillips.

Das, S.C. 1893. "The marriage customs of Tibet," *Journal of the Asiatic Society of Bengal*, LXII(I):8–19.

Das-Gupta, Hem Chandra. 1921. "A short note on polyandry in the Jubbal State (Simla)," *The Indian Antiquary* 50:146–48.

deVoe, Dorsh Marie. 1981a. "The refugee problem and Tibetan refugees," *The Tibet Journal* VI(3):22–42.

—— 1981b. "Framing refugees as clients," *International Migration Review*, 15(1):88–94.

Diehl, Kiela. 1996. "The wedding hostesses of Central Tibet," *Chö Yang*, 7:102–5.

—— 1997. "When Tibetan refugees rock, paradigms roll: echoes from Dharamsala's musical soundscape," in Frank J. Korom (ed.), *Constructing Tibetan Culture: Contemporary Perspectives*. Quebec: World Heritage Press,122–59.

(DIIR) Department of Information and International Relations. 1999. *Dharamsala: Little Lhasa in India*, Dharamsala: Department of Information and International Relations.

Dillingham, Beth W. & Barry L. Isaac. 1975. "Defining marriage cross-culturally," in Dana Raphael (ed.), *Being Female: Reproduction, Power, and Change*. The Hague: Mouton, 55–63.

Dumont, Louis. 1968. "The Marriage Alliance," in Paul Bohannan and John Middleton (eds.), *Marriage, Family, and Residence*. Garden City, New York: The Natural History Press, 203–11.

Dunham, Carroll. 1991. "Nooit jaloers! Veelmannerij in Humla," *Himalaya* 4:16–20.

Dunham, Carroll, and Ian Baker. 1993. *Tibet: Reflections from the Wheel of Life*. New York: Abbeville Press.

Dunham, Carroll, Sedhar Chozam, and Joanna Head. 1993. "The dragon bride" (Anthropological documentary), in *Under the sun*, June 10, 1993 (50 min.). London: BBC-TV with The National Geographic Society.

Ekvall, R.B. 1972. "Demographic aspects of Tibetan nomadic pastoralism," in Brian Spooner (ed.), *Population Growth: Anthropological Implications*. Cambridge: MIT Press, 265–85.

Fielding, William J. 1942. *Strange Customs of Courtship and Marriage*. Philadelphia: The Blakeston Company.

Fischer, H.Th. 1942. *Huwelijk en Huwelijksmoraal bij vreemde volken*. Utrecht: De Haan.

—— 1952. "Polyandry," *International Archives of Ethnography* 46:106–15.

Fisher, Helen E. 1992. *Anatomy of Love: The Natural History of Monogamy, Adultery and Divorce*. New York: Norton.

Fisher, J.F. 1987. *Trans-Himalayan Traders: Economy, Society, and Culture in Northwest Nepal*. Delhi: Motilal Banarsidass.

French, Rebecca Redwood. 1995. *The Golden Yoke: The Legal Cosmology of Buddhist Tibet*. New York: Cornell University Press.

Fürer-Haimendorf, C. von. 1975. *Himalayan Traders*. London: John Murray.

—— 1990. *The Renaissance of Tibetan Civilization*. Oracle (U.S.A.): Synergetic Press.

Goldstein, M.C. 1971a. "Taxation and the structure of a Tibetan village," *Central Asiatic Journal*, XV(1):1–27.

—— 1971b. "Serfdom and mobility: An examination of the institution of 'Human Lease' in traditional Tibetan society," *Journal of Asian Studies*, 521–34.

—— 1971c. "Stratification, polyandry and family structure in Tibet," *Southwestern Journal of Anthropology*, 27:64–74.

—— 1973. "The circulation of estates in Tibet: Reincarnation, land and politics,"*Journal of Asian Studies*, XXXII(3):445–55.

—— 1976. "Fraternal polyandry and fertility in a high Himalayan valley in northwest Nepal," *Human Ecology*, 4:223–33.

—— 1978a. "Adjudication and partition in the Tibetan stem family," in David C. Buxbaum (ed.), *Chinese Family Law and Social Change in Historical and Comparative Perspective*. Seattle: University of Washington Press.

—— 1978b, "Ethnogenesis and Resource Competition among Tibetan Refugees in South India," in J. Fisher, *Himalayan Anthropology: The*

Indo-Tibetan Interface. The Hague, Paris: Mouton Publishers, 395–420.

—— 1981. "New perspectives on Tibetan fertility and population decline," *American Ethnologist,* 8:721–38.

—— 1987a. "When brothers share a wife," *Natural History,* 96:3:39–49.

—— 1987b. "Pahari and Tibetan polyandry revisited," in M.K. Raha and P.C. Coomar (eds.), *Polyandry in India*. Delhi: Gian Publishing House, 198–219.

—— 1989. "The impact of China's reform policy on the nomads of Western Tibet," *Asian Survey,* 29(6):619–41.

—— 1993. *A History of Modern Tibet, 1913–1951: the Demise of the Lamaist State*. Delhi: Munshiram Manoharlal Publishers.

Goldstein, Melvyn C. and Cynthia M. Beall. 1982. "Tibetan Fraternal Polyandry and Sociobiology: A Rejoinder to Abernethy and Fernandez," *American Anthropologist,* 84(4):898.

—— 1990. *Nomads of Western Tibet*. Berkeley: University of California Press.

Goldstein, Melvyn C., Paljor Tsarong, and Cynthia M. Beall. 1983. "High altitude hypoxia, culture and human fecundity/fertility: a comparative study," *American Anthropologist,* 85(1):28–49.

Gombo, Ugen. 1985. *Tibetan Refugees in the Kathmandu Valley*. Ann Arbor: University Microfilms International.

Goody, Jack. 1990. *The Oriental, the Ancient, and the Primitive: Systems of Marriage and the Family in the Pre-industrial Societies of Eurasia*. Cambridge: Cambridge University Press.

Gough, E. Kathleen. 1968. "The Nayars and the definition of marriage," in Paul Bohannan and John Middleton (eds.) *Marriage, Family and Residence*. Garden City, New York: The Natural History Press, 49–71.

Henneman, Joseph. 1954. "Polyandrie im vorislamischen Arabien," *Anthropos* 49:314–22.

Hermanns, M. 1953. "Polyandrie in Tibet," *Anthropos* 48:637–641.

Hiatt, Lester R. 1985. "Polyandrie in Sri Lanka," in Gisela Völger und Karin von Welck (eds.), *Geliebt-Verkauft-Getauscht-Geraubt. Zur Rolle der Frau im Kulturvergleich*. Köln: Rautenstrauch-Joest Museum, 620–24.

Herbert, Jeanne. 1997. *Tibetan marriage: old customs and new traditions*. Unpublished paper.

Jain, K.S.D. 1980. "Woman's status in marriage and family in a poly-androus society," in S.M Dubey, P.K. Bordoloi, and B.N. Borthakur (eds.), *Family, Marriage and Social Change on the Indian Fringe*. New Delhi: Cosmo Publications, 83–90.

Kapadia, K.M. 1990. *Marriage and Family in India*. Calcutta: Oxford University Press.

Kawaguchi, Ekai. 1909. *Three Years in Tibet*. Benares & London: Theosophical Publishing Society.

Klieger, P. Christiaan. 1992. *Tibetan Nationalism*. Berkeley: Folklore Institute.

—— 2001. "Engendering Tibet: Power, self, and change in the diaspora," in P. Christiaan Klieger (ed.) (this volume).

Kloos, Peter. 1991. *Culturele Antropologie: Een Inleiding*. Assen (NL): Van Gorcum.

Kolas, Ashild. 1996. "Tibetan nationalism: the politics of religion," *Journal of Peace Research*, 33(1):51–66.

Korn, Evelyn. 2000. "On the formation of family structures," *Public Choice*, 105:357–72.

Korom, Frank J. (ed.). 1997a. *Constructing Tibetan Culture: Contemporary Perspectives*, Quebec: World Heritage Press.

—— 1997b. *Tibetan Culture in the Diaspora*, Wien: Österreichische Akademie der Wissenschaften.

Kurian, George (ed.). 1979. *Cross-Cultural Perspectives of Mate-Selection and Marriage*. London: Greenwood Press.

Kvaerne, Per and Rinzin Thargyal. 1993. *Bon, Buddhism, and Democracy: The Building of a Tibetan National Identity*, NIAS Report, no. 12. Copenhagen: Nordic Institute of Asian Studies.

Leach, E. 1955. "Polyandry, inheritance and the definition of marriage," *Man*, December 1955:182–86.

—— 1991. "The social anthropology of marriage and mating," in V. Reynolds and J. Kellett (eds.), *Marriage and Mating*. Oxford: Oxford University Press.

Levine, N. E. 1978. "The theory of Rü kinship, descent and status in a Tibetan society," in C. von Fürer-Haimendorf (ed.), *Asian Higland Societies in Anthropological Perspective*. New Delhi: Sterling Publishers, 52–78.

—— 1980. "Nyinba polyandry and the allocation of paternity," *Journal of Comparative Family Studies*, XI(3):283–98.

—— 1981a. "Law, labor and the economic vulnerability of women in Nyinba society," *Kailash*, 8:123–53.

—— 1981b. "Perspectives on love: morality and affect in Nyinba interpersonal relationships," in: A.C. Mayer (ed.), *Culture and Morality: Essays in Honour of C. von Fürer-Haimendorf*. Delhi: Oxford University Press,106–25.

—— 1988. *The Dynamics of Polyandry*. Chicago and London: The University of Chicago Press.

—— 1994. "The demise of marriage in Purang, Tibet: 1959–1980," in Per Kvaerne (ed.), *Tibetan Studies*. Oslo: The Institute for Comparative Research in Human Culture, 468–80.

—— 1997. "Why polyandry fails: Sources of instability in polyandrous marriages," *Current Anthropology*, 18(3):375–98.

Levine, Nancy E. and Lopsang Geleg. 1990. "Ethnic variation and cultures of Tibet," in Carole Elchert (ed.), *White Lotus: An Introduction to Tibetan Culture*. Ithaca, NY: Snow Lion, 56–65.

Levine, N.E., and W.H. Sangree. 1980. "Conclusion: Asian and African systems of polyandry," *Journal of Comparative Family Studies*, XI(3):385–410.

Lopez, Donald S. 1997. *Religions of Tibet in Practice*. Princeton, NJ: Princeton University Press.

Macartney, Jane. 1994. "China lashes out at resurgence of Tibet polyandry," *World Tibet Network News*, December 28, 1994. http://www.tibet.ca/wtnarchive/1994/12/28_1.html.

Mahmoudi, Kooros. 1996. "Defining refugees, examining refugee adjustments: the case of Tibetans in India," *Guruk Nanak Journal of Sociology*, 49–71.

Majumdar, D.N. 1960. *Himalayan Polyandry: Structure, Functioning and Cultural Change: A Field Study of Jounsar*. Bombay: Asia Publishing House.

Mandelbaum, David G. 1938. "Polyandry in Kota society," *American Anthropologist*, 40:574–583.

Mukherji, Anima. 1950. "The pattern of a polyandrous society with particular reference to tribal crime," *Man in India*, 30:56–65.

Muller, J.C. 1980. "On the relevance of having two husbands: contribution to the study of polygynous/polyandrous marital forms of the Jos Plateau," *Journal of Comparative Family Studies*, XI(3):359–69.

Nakamura, Hajime and Philip P. Wiener (eds.). 1981. *Ways of Thinking of Eastern Peoples: India, China, Tibet, Japan*. Honolulu: University of Hawaii.

Nandi, S.B. 1987. "Status of women in polyandrous society," in M.K. Raha and P.C. Coomar (eds.), *Polyandry in India*. Delhi: Gian Publishing House, 422–34.

Nowak, Margaret. 1978. "Liminal 'Self', Ambigious 'Power': The Genesis of the 'Rangzen' Metaphor among Tibetan Youth in India." University of Washington Doctoral dissertation.

—— 1980. "Change and differentiation in Tibetan sex roles: the new adult generation in India," in M. Aris and Aung San Suu Kyi (eds.), *Tibetan Studies in Honour of Hugh Richardson*. Warminster: Aris and Phillips Ltd.

—— 1984. *Tibetan Refugees*. New Jersey: Rutgers University Press.

Otterbein, Keith F. 1968. "Marquesan polyandry," in Paul Bohannan and John Middleton (eds.), *Marriage, Family and Residence*, Garden City. New York: The Natural History Press, 287–96.

Pakrasi, K. 1987. "A note on differential sex-ratios and polyandrous people in India," in M.K. Raha and P.C. Coomar (eds.), *Polyandry in India*. Delhi: Gian Publishing House, 377–93.

Palakshappa, T.C. 1978. *Tibetans in India*. New Delhi: Sterling Publishers.

Park, Willard Z. 1937. "Paviotso polyandry," *American Anthropologist* 39:366–68.

Parmar, Y.S. 1975. *Polyandry in the Himalayas*. New Delhi: Vikas.

Pathak, Nupur. 1997. "Continuity and change in education amongst immigrant Tibetans in India," in H. Krasser, M.T. Much, E. Steinkellner, and H.Tauscher (eds.), *Tibetan Studies: Proceedings of the 7ʰ Seminar of the International Association for Tibetan Studies, Graz 1995*, II:745–50.

Perentidis, St. 1997. "Réflexions sur la polyandrie à Sparte dans l'Antiquité," *Revue historique de droit français et étranger*, 75 (1):7–32.

Peter, Prince of Greece and Denmark. 1956. "For a new definition of marriage," *Man*, March:48.

—— 1957. "For a new definition of marriage," *Man*, February:32.

—— 1963. *A Study of Polyandry*. The Hague: Mouton.

—— 1965. "The Tibetan Family System," in M.F. Nimkoff (ed.), *Comparative Family Systems*, 192–208.

—— 1980. "Comments on the social and cultural implications of variant systems of polyandrous alliances," *Journal of Comparative Family Studies*, XI(3):371–75.

Planning Council. 2000. *Tibetan Demographic Survey 1998*. Dharamsala: Central Tibetan Administration.

Quale, G.R. 1988. *A History of Marriage Systems*. Westport (U.S.A.): Greenwood Press Inc.

Reynolds, V. and J. Kellett (eds.). 1991. *Marriage and Mating*. Oxford: Oxford University Press.

Russell, Jeremy. 2000. *Dharamsala: Tibetan Refuge*. New Delhi: Lustre Press & Roli Books.

Saklani, G. 1984. *The Uprooted Tibetans in India*. New Delhi: Cosmo Publications.

Saksena, R.N. 1954. *Social Economy of a Polyandrous People*. Agra University Press.

Samuel, Geoffrey. 1993. *Civilized Shamans: Buddhism in Tibetan Societies*. Washington & London: Smithsonian Institution Press.

Sangree, Walter H. and Nancy E. Levine. 1980. "Introduction," *Journal of Comparative Family Studies*, XI(3):i–iv.

Schuler, S. 1978. "Notes on marriage and the status of women in Baragaon," *Kailash*, 6:141–52.

—— 1983. *Fraternal Polyandry and Single Women: A Study of*

Marriage, Social Stratification and Property in Chumik, a Tibetan society of the Nepalese Himalayas. Harvard Unversity thesis.

—— 1987. *The Other Side of Polyandry*. Boulder: Westview Press.

Seng, Yvonne J. and Betty Wass. 1995. "Traditional Palestinian Wedding Dress as a Symbol of Nationalism," in Joanne B. Eicher (ed.), *Dress and Ethnicity*. Oxford: Berg, 227–54.

Shakabpa, W.D. 1988. *Tibet. A Political History*. Singapore: Potala Publications.

Shakya, Tsering. 1999. *The Dragon in the Land of Snows: A History of Modern Tibet since 1947*. London: Pimlico.

Shastri, Lobsang. 1993. "The Marriage Customs of Ru-thog Khyung-rDzong dKar-po," in Per Kvaerne (ed.), *Tibetan Studies*. Oslo: The Institute for Comparative Research in Human Culture, 755-67.

Singh, K.S., B.R. Sharma, and A.R. Sankhyan. 1996. *People of India, State Series: Himachal Pradesh, Vol.XXIV*. New Delhi: Manohar Publishers, on behalf of Anthropological Survey of India.

Singh, Sarva Daman. 1988. *Polyandry in Ancient India*. Delhi: Motilal Banarsidass.

Skolnick, Arlene. 1973. *The Intimate Environment. Exploring Marriage and the Family*. Boston: Little, Brown and Company.

Smith, Eric Alden. 1998. "Is Tibetan polyandry adaptive?: Methodological and Metatheoretical Analyses," *Human Nature*, 9(3):225–62.

Smith, Warren W. 1997. *Tibetan Nation: A History of Tibetan Nationalism and Sino-Tibetan Relations*. New Delhi: Harper Collins.

Stein, R.A. 1972 (1962). *Tibetan Civilization*. Stanford: Stanford University Press.

Stephens, M.E. 1988. "Half a Wife Is Better Than None: A Practical Approach to Nonadelphic Polyandry," *Current Anthropology*, 29(2):354–56.

Stevens, John. 1994. *Boeddhisme en Sex*. Katwijk: Panta Rhei.

Stewart, Omer C. 1937. "Northern Paiute polyandry," *American Anthropologist* 39:368-9.

Subba, T.B. 1990. *Flight and Adaption: Tibetan Refugees in the Darjeeling-Sikkim Himalaya*. Dharamsala: Library of Tibetan Works and Archives.

Tambiah, S.J. 1966. "Polyandry in Ceylon," in C. von Fürer-Haimendorf (ed.) *Caste and Kin in Nepal, India, and Ceylon*. Bombay: Asia Publishing House, 264–360.

Taring, R.D. 1978. *Daughter of Tibet*. New Delhi: Allied Publishers.

Thurman, Robert A.F. 1996. *Essential Tibetan Buddhism*. New Delhi: Harper Collins.

Trevithick, Dalan. 1997. "On a panhuman preference for monandry: is polyandry an exception?," *Journal of Comparative Family Studies*, 28(3):154–81.

Tucci, G. 1967. *Tibet*. London: Elek Books.

Vajda, László'. 1985. "Polygynie und polyandrie. Zwei formen der Vielehe," in Gisela Völger und Karin von Welck (eds.), *Geliebt-Verkauft-Getauscht-Geraubt: Zur Rolle der Frau im Kulturvergleich*. Köln: Rautenstrauch-Joest Museum, 80–87.

Vangeenberghe, F.P.J. 1957. "Mariage pama, polyandrie et ordre public," *Problèmes d'Afrique Centrale*, 10(35):3–22.

Walker, A.R. 1986. *The Toda of South India*. Delhi: Hindustan Publishing Corporation.

Westermarck, Edward. 1903. *The History of Human Marriage*. London: MacMillan.

Yeh, Emily. 2001. "Will the *real* Tibetan please stand up!": Identity politics in the Tibetan Diaspora," in P. Christiaan Klieger, (ed.) (this volume).

CHAPTER FIVE

ENGENDERING TIBET: POWER, SELF, AND CHANGE
IN THE DIASPORA

P. CHRISTIAAN KLIEGER (CALIFORNIA ACADEMY OF SCIENCES)

INTRODUCTION

The construction of gender-based identities among Tibetan groups is a subject of growing interest in Tibetology, especially within the last decade. This paper examines how some of the expressions of the modern Tibetan Self in India are enacted through gender and how these presentations are related to ethnic and national categories of identity. It is based recent empirical research in the large Tibetan communities of Delhi performed in the year 2000.[191]

Diaspora Tibetan culture is often chosen by social scientists to help demonstrate the phenomena of sociocultural change and assimilation, and their opposites, resistance to change and enclavement. As some scholars have suggested, Tibetan exiles' uniquely configured constructions as actors in a globally dispersed culture serve as a challenge to the essentialising notions of the traditional, locale-based ethnographic record. Because gender is so intimately associated with constructions of the Self, its study can be illustrative of various dynamic process impacting individuals in exile, including modernisation, acculturation, Western-inspired 'reflexivity', and international positioning.

Despite, or perhaps because, of this globally dispersed culture, essentialising agents are created and maintained by the Tibetan government-in-exile. In the hyperconscious world of Dharamsala, culture change is of course what is not supposed to happen. Social institutions are critically designed to preserve Golden Age traditions and foster strong notions of pan-Tibetan identity, until some un-

[191] I wish to thank Tsering Paljor and Jampa Lhawang of Delhi for their help on this project.

defined time that the country is liberated. So agency, innovation, and artifacts of change tend to be immediately suspect and potentially polluting. Variations in gender categories or role expectations may thus be referenced as Western or Chinese affectations.

For numerous historical reasons, including the perpetuation of the adamantine essentialist paradigm of Shangri-La, the study of gender and variation in Tibetan society has slowly developed. As Barbara Aziz once put it, the relative absence of gender-based field studies has made if difficult to use Tibetan data in cross-cultural comparisons (Aziz, 1987:76). There are notable exceptions: the late Beatrice Miller was a pioneer in studying the role of women in Tibetan society (see Miller, 1998), and Goldstein's 1964 work on *ldab ldob* gender role variation in monasteries are at variance to most ethnographer's rather clear cut division of male and female worlds in Tibetan society and Tibetological scholarship. These are not necessarily categories based in Western social science. Rather, the strong binary divisions of male/female and householder/renunciate found so often in this ethnographic literature may be largely artifacts of the ideological constructs of Buddhist and Brahmanic philosophy. Many Tibetan informants, in Tibet and in the South Asian diaspora, are keen to provide exegeses of their ideal social structures, especially to outsiders.

Since the 1980s, however, the exciting works of Janice Willis (e.g., [ed.], 1987), Janet Gyatso, Karma Lekshe Tsomo, and others on the role of Tibetan nuns and religious women in history have been indicative of an exponential expansion in women studies and more general gender based analyses. Barnett, Upton, Makley, Diemberger, Heller, Shaw, Uebach, and many others currently are working in the realm of Tibetan women and gender studies. Stimulated by this scholarship, there is now an increasing facility to construct models of gender, gender performance, gender variation, sexuality, and power relations in Tibetan society, and not just of women but of men too. This would leave us with, as Aziz might say, a true sociology of Tibet, one that could be a resource for comparison of Tibetan communities around the world and in cross-cultural studies.

Have traditional categories and expectations of gender changed through the passage of time and in the experience of exile? These questions were asked of a sample of young Tibetan residents of Delhi. I suggest that the basic categories of Tibetan gender expression have been changing in response to various agents, including idealisation of Western patterns of behaviour; different socio-economic conditions; revised societal expectations; and 'selective assimilation' of categories from Indian or Western models of gender categorisation.[192] As there has been some evidence that the inde-pendent-living, nuclear family is strengthening as an ideal in many Tibetan refugee communities, even among those groups with a strong history of polyandry or polygyny, one may theorise that gender categories and role expectations have also markedly changed from those of pre-diaspora Tibet. The purpose of my research has been to gather empirical data on ideal and actual behaviours relating to gender presentation of Self in an exile community. It is really a preliminary analysis, to begin to answer questions about gendered life in modern Tibetan society. With the assumption of change, then, I challenge both the essentialist positions in Tibetan studies, and the applied essentialist constructs of the Dharamsala/TCV/Welfare Office system.

METHODS

The Delhi survey has two components: a written questionnaire and focused interviews. Two sites in Old Delhi, India were chosen, Majnukatilla and Rohini. Majnukatilla (Figure 5.1)

---

[192] I am reminded here mostly of the work of Kalon Rinchen Khando Choegyal and the Tibetan Women's Association.

Figure 5.1: The Tibetan Temple at Majnukatilla, Delhi. Tsering Paljor.

refers to a neighborhood around an old Sikh temple, and is one of the most established urban Tibetan refugee settlements throughout the diaspora. The area is situated between the national highway to the Punjab and the banks of the Yamuna River. It is broken into two camps, old and new. According to the Tibetan Welfare Office, there are 378 large family groups comprising about 2,500 individuals re- siding in Majnukatilla. Most of the Tibetan families are involved in the seasonal sweater trade, while others are restaurateurs and shop- keepers. The neighborhood has somewhat of a notorious reputation as being rich with chang shops and a haven for prostitution. The other site is Rohini, in northwestern Delhi. The residents of the S.O.S. Tibetan Youth Hostel (Figures 5.2 and 5.3) were selected. The hostel inhabitants are mostly young Tibetan college students from all around India, Nepal, Bhutan, and the Tibet Autonomous Region (T.A.R.) of China. I wanted to interview a sample of

Figure 5.2: S.O.S. Tibetan Youth Hostel, Rohini, Delhi. Jampa Lhawang.

Figure 5.3: Student Residents, Rohini, Delhi. Jampa Lhawang.

the first generation of Tibetans born in exile, and recent arrivals from Tibet—all relatively young adults with ages ranging 18—40.

Using college-age Tibetan survey workers, we distributed a questionnaire with 47 questions. Topics included marriage arrangements, residence preference, gender conceptual-isations and expectations, self-identity, religious practice, and educational levels. Of the 258 respondents, 103 were gathered from Majnukatilla and 155 from Rohini. About 2% of the responses were eliminated, as they did not fit the age parameters or were otherwise compromised. The survey was followed up with 20 in-depth, recorded interviews on the subjects of marriage, dating, *rang bstan* (freedom) and other activities possibly related to the construction of Tibetan identity. Conversations were recorded in Tibetan at Majnukatilla, in English in Rohini.[193]

RESULTS

Majnukatilla is the older refugee settlement. Here, almost all respondents' families went into exile with the Dalai Lama in 1959–60, whereas about 22% of Rohini respondents' families left Tibet after the 1970s. Conversely, the Rohini population has been more mobile, with about 8% of the sample having traveled back and forth to Tibet in recent years.

MARRIAGE PATTERNS

Considering how infrequent polyandry and polygyny actually were in Tibet, it is surprising to note that 18% of the Majnukatilla males and females claim descent from polygamous families. Fully 19% of the males and 5% of the females at Rohini are descended from polygamous families. In both neighborhoods, polygamous marriages ended in their families an average of 22–24 years ago, about at the birth time of the respondents, and usually after the parents had left Tibet. Polygamous marriages still exist in elderly populations, but the marriage practice is apparently disappearing in modern diaspora society.[194] Said one woman in Rohini, "too many husbands are a problem."

---

[193] The difference in the language usage may indicate not only the greater bilingual competence of the Rohini students, but an English-speaking preference as well.

[194] Nellie Grent, in her 2000 Leiden IATS paper (this volume), suggests that in Dharamsala at least, polyandry is still practiced, but done so rather clandestinely. It appears that polyandry has assumed the status of a less favorable marriage option

Marriage & Locality

Another surprise in the data from the two Tibetan settlements in Delhi was the apparent disparity between verbal responses that Tibetan refugees prefer neolocal marriage residence, and the questionnaire data that indicate that for themselves, they prefer to live with their parents after marriage. One Rohini woman said that neolocality was preferable, but it was due to Western influence. Typical of the responses was the sentiments of one man, who was the only male left at home with his parents. Since his brothers and family worked to assure that he had an education, he may need to leave in order to optimise his advantages. And, in fact, he would prefer to stay with his wife away from home and make is own way through life. Others conditioned their response by saying that it was their responsibility to take care of their parents, even though they would like to establish an independent household. Several men stated flatly that they didn't believe in marriage: "I'm living life with my friends only, not with my wife and all." In Majnukatilla, fully 63% of the males wish to live with their parents after marriage, 40% of the females. Only 8% of the females preferred patrilocality, which was perhaps the most common practice in traditional Tibetan society. In Rohini, about 68% of both the males and females wished to live with their parents after marriage.

In both Majnukatilla and Rohini, all people surveyed labeled themselves 100% ethnically Tibetan, with both parents being either born in Tibet or born in exile of Tibetan parents. Most astonishing, all respondents who answered the question in Rohini and all but one in Majnukatilla said they prefer to marry another Tibetan. A single female listed a German, which leads me to believe she was referring to her specific situation and not the ideal for all Tibetans. Many informants said in the interviews that while marriage with foreigners should ideally not make a difference, it is important for the survival of the Tibetan race to marry Tibetans. Several said that there was a positive side to marrying a foreigner, especially if "one could make that person Tibetan." One man in Rohini said:

---

under the experience of exile, accomplished with the sentiment of shame and the feeling of anachronism.

> It couldn't hinder our own struggle for independence if the girl [from another race] is suited for oneself. If [she] is able to lift up the culture of me, then I don't consider it a hindrance.

Another stated:

> I will marry a Tibetan. But I don't have any objection of people marrying foreigners. I think that will be [very helpful] if we are able to make them [into] Tibetans.

A similar response also touched on the 'acquisitional' nature of Tibetan identity:

> There is not much effect on Tibetan society marrying outsiders; there is both positive and negative effect. As far as positive side is concerned we can spread the Tibetan tradition and culture to other people.

These responses tend to reinforce the achievement-based model of Tibetan identity formation that I discussed in *Tibetan Nationalism* (1992). A different sentiment, however, is seen in the official Government-in-exile press, which specially views Han/Tibetan intermarriage and general Han resettlement in Tibet as the most serious threats to Tibetan culture in the homeland. There are not similar published concerns about Tibetan refugee-foreigner unions, however. Unions with Indians, according to one young woman, are generally looked down upon by refugee society:

> I've noticed one funny thing. There are many people who are getting married with foreigners in like Western country and there are many other people who marry Indians; the irony is these who marry to foreigners, they are okay, fine; but those who are married to Indians, they are like, "Oh, she has married an Indian," they look down upon it.

Surprisingly, going abroad to live is generally looked down upon in the surveyed Delhi communities.[195] By going abroad, one may develop a facility to disseminate truth to global audiences, according to the respondent. One interlocutor said,

> there is a difference in unity when abroad and the unity of Tibetans in India due to the Tibetan government-in-exile being here.

---

[195] This is contrary to the sentiments generally associated with many refugees in Dharamsala, Kathmandu and other places with heavy Western tourism patronage. Here, the West often is constructed as a sort of a "reverse Shangri-La." See Klieger (2000).

In general, to go abroad and study is good, otherwise it was widely felt that permanent settlement abroad would have a negative consequence on the Tibet freedom movement.[196]

GENDER AND IDENTITY

Identity is a layered set of boundaries inextricably linked with gender. In exiled communities, traditions are not taken for granted, rather they are often consciously articulated with those on the outside. In Majnukatilla, males and females had gender-specific ways to express what it means to be Tibetan. Nearly all were deeply convinced that it was important to show oneself as Tibetan to the outside world. "We have lost our rosy cheeks," said one woman explaining the exodus to India; it was therefore necessarily to consciously articulate that which once was taken for granted. "Yeah, this is an instinct," said one young man in Rohini. He further clarified an important, highly conscious element in the portrayal of Tibetan cultural identity to foreigners:

> Yeah, there will be a lot of people from outside who will be looking into the Tibetan community who are all the time in touch with the Tibetan community. They have lots of concerns on us — if these people are doing something for our country, then of course it is important to be a perfect citizen, a perfect Tibetan, with a Tibetan identity. I think this is very important.

When asked what picture he would give to a foreigner about Tibet, one young Rohini student expressed the Shangri-La version of Tibet:

> In my mind I give a very turquoise sea, with clear air, green park, with a snowy mountains and all. Like something like equal to heaven, which I haven't been but my parents keep on talking about such things during my childhood.[197]

Distinctive dress is a traditional and important marker of ethnic affiliation throughout Asia. And female gendered bodies are often the medium that communicates ethnic difference of the group to the

---

[196] Again, this viewpoint is generally contrary to the well-known Tibetan government-in-exile and foreign NGO programs for selective resettlement of a small population of refugees in Europe and America (e.g. U.S.-Tibet Resettlement and Swiss resettlement projects).

[197] Mytho-historical descriptions of a homeland that Tibetan refugees have not directly experienced are further discussed by Yeh (this volume).

outside world. Are young Tibetan women really dispensing with the chupa in hot India? The survey indicates that 68% of the Majnuka-tilla females feel the most important way of showing Tibetan-ness is by wearing the chupa and pang den. In Rohini, however, only 31% of the females indicated the primacy of chupa as a marker of identity. There were many other responses—one woman said, "by not marry-ing a foreigner." The majority of Majnukatilla men who commented on female ethnic markers indicated that the chupa was most important, in contrast to a much more mixed response in Rohini.

The most frequent way Majnukatilla males said they communi-cated their Tibetan-ness was through action rather than passive display. A typical response:

> I'll try to maintain and propagate the religious tradition, which [demonstrates] our non-violence, ahimsa.

Fully 31% of the respondents indicated a preference for displaying active kindness, humbleness, and polite behaviour, all of which demonstrate a compassionate nature (*snying rje*). Similarly, 22% of the males suggested that the active telling of the truth of Tibet to outsiders was most important. Data outliers included one respondent mentioning the possession of the refugee registration card (RC), another the wearing of an earring.

Outward identity responses were broader in Rohini, with 21% suggesting *snying rje* and 12% political activism. Going against the older assumptions of Buddhist practice as paramount for the con-struction of nang ba inclusiveness, only a handful of young men and women in both locations indicated that religious practice was most important for demonstrating their cultural identity. Nearly all of the responses were conditioned by statements reflecting the sentiments that there is a nation called Tibet, and that all individuals should be proud to be Tibetan.

How are these ideal markers represented in actual practice? Seventy-two percent of the Majnukatilla males indicated that they wore Tibetan clothing only 0–20% of the time (including monks). This was qualified in the oral interviews—informants suggested that ethnic clothing was worn exclusively at Lo Sar or the Dalai Lama's birthday. However, almost half the females indicated wearing chupa over 40% of the time. Figures were similar in Rohini. Ideal state-ments and real practice seem to coincide on this topic.

Food preference is also a popular index of cultural affiliation, especially in communities exposed to assimilation.[198] In Majnukatilla, the majority of all respondents stated that they eat Tibetan food most of the time. In Rohini, 70–80% of the females prefer Tibetan food; males were fairly evenly split between Tibetan, Indian, and other types of cuisine. In assessing the Rohini figures, however, we should take into account the fact that many youth live in dormitories and they eat at commissaries where choice of cuisine is not always possible. In Majnukatilla, momo are slightly more popular than thenthuk and thukpa. In Rohini, thukpa and thenthuk edge out momo as favorite foods.

Another widely accepted index of ethnic solidarity is the frequency of friendships and other associations with people of one's group. When asked what percentage of their friends were Tibetan, 60% of the females and 57% of the males of Majnukatilla said that 80–100% of their friends were Tibetan. In Rohini, the percentages were 74 and 71%, respectively, between genders. These numbers dropped when the term 'associates' rather than 'friends' was used. There appeared very little gender difference in this response at both research sites.

Tibetan language use is a major issue of identity performance among the survey respondents. Although the vast majority of all respondents indicated that the use of the Tibetan language was very important for maintaining Tibetan identity, it was surprising to learn that many of the Rohini students said their literary language was English, not Tibetan. Similarly, others indicated that English was their primary language in general. All expressed concern that Tibetan youngsters were beginning to lose their abilities in Tibetan language, especially those in the northeast (Darjeeling, Kalimpong, Sikkim, etc.) where Nepali is the primary language.

GENDER RELATIONS, WORK AND RELIGION

In Majnukatilla, women strongly believed in equal aptitude between the sexes, that they have just as much ability as men do. The frequency of this response was a bit lower when men were surveyed about feminine equality. Surprisingly, the split between genders on this question was wider in Rohini. As to what type of job would be considered inappropriate for women, few career-minded college stu-

---

[198] In the immigrant rich nation of the United States, for example, ethnic food preferences often have remained long after material culture, language, marriage patterns, and other aspects of the original culture have disappeared.

dents in Rohini chose to answer the question at all. Those that did tended to indicate that any job was suitable. However, in Majnuka-tilla, most respondents, male and female, said that prostitution and chang selling were occupations that women should not do. It is inter-esting that those are the very professions that are allegedly prevalent in the Majnukatilla neighborhood. Across the board, men and women felt strongly that women should and were going out into the work-place, especially as long as they didn't neglect home. This perhaps reflects one of the most significant changes in Tibetan society in general, in the urban homeland as well as urban exile. When asked whether men actively participated in household duties, the majority of those not living in communal dormitories said they did.

Respondents were asked to rate lay men and women, nuns, and monks relative to perceptions of accumulated merit (*sonam*). In many homeland accounts, including the current work of Charlene Makley (1999) in Labrang village in A mdo, the clergy, with its divi-sions of nuns and monk, are usually considered ideally higher in merit than the laity. Within each of the sacred and profane catego-ries, the female element is traditionally considered inferior. In many social configurations, however, nuns appear to be at the bottom, as Karma Lekshe Tsomo, Makley, and others have attested. What is the attitude in urban Delhi towards the monastic institutions?

In Majnukatilla, 85% of the females and 90% of the males put monks in the first category of merit ranking, in contrast with the re-sponses at Rohini. In the latter neighborhood, only 80% of the females and 71% of the males considered monks as having the high-est merit. None of the women and only 3% of the males of Majnuka-tilla felt that monks and nuns shared the same merit. In Rohini, how-ever, 11% of the females and 13% felt that nuns and monks as a religious cohort were equal. Quite a few respondents stated that all categories of religious practitioner are equally meritorious. Rohini, then, seems to show a stronger sentiment of gender equality than in Majnukatilla, and the Delhi communities themselves seem to be more gender neutral in religious matters than that reported by Makley in A mdo. This suggests a correlation between educational levels and occupational expectations. It is clearly seen in the data comparing scholastic Rohini and tough-and-tumble Majnukatilla.

It appears that both groups still identify as being very religious, and this is supported by frequencies of going to *gompa*, reciting *mani* doing *khor ra*, etc. However, the traditional prestige of the monastic community appears to be declining, especially in Rohini. Many informants talked rather disparagingly of the modern monks in exile. With the exception of the Dalai Lama himself, I did not get the sense that the refugee monastic community was much respected:

> Fifty percent of our monks love money, they're after money you can say, and they pray and all but deep in their heart they don't have spiritual, *he na*? They are pretty corrupt.

One woman from Rohini said: "I'm sad to say I have a very bad picture about them. They're not practicing their monastic life strictly." Another reported: "they do a lot of things that aren't needed for them."

The tendency of reporting only ideal behaviour, especially to outsiders, has contributed to the general notion that homosexuality is largely unknown in both traditional Tibetan and diaspora societies. The survey figures in the Delhi population, at least, demonstrate otherwise. In worldly Majnukatilla, fully 23% of the female respondents and 37% of the males indicated that they had heard stories of homosexual practice in the monasteries. The figures were slightly lower for Rohini. When asked if they were aware of this practice by lay Tibetan males, 37% of both men and women of Majnukatilla said they were aware. Many responded that it was well known in the Tibetan regiments of the Indian army. These figures were considerably lower in Rohini. Lesbian Tibetan awareness existed in small numbers in both groups. Interestingly, many who did respond that they knew nothing about homosexuality, said that the practice was nevertheless sinful. Many informants considered such sexual identity a Western affectation, and that the Tibetans were lucky not to have 'contracted' it. Some informants concluded that homosexuality in single-sex communal situations, such as monasteries and the military, were only due to necessity, not choice.

Young Tibetans in Delhi also seem to segregate themselves from the senior refugee generation(s). When Tibetan men were asked if they would share a social drink with their fathers, nearly all expressed either the negative or conditioned their responses by referring to a time when they were older, more independent, etc. Similarly, the Tibetan youth who smoked did so without the knowledge of their parents. These responses seem in line with other statements of respect and fear expressed by the young Tibetan adults in reference to the older generation(s). Throughout the sample, and at both sites, the genre of 'youthful defiance' so common in the West seemed conspicuously absent.

CONCLUSIONS

I was surprised that statistically valid information on gender variance and sexuality was obtained in the Delhi communities. Gender seems so basic, or essential, in Tibetan society as to be taken for granted. An overwhelmingly prosaic notion of gender and sexuality in Tibetan society seems to suppress overt discussion on the topic. This, in turn, has affected generations of scholarship in Tibetan social studies. As Makley (1999:27) eloquently speaks on the dangers of the subject matter, "international interest in Tibet had meant that a research focus on gender (versus 'women') can be viewed as at once trivial and intensely threatening." Makley has discussed her own position as a foreign woman in day-to-day gender discourse, as has Yeh (this volume). Some of reluctance of Tibetans to speaks about gender dynamics and sexuality to outsiders may have been overcome in this study by using local Tibetan students as survey-takers.

It is consistent with Shangri-La orientalism to gravitate towards extremes: either to eroticise or neuter the object of study. Indeed, Tibetans have been neotonised and their 'potency' diminished throughout much of the Western colonial experience in South and Central Asia (see Klieger, 1997). Over the last few centuries, Tibetans, especially males, were transformed from the blood-thirsty kin of the Mongols and the Tartar hordes to the peace-loving, spiritual ascetics now most often experienced with the current Dalai Lama.

Modern Tibetan women studies, as distinct from gender, are much more popular in Western scholarly circles than they appear to be in the exile communities because they tend to be articulated within a realm of relative marginality and power-lessness. Women studies were not necessarily a challenge to the widely held notions of either the 'heroic male' ideal or the common 'celibate monastic' stereotype prevalent in traditional Tibet and diaspora studies.

It is especially interesting to note the heroic male archetype (see Goldstein, 1964; Paul, 1982; and Makley, 1999), a Tibetan 'macho', articulates a widely held sentiment that young men in the homeland can show their masculinity by fighting with each other, pursuing women, and drinking alcohol. This ideal seems to have been transformed by the young exiles into an active *snying rje*, the 'going forth' to tell the true story of Tibet. This may be an internalisation of the non-violent teachings of the current Dalai Lama and demonstrative the effectiveness of the refugee education system. After all, 'active' compassion is an attribute of the godhead, Avalokitesvara/Chenrezig, manifest in the Dalai Lama.

Other than a strong correlation between educational levels and career expectations, in general I found little difference between the young adult working class in Majnukatilla and the education-oriented youth of Rohini. The most expressed difference between the young generation of Tibetan refugees and the first generation of exiles is a change in marriage preference from arranged to love matches. Great concern for aging parents is still a major commitment, however, in modern urban society and seemingly continuous with traditional ideal. Rather than show marked signs of cultural loss, both groups seem to have a very clear idea what it is to be Tibetan, and most have not abandoned the notion that Tibetan will one day be free. A theme that was woven throughout both the written and oral interviews at both sites was an obvious pride in being Tibetan.

Studies of maleness and femaleness and alternative sexualities are a distinctive challenge, allowing perhaps some researchers to commiserate with the idea that the most guarded secrets of Tibetan culture are not those of tantric esoterica, but rather the mundane world of the gendered Tibetan self. It is nevertheless encouraging by preliminary data that Tibetans are indeed actively negotiating gender and other forms of self-presentation in exile. It is hoped that this survey may be expanded to include other urban centers in South Asia with substantial Tibetan settlement.

BIBLIOGRAPHY

Aziz, Barbara Nimri. 1989. "Moving towards a Sociology of Tibet," in Janice Willis (ed.), *Feminine Ground*. Ithaca, New York: Snow Lion Publications.

Goldstein, Melvyn. 1964. "A Study of *the Ldab Ldop*," *Central Asiatic Journal*, 9.

Klieger, P. Christiaan. 1997. "Shangri-La and Hyperreality: A Collision in Tibetan Refugee Expression," in Frank J. Korom (ed.), *Tibetan Culture in the Diaspora*. Volume 4, Proceedings of the 7th Seminar of the International Association for Tibetan Studies, 18–24 June, 1995, Schloß Seggau. Ernst Steinkellner [General Editor]). Wien: Österreichsche Akademie Der Wissenschaften.

—— 2000. "Anthropologist as Hero," in Terry Stocker (ed.), *Incidents*. Tempe, Arizona: Franklin Press.

Makley, Charlene Elizabeth. 1999. *Embodying the Sacred: Gender and Monastic Revitalization in China's Tibet*. University of Michigan doctoral dissertation. UMI, Ann Arbor.

Miller, Beatrice. 1997. "Tibetan Women Across Time, Space, and Political Boundaries." Paper read at the 8th Seminar of the International Association of Tibetan Studies, Bloomington, Indiana.

Paul, Robert. 1982. *Tibetan Symbolic World*. Chicago: University of Chicago Press.

Willis, Janice (ed.). 1987. *Feminine Ground*. Ithaca, New York: Snow Lion Publications.

CHAPTER SIX

NEW AGE NAMTAR:
TIBETAN AUTOBIOGRAPHIES IN ENGLISH

Laurie Hovell McMillin (Oberlin College)

Historically Tibetan culture has been rich with life stories, 'full liberation' stories told both as *namtar* (*rnam thar*, biography), and as *rangnam* (*rang rnam*, autobiography). As Janet Gyatso demonstrates (1998:101), despite the suggestion of some European literary critics that the autobiography is a distinctly Western phenomenon, Tibetan autobiographies have a rich tradition. Using the life of the Buddha as a kind of blueprint, these stories traditionally relate the exploits and the development of exemplary religious agents such as saints, bodhisattvas, purveyors of crazy wisdom, and other enlightened beings. They are designed to inspire and instruct their readers and listeners.

But in the contemporary situation of Tibetan diaspora, in which Tibetans have made new homes in India, Nepal, Australia, Europe, and the U.S., new forms of autobiography have appeared—other figures have emerged to tell their life stories—this time in English. Thus, in addition to the two autobiographies of the Fourteenth Dalai Lama, Anglophone readers also have access to the autobiographies of two of his siblings, of women of aristocratic birth, run-of-the-mill monks, torture victims, educated young men, and even a one-time exile who returned to live and work in Chinese-occupied Tibet.

Published in English in generic forms that are familiar to English readers, these texts address new audiences and offer versions of Tibetan-ness to an eager portion of what is largely an American and sometimes British audience. How might we think about these Tibetan autobiographies in English? Should we see them as participants in the Tibetan tradition of creating *rangnam*? Or are they simply a kind of capitulation to Western desires, telling readers the stories they want to hear in a way they want to hear them? Or might they be still something else?

In *Prisoners of Shangri-La*, Donald S. Lopez, Jr. offers a metaphor and a way of thinking about Tibetan self-presentation that has shaped my approach to these autobiographies. He writes that when Tibetans came into exile, they

> stepped into a world in which they were already present, and since their belated arrival . . .they have merged seamfully [sic] into a double that had long been standing. . . .[W]hat has occurred since 1959 has been a sometimes fitful accommodation of this double; as though mimicking a phantom, the Tibetans' self-presentation, as in a science fiction film, sometimes merges with its evil twin and sometimes stands alone, while the observer is rarely able to tell them apart. (Lopez, 1998:200)

As I understand it, then, the making of Tibetan autobiography in English emerges from a tangled and complex set of circumstances, conventions, and expectations. In some ways, the autobiographies come out of a deeply Tibetan impulse to tell life stories; in some ways, the phenomenon is one of diaspora, and a response to what I call the Western myth of epiphany — the dream that contact with Tibet and/or Tibetans might transform Westerners.[199] As I see it, the making of Tibetan autobiographies in English is inevitably a mixed phenomenon, one that is intertwined with both Western expectations and with some Tibetans' desires to represent what might be seen as the authenticity of their experience. Here I will discuss how these texts operate as a kind of exchange between Western readers and Tibetan writers. Because this paper comes out of a larger study of Tibetan autobiography in English in this space I will outline some of the key points.[200]

So first: what do Anglophone readers want from these texts? What do they get?

Although the subjects of these rangnam show a new diversity, there are nonetheless several features common to almost all Tibetan autobiographies in English, of which there are about 30 published[201]: almost all are written by Tibetans who identify themselves as

---

[199] See Laurie Hovell McMillin (1999:49-69).

[200] For further discussion of the myth of epiphany developed in British texts of travel as well as for an extended discussion of Tibetan autobiographies in English, see my *English in Tibet, Tibet in English* (2001. New York: Palgrove).

[201] Because some books contain two or more autobiographies and because more appear all the time, the count cannot be exact.

Buddhist, as nationalist, and as exiles. These, apparently, are the exemplary Tibetans who can inspire readers in English.

Such a profile — Buddhist, nationalist, exile — cannot begin to tell the story of the diversity of ethnic Tibetans' experiences and aspirations, of course. But such a profile, I think, does tell us something about the ways in which Tibetan exiles' self-identifications and Western perceptions of Tibetan-ness sometimes come together. These identities — Buddhist, Tibetan nationalist, and exile — all combine to create something I will call, after Vincanne Adams, the 'authentic Tibetan'[202] — one who is thought to embody these ideals in a kind of simple, unassuming way.

Given the desire for the authentic Tibetan, there is little market, apparently, for the Tibetan who is secular,[203] or for the Tibetan who does not question Chinese rule of Tibet. And because exile is closely tied to nationalism in the Tibetan diaspora, there is even little room for the life-stories of Tibetans who live in Tibet. (There is one autobiography that is an exception to each of these things, but it is clearly in the minority).[204]

Similarly, given this notion of the authentic, there is little room for the stories of Tibetans whose lives suggest compromise, what some might see as an undesirable hybridity or mixedness of 'pure' Tibetan culture with either a tainted Western one or a tainted Chinese one.

For example, because some exiles and their Western supporters believe that, as Jetsun Pema puts it, "[Tibetan] culture is alive only in exile" (Jetsun Pema with Gilles van Grasdorff, 1997:217). Tibetans who live in Tibet can be seen as not fully authentic. The unspoken logic here is that if the situation in Tibet were really unlivable, then real Tibetans couldn't live there. At other moments, however, authenticity is differently defined, and it is precisely those Tibetans who have come into exile in the West who are seen as tainted: in my interviews with him, a white collar, German-speaking, Tibetan exile in Switzerland, for example, tended to locate authentic Tibetan-ness

---

[202] See *Tigers of the Snow and other Virtual Sherpas* where Adams refers to the notion of the authentic Sherpa (1996. Princeton: Princeton University Press).

[203] One exception to this is Dawa Norbu's *Red Star Over Tibet*, where he presents himself as a secular intellectual (1987. New York: Envoy).

[204] See Melvyn Goldstein, William Siebenschuh, and Tashi Tsering, *The Struggle for a Modern Tibet: The Autobiography of Tashi Tsering* (discussed in Part Two, Chapter VIII. 1997. New York: M.E. Sharpe).

elsewhere; as a non-Buddhist, he knew he didn't have it; instead it was among those of "simple strong belief"—usually in Tibet or in India.[205] These are the kind of Tibetans we usually meet in Tibetan auto-biography in English, for most Tibetan autobiographies in English present a relatively untroubled version of their subject, one that accords with extant Western notions of what makes a real or authentic Tibetan.

To represent such a Tibetan (as in an autobiography) is to offer a presence that promises to transform western readers. I am using the term presence in two ways here: one refers to the way the term has been used in Western literary theory: presence refers to a reader's desire to accept the representation of the text for the real—for the thing itself. The second usage refers to the Kundun kind of presence.

Kundun, or presence as it is often translated, is, as you know, an epithet of the Dalai Lama, who is seen by Tibetan Buddhists as the presence of enlightenment on earth, an incarnation of Chenrzig, the dynamic and recurring emanation of the union of wisdom and compassion. So beneficent is the presence of the Dalai Lama (and other lamas) that devotees will touch the place where they have sat and perform rituals to request that they live long amongst us.

And in a sense, both kinds of presence are what Tibetan auto-biographies in English proffer. For some readers, these texts do not just offer the story of a real Tibetan as told by that Tibetan. They offer the presence of that Tibetan, the emanation of that Tibetan in a (Western) reader's life, and it is through such presence that the reader is educated or even transformed.

That might sound far-fetched, but this is made possible by Western habits of reading that include the cult of the author and the tendency to identify the speaker of the autobiographical narrative with the spoken—to identify the narrator with the subject of the writing; similarly, the name of the author is thought to refer to a 'real person' in the world. This confusion of narrator, protagonist, author and person in the world is marked in the case of Tibetan auto-biographies in English by the frequent inclusion of the subject's portrait on the cover of the book.

---

[205] Tashi [pseud.], a 27-year-old Tibetan male, interview by author in English, tape recording, Horgen, Switzerland, June 1996.

So Lobsang Gyatso in his maroon monk's robes grins at us from the cover of his book; similarly, the Dalai Lama graces the cover of his two autobiographies. On her book, Jamyang Sakya is bedecked in jewels and brocade. The clothbound edition of Palden Gyatso's life story not only boasts photos of the author/narrator/protagonist inside, the entire volume is clothed in monastic red and gold, colours the imprisoned monk was long forbidden to wear. All of these images and inclusions combine to suggest: what we have here is the real thing.

That readers frequently confuse the representation of a life with people in the world is suggested by their comments on Amazon.com's Website; there readers often give the highest 5-star rating to Tibetan autobiographies that (at least in my opinion) seem to be very boring or poorly edited. To criticise the book would seem like criticising the person 'in the world'. This seems particularly ironic given that many of these books are not really written by Tibetans at all, but are instead ghostwritten.

The dream of presence is enhanced by the very genre of auto-biography: given that the narrative is told in the first person, by an 'I', readers are invited to take up the position of the second person, 'you'. Reading thus seems to be a kind of dialogue. One reader's comments bear this out: "As I read Freedom in Exhile [sic] I had to keep reminding myself that it was a book and not a letter from His Holiness to myself."[206]

Because Tibet was perceived as the 'forbidden land' for so long and because Tibetans were long considered mysterious and isolated others, the fantasy of having a Tibetan right in one's home, one's hands, one head is too much to resist. And while it used to be that travel to Tibet was thought to transform Westerners, in recent years it seems that even contact through reading is enough to invoke the myth of epiphany; reading the life of a Tibetan—seeming contact with that Tibetan—becomes something that can transform readers, making them into a new 'you'.

And thus, other readers' comments on Amazon.com claim the potential of Tibetan autobiographies to change readers. One reader from California writes, "I started reading [*Freedom in Exile*] out of

---

[206] Amazon.com: Customer comments: *Freedom in Exile: The Autobiography of the Dalai Lama*, July 3, 1999.

interest and finished the book a wiser person."[207] Or as another reader
writes of Palden Gyatso's story, this book "must be a compulsory
read for anyone trying to be a better person...;"[208] and yet another
writes, "You'll be a better person for reading this book."[209] And
while it is useful to have an autobiography to access for such
transformation, for some readers the very existence of Tibetans in the
world can bolster Western lives. As one reader comments, "It's not
the Dalai Lama that [sic] is great. It is the Tibetan people. Everytime
[sic] one of those bodhisattvas dies, it affects us all."[210] The notion at
work here is that Tibetans are the 'good' and even 'enlightened'
people who by their very existence ennoble the lives of all the rest of
us poor souls.

If travel to Tibet once promised epiphany to Western travelers,
now in the situation of exile and diaspora, reading Tibetans' life
stories is enough to transform readers. But what do Tibetans get out
of the exchange? Some readers' comments on Amazon.com suggest
that in exchange for personal growth, Tibetans get support. As one
reader from Texas comments, "I can't imagine reading this book and
not being moved to support Tibetian [sic] independence."[211] That
Tibetan autobiographers encourage readers to take up such political
commitments is evident in a number of texts. As Heinrich Harrer
notes, Thubten Jigme Norbu was only persuaded to tell his story
when Harrer told him that "with such a book he could help his
country and his people," (Harrer, 1986:15). While some may see these
indirect pleas for Western support as a participation in crass Western
commodification of Tibet, such a plea for support also have Tibetan
sources; in this case, Tibetan autobiographies participate in a model
of patronage.

As both Lopez (1998:206) and Klieger (1992:19) have argued, in
the situation of Tibetan diaspora the standard patronage models—
choyon (*mchod yon*) and *jinda* (*sbyin bdag*)—have been transformed.
These models, which date back to the 13th century and significantly

---

[207] Amazon.com: Customer comments: *Freedom in Exile: The Autobiography of
the Dalai Lama*, July 3, 1999.
[208] Amazon.com: Customer comments: *The Autobiography of a Tibetan Monk*,
July 3, 1999.
[209] Ibid.
[210] Customer comments: *Freedom in Exile: The autobiography of the Dalai
Lama*, July 3, 1999.
[211] Ibid.

structured Tibetan relationships with Mongol and Manchus, have
taken on new incarnations since 1959. Lopez argues that, in many
ways, Westerners are now the patrons of Tibetan lamas, and Klieger
goes even further to argue that in the diaspora, all Tibetan exiles
have become objects of Western patronage—all have become worthy
fields of merit.

Interestingly, one of the first times that Tibetans told their stories
for the larger world occurred in 1959, after many had made their way
to India; it was then, perhaps, that the system of patronage began to
be redefined. When they arrived in India, many exiles were asked to
recount the atrocities they had witnessed in Tibet. The Dalai Lama's
brother, Gyalo Thondup, organised the interviews; one of the
interviewers sent to the camps in Assam was Tashi Tsering. He
writes:

> [Gyalo] wanted the world to know how the Tibetans had suffered at
> the hands of the Chinese and said he needed me to help him collect the
> narratives of the refugees so we could tell their story to the world. I
> was to interview as many people as I could and write down what I
> learned. . . . I tried to get as many eyewitness accounts of the uprising
> and flight as possible, taking careful notes in Tibetan. But it turned out
> to be more difficult than I expected. Most of the people I spoke to
> were illiterate and did not have an orderly or logical way of controlling
> and expressing their thought. (Tashi Tsering, 1997:56f.)

According to Tsering, because the refugees were unused to speaking
of themselves and their lives in this way—because, in effect, they
lacked appropriate narrative models—their stories had to be fash-
ioned for them. And because what little they said did not strongly
support the theme of Chinese oppression, their stories had to be
recast by those with a stronger sense of what the larger world needed
to know. Eventually these narratives became part of the evidence for
the International Commission of Jurists' report, which in 1960
condemned the Chinese occupation of Tibet. While little of real
political value came out of the Jurists' report, the sense that the life-
stories of ordinary Tibetans mattered was born on the Tibet-Indian
border. And there too was born the need for and the intervention of a
ghostwriter—someone who shaped these exiles recollections into a
compelling story. It was through these stories that 'the world' would
come to know of the situation in Tibet. It was through these stories
that the West was called on to act on behalf of Tibet. In this reinter-

pretation of patronage, to be worthy of support is another way of being authentic; to receive support is to have one's Tibetan-ness affirmed.

We might also note at this point that, just as the exiles' stories had to be refashioned by others in order to make a certain kind of sense, when Tashi Tsering told his own story in the 1990s, it was also shaped—this time by two interlocutors, Melvyn Goldstein and William Siebenschuh. These interlocutors, no doubt, differed from Gyalo Thondup in their sense of what the world needed to hear about Tibet. Tsering's account of being beaten by his Tibetan teacher (instead of by Chinese prison guards), his conscription as homosexual lover to a high-ranking monk, and his desire to work within Chinese-occupied Tibet all serve to intervene in idealised Western versions of Tibet. While the recent exiles' stories were designed to encourage patronage, Tashi Tsering's oppositional narrative is designed to problematise it. But both sets of narratives are intimately linked with Western desires. As Lopez wrote (1998:200), "Tibetans' self-presentation[s] . . . sometimes merge with [their] evil twin[s] and sometimes stand alone. . . . [T]he observer is rarely able to tell them apart."

What I try to do in my study of these texts is to analyze the significance of these mergings and intertwinings. I also want to suggest that such mixedness does not point to the degradation of Tibetan culture but rather to culture as usual. For I would even say that all these attempts to represent the 'pure' and 'authentic' Tibetan are themselves intercultural productions.

I'm interested in developing a more reflective and critical approach to these autobiographies as well as in intervening in commonplace views of Tibetans and Tibetan-ness. For even in some autobiographies that seem not to challenge images of the authentic Tibetan it is possible to read against the grain and thus discover or construct other versions of Tibetan identity.

Because the desire for the authentic Tibetan and the tendency to demonise the Chinese are strong impulses in popular American culture, it's not easy to produce an alternative reading. The notion that Tibetan identity is mixed, indeterminate, and often strategically deployed threatens established structures in Tibetan-Western relations. (Perhaps this is why an exhibition of Tibetan culture and folkways in Washington D.C. was scheduled at the same time as the conference for the International Association of Tibetan Studies: critical voices are not particularly welcome in this exchange.)

Although I don't have a program that would save us from all of this, I would suggest that readers of Tibetan autobiographies in English need to be watchful of our desires for presence and for the authentic Tibetan. As I see it, Tibetans need not be angels in order to be entitled to human rights; as Lopez writes (1994:92), "[t]he ravages wrought by China's policies in Tibet, resulting not only in the destruction of monasteries, temples, texts, and works of art, but in the deaths of hundreds of thousands of Tibetans, would seem enough to sustain the clear contrast with life in Tibet prior to the invasion" and thus also to support Tibetan aspirations for self-determination. Although my goal here is not to develop a coherent activist program, disbanding the myth of the authentic Tibetan may be the only way to salvage an effective pro-Tibetan politics. In any case, only by working against the old stories, reading against the entrenched notions of Tibetan-ness, can something else happen—a different story can be told, one in which ethnic Tibetans are allowed to play roles other than that of authentic Tibetan, one in which they are allowed to take up other tasks than the bearing of Western desires.

BIBLIOGRAPHY

Adams, Vincanne. 1996. *Tigers of the Snow and other Virtual Sherpas.* Princeton: Princeton University Press.

Goldstein, Melvyn, William Siebenschuh, and Tashi Tsering, 1997. *The Struggle for a Modern Tibet: The Autobiography of Tashi Tsering.* New York: M.E. Sharpe.

Gyatso, Janet. 1998. *Apparitions of the Self: The Secret Autobiographies of a Tibetan Visionary: A Translation and Study of Jigme Lingpa's Dancing Moon in the Water and Dakki's Grand Secret-talk.* Princeton: Princeton University Press.

Harrer, Heinrich. 1986. "Preface," in Dalai Lama's *Tibet is My Country.* London: Wisdom, 1986.

Lopez, Donald. 1994. "New Age Orientalism: The Case of Tibet," *Tricycle*, Spring.

—— 1998. *Prisoners of Shangri-La: Tibetan Buddhism and the West.* Chicago: University of Chicago Press.

Klieger, P. Christiaan. 1992. *Tibetan Nationalism: The Role of Patronage in the Accomplishment of a National Identity.* Meerut: Archana.

McMillin, Laurie Hovell. 1999. "Enlightenment Travels: The Making of Epiphany in Tibet," in James S. Duncan and Derek Gregory (eds.), *Writes of Passage: Reading Travel Writing.* London: Routledge.

Norbu, Dawa. 1987. *Red Star Over Tibet.* New York: Envoy.

Pema, Jetsun, with Gilles van Grasdorff. 1997. *Tibet: My Story.* Boston: Element.

Tsering, Tashi. 1997. *Struggle for a Modern Tibet: The Autobiography of Tashi Tsering.* New York: M.E. Sharpe.

CHAPTER SEVEN

LION OF THE SNOWY MOUNTAINS
THE TIBETAN POET YI DAM TSHE RING AND HIS CHINESE POETRY: RECONSTRUCTING TIBETAN CULTURAL IDENTITY IN CHINESE

LARA MACONI (LANGUES 'O INALCO — PARIS)

Quant à moi, si vous ne le savez pas
Je suis le roi, Grand Lion du monde! [...]
Je suis l'elu des dieux d'en haut
C'est moi, le Grand Lion joyau qui dompte les ennemis

Chant de Gesar d'apres le *Livre de la course de cheval*[212]

詩是詩人心靈里流出的心汁，不是隨口唾棄的唾沫
Poetry is like essence flowing from the poet's soul
It is not spittle blurted out absent-mindedly

Yi dam tshe ring, no.5 fragment on poetry[213]

The A mdo ba poet Yi dam tshe ring (b.10/2/1933) or Yidan Cairang 伊丹才讓 (phonetic transposition of his name in Chinese) is one of the first generation of sinophone writers from 'post-Liberation' Tibet whose work and reputation I have often come across during fieldwork in the PRC.[214] Yi dam tshe ring is widely known in China,

---

[212] Cf. Mirelle Helfer, *Les chants de l'epopee tibetaine de Gesar d'apres le livre de la course de cheval. Version chantee de Blo bzang bstan jin.* (Geneve-Paris : Librairie Droz, 1977:346, 350).

[213] In "Wo huhuan zhencheng de shihun. Guanyu shi de duanxiang" ("Myself, A Poetic Soul Calling for Truth. Fragments on Poetry"), in Yi dam tshe ring (1991:248). Tibetan translation by Bkra shis tshe ring in *Rtsom dpyad gtam tshog (Compendium of Literary Criticism)*, 'Gyur med ed. (1993:445–74).

[214] Since 1995 fieldwork research has constituted an important aspect of my doctoral research project on Tibetan post-Liberation literature in the PRC. My project focuses mainly on the works by Tibetan authors writing in Chinese and on the problem of cultural identity connected with their work and with the language they use. I have kept regular contact with Yi dam tshe ring since July 1996 when I

Tibet and the diaspora as one of the most vigorous and unconditional spokesmen on Tibetan identity today. He is reckoned among the most representative and original figures in the present day Tibetan literary world, both for his work and for his outspoken views on Tibetan cultural revival and renewal. Yi dam tshe ring considerably stresses the importance of the development of literature in the Tibetan language. What makes such advocacy particularly interesting is that he writes in Chinese.[215]

This paper seeks to analyse Yi dam tshe ring's Chinese poetry in terms of what I call 'Tibetan sinophone literature in post-Liberation Tibet'. My goal is to demonstrate the poetic devices Yi dam tshe ring uses in his ardent attempt to express an authentic Tibetan sensibility through poetry written in Chinese. Yi dam tshe ring's project relative to Tibetan tradition appears to be one of recollection, recuperation, (re)-construction but also invention. Reading his work within a cross-cultural perspective is useful to avoid simplistic approaches to contemporary Tibetan culture and literature, making room for otherness, variety and complexity.

This paper is divided in the following way:

1) An explanation of the theory and methodology used, and a description of the context of Tibetan sinophone literature in 'post-Liberation' Tibet.

2) A presentation of Yi dam tshe ring's life and work, and his poetic awakening to the question of Tibetan national identity. This presentation is divided into two sections. The first section focuses on Yi dam tshe ring's political and artistic activities until the end of the Cultural Revolution. The second section deals with Yi dam tshe ring's philosophical and poetic evolution since the end of the Cultural Revolution up to the present day.

---

met the poet for the first time and interviewed him during a conference on his poetry (*Bod kyi snyan ngag mkhan po Yi dam tshe ring gi snyan rdzom zhib dbyad tshogs 'du*; ch. *Zhuming zangzu shiren Yidan Cairang chuangzuo chengjiu yantaohui*, in A mdo, Hezuo county, Gannan Tibetan autonomous prefecture, Gansu province, 10–11 July 1996). At the conference, I gave a paper in Chinese, cf. Ma Lan (Maconi Lara), (1996.1:61f.), abridged version.

[215] Many of Yi dam tshe ring's poems have been translated into Tibetan. Nine translated poems appear in *Sprin gyi sgra dbyangs* and *Lang tsho'i rbab chu*, 'Gyur med', ed. (1991:49–91,225–29 and 1993:83).

3) An analysis of Yi dam tshe ring's poetic (re-)construction of Tibetan national identity. My analysis is divided into three sections. Each section takes into consideration a literary device that Yi dam tshe ring uses to realise his poetic project: the use of highly symbolical images, the practice of poetic 'pilgrimages' to important sites of Tibetan culture, the 'Tibetanisation' of the Chinese language.

1 TIBETAN SINOPHONE LITERATURE IN 'POST-LIBERATION' TIBET

1.1 THEORETICAL ISSUES

The expression 'Tibetan sinophone literature in post-Liberation Tibet' needs to be explained. My use of the term 'post-Liberation' is related to a specific interpretation of the term 'post-colonial'. Recent post-colonial studies have focused on the phenomenon of literature written in an imported language by a society experiencing diglossy and culture shock as a consequence of external political occupation. Thus, for example, we hear of 'anglophone/francophone post-colonial literature'. Originally, historians after the Second World War used the term 'post-colonial' in a chronological way, to designate the post-independence period. However, since the late 1970s, the term has been appropriated by literary critics to discuss the various cultural effects stemming from a process of colonisation that continues.[216]

According to B. Ashcroft, G. Griffiths and H Tiffin (1991), the characteristic that post-colonial literatures share in common—beyond their distinctive features—is their development in a climate of multi-layered tensions (self-other, native-foreigner, tradition-modernity, past-present, centre-periphery-marginality) created by the experience of political domination. There are a number of major features of post-colonial literature, including: linguistic considerations (marginalisation of native language, domination of the imported language), preoccupations with place, displacement (identifying relationship between self and the place), a pervasive attention to myths of identity, tradition, history, authenticity and a manifestation of cross-cultural phenomena. These same elements figure prominently in Tibetan literature written after the 1950s in

---

[216] For an exhaustive explanation of this debate in the field of post-colonial studies see, for example, B. Ashcroft, G. Griffiths, and H. Tiffin (1991).

Chinese, in general, and in Yi dam tshe ring poetry in particular. The idea of looking for new comparative literary frameworks in the field of post-colonial literatures was suggested to me by the Tibetan authors themselves who, during interviews, often mentioned writers and literary characteristics from 'Third World literature' or 'dominated country literature' (Indian, African, Jewish, socialist country literatures). However, the attempt of applying a post-colonial framework to Tibetan 'post-Liberation' literature must take into account the subject of the next part of this first section, the particularities of the socialist transformation of Tibet.[217]

1.2 THE SOCIALIST TRANSFORMATION OF TIBETAN LITERATURE

Yi dam tshe ring's poetry has emerged from within a very specific context that needs to be taken into consideration, by which I mean the substantial enthusiasm on the part of a new progressive Tibetan intelligentsia that had begun to emerge under the 13th Dalai Lama (1876–1933) for change, modernisation, republican ideals and

---

[217] This attempt to view post-1950s Tibetan literature in a post-colonial perspective needs further investigation that I am currently carrying out in view of my doctoral thesis. In this paper, it suffices to point out that there is a need to understand and approach Tibetan post-1950s literature with more relevant methodological bearings and terminology. The debate on the validity of established literary labels in the PRC is nowadays open even in mainland China and dealt with in some Tibetan articles (See Zi Duo, "Lun zangzu wenxue" ["On Tibetan Literature"], unpublished article). Thus, for example, in this article, my use of the expression 'post-Liberation' instead of 'contemporary' allows me to avoid a simplistic use of the word 'contemporary' (ch. *dangdai* 當代), a word that, as it is used in political and cultural discourses in the PRC, not only contains temporal denotations, but also, normative connotations. According to socialist evolutionist theories, *dangdai* means not only 'contemporary' (that is, the 'present period') but also the new socialist epoch, a step forward on the road to revolution. In the same way, *dangdai wenxue* 當代文學 means not only 'contemporary literature' (that is 'present-day literature'), but also the 'new', 'more advanced' socialist literature after the 1950s. Equally, the Tibetan word *deng rabs*, as it is used in the PRC to designate post-1950s politics, culture, and literature, is supposed to translate *dangdai* and to render its socialist connotations (as, for instance, in 'Gyur med, ed., 1990–93, *Bod kyi deng rabs rtsom rig dpe tshogs* translated as *Zangzu dangdai wenxue congshu*, etc). A glance at Tibetan and Chinese literary publications bears witness to the fact that the evolutionist socialist orientation of Maoist discourse is embedded in the use of literary terminology in the PRC. On the use of 'modern' and 'contemporary' in China, see Hong Zicheng (1998, 6:38–49). See also Isabelle Rabut (2000:140–62).

socialist values.[218] As Heather Stoddard remarkably points out, "Tibetan society on the eve of the Chinese invasion was not quite as homogeneously traditional as we sometimes might like to believe" (Stoddard, 1994:121-56; see also Stoddard, 1985). In exploring the context that gave birth to Yi dam tshe ring's work, it is essential to stress how socialism as an international set of aspirations not specifically identified with Chinese domination appealed to certain intellectuals. Nevertheless, it is also important to stress how the actual political and cultural changes brought about by the Chinese occupation affected Tibet in a substantial way. In the intention of the new Chinese political establishment, the construction of socialism in Tibet was to eradicate the 'old' and 'feudal' germs of the Tibetan tradition. Tibetans became one of the 56 Chinese National Minorities of the PRC. Early in the 1950s, the long-term Chinese policy for the Socialist transformation of Tibet (as it was expressed both in the Common Programme and, later, in the 17-Point Agreement) included nationality issues that only very broadly concerned culture, language, and religion.[219] Items such as national minority literatures were hardly taken into consideration. Priority was given to political, social and economic issues. Propaganda work became paramount. Beginning in the early 1950s, the Chinese Communist Party attached great importance to translations into Tibetan of Marxist literature and bureaucratic memoranda. Tibetan scholars and monks were especially recruited for translation work.[220]

---

[218] Among the young intellectuals of that period we find: Rab dga' spom mda' tshang (one of the three brothers Spom mda' tshang, from Khams. Very politically and culturally engaged in the first half of the century, he was a Guomindang member, founder of the Tibet Progressive Party, translator (by the early 40s) of Sun Yat-sen's *sanminzhuyi* (The Three Principles of the People); dge bshes Shes rab rgya mtsho (from A mdo, he was to become Chairman of the China Buddhist Association of the PRC, translator of Tsong kha pa's *Lam rim chen mo* into Chinese); Phung tshog dbang rgyal (alias Min Zhicheng, from 'Ba' thang, one of the first Tibetan communists, author of a reform project proposed to the Tibetan government in 1949, he led the PLA into Lhasa in 1950); and the emblematic figure of Dge 'dun chos 'phel, the great modern Tibetan scholar who died in 1951.

[219] See Point 9 in 17-Point Agreement: "The spoken and written language and school education of the Tibetan nationality shall be developed step by step in accordance with actual conditions of Tibet," quoted in Tsering Shakya (1999: 451).

[220] The Eight-Point Contract (a manifesto outlining the policies the Communists intended to pursue after their victory, proclaimed by Mao Zedong and Zhu De on 25 April 1949) was the first Communist document translated into Tibetan by the monks of Labrang in 1950. See Tsering Shakya (1999:35).

Early in 1942, Mao proclaimed his "Talks at the Yan'an Conference on Literature and Art," which were to become the future-PRC's socialist literary theory. In July 1949, at the First National Congress of Chinese Literature and Art Workers, the 'Talks' were officially accepted as the uniquely correct line of guidance for the literary and art world for the whole of China. They were not discarded during the Cultural Revolution, they were not abrogated at the end of the 1970s when Beijing's new power-holders levelled criticism at the Gang of Four. They still have not been discarded.[221]

With the Chinese occupation of Tibet, previously unheard-of socialist conceptions of literature and art began to spread in the Land of Snow. Mao's slogans promoting and imposing a combination of Socialist Realism and Revolutionary Romanticism[222] as a creative method, and the *er wei* 二爲 (two services) directive[223] as a literary guideline were to upset the Tibetan traditional literary and artistic outlooks. While traditional Tibetan written literature was mainly an elitist activity, refined in taste and rich in religious meaning, the new Maoist policy promoted the complete secularisation and politicisation of literature. Created by the masses, for the masses, in the language of the masses, the new literature had to eulogise the heroic constructions of socialism. Moreover, national minorities, in accordance with the new nationality policy condemning *han* 漢 chauvinism, were encouraged to emphasise *minzu tese* 民族特色 (national characteristics) in literary works.[224] In Tibet, to emphazise *minzu tese*

---

[221] In a notice issued in May 1979, Beijing's Ministry of Culture abrogated Jiang Qing's positions on literature and art but reaffirmed Mao's Yan'an 'Talks'. See Hsuan Mo (1981:33–46).

[222] Socialist Realism was proposed in the USSR in 1932. In November 1933 Zhou Yang (a leader of left-wing literary circles in Shanghai) promoted it in China with his article "On Socialist Realism and Revolutionary Romanticism;" see Yu Yan, "Geming de xianshizhuyi he geming de langmanzhuyi xiang jiehe wenti de taolun" ("The Discussion on the Combination of Revolutionary Realism and Revolutionary Romanticism"), *Wenxue Pinglun* (1959.2).

[223] *Er wei* directive: *Wei shehuizhuyi fuwu, wei renmin fuwu* (In service of Socialism, in service of the masses). Nowadays the *er wei* directive is still promoted in the official discourse on literature throughout the PRC, but the expression has been reversed, and *renmin* (a term that nowadays has lost its revolutionary meaning) means the 'people' more than the 'masses'. The slogan is basically as follows: In service of the people, in service of Socialism.

[224] According to Li Jiajun (1989:17), a piece of literature can be considered national literature if it possesses three characteristics: "the social life of a nationality,

was particularly recommended, especially for Tibetan literature written in Chinese.[225]

Socialist Revolutionary literature in Tibet was clearly an imported phenomenon from Inland China. There, socialist literary theories were known among left-wing intellectuals ever since the 1930s, and a socialist literature was already quite developed by the 1950s. Thus, it was via Chinese compositions that Tibetan intellectuals became acquainted with Socialist Realism. The Chinese PLA soldier-writers on a mission in Tibet played a crucial role in this. Inspired by the interesting and exotic Tibetan environment, soldiers from the PLA propaganda sections wrote and diffused in Tibet the first socialist literary works accessible to Tibetans.[226] These works served as models for the first Tibetan authors writing under the new Maoist establishment, both in Tibetan and in Chinese.

It was in this new socialist cultural environment that Tibetan advocates of the revolution started writing about their political enthusiasm and revolutionary spirit, their confidence in mass democracy and the fraternity among nationalities. The very first Tibetans who started writing under the new regime were highly educated intellectuals, often of noble origin, trained in pre-1950 Tibet with a traditional Tibetan education. They mainly wrote poetry, and in the Tibetan language.[227]

---

the artistic form of a nationality, the psychological specificities of a nationality." No official mention of language as a national characteristic of literature is made.

[225] The results of this practice are works emphasising presumed Tibetan national characteristics by superficially adding so-called "high mountain and grassland flavours." This literary style is said to have *suyou zampa wei* (butter and *rtsam pa* taste).

[226] Xu Huaizhong's novel *Women bozhong aiqing* (*We Sow Love*) is considered as the most representative work of Chinese military literature on Tibet by the 1950s. It was translated into Russian, English, and German. Other 1950s well-known works are: Liu Ke's short novel "Yang Jin" ("Dbyangs can;" Tibetan translation in *Bod kyi rtsom rig sgyu rtsal*, 1980.1. The anonymous translator is Chab spel tshe brtan phun tshogs, personal communication); and Gao Ping's lyric poem "Daxue fenfei" ("The Snow Flakes Fall Thick and Fast"), etc. See Li Jiajun (1989:12-14).

[227] Among them there were: the Sera Monastery *dge bshes lha ram pa* Tsha sprul mnga' dbang blo bzang *rin po che* (1880–1957) who eulogised technology (cf. "Lcags kyi phug ron dngul skya mdog", "The Silvery Iron Pigeon", in *Bod ljongs nyin re'i tshags par*, 12/4/1956); Lcang can bsod nams rgyal po, who advocated fraternity among nationalities through the symbol of Srong btsan sgam po's Chinese consort Rgya bza' (Wencheng Gongzhu); Chab spel tshe brtan phun tshogs (b.1922) whose literary activity (started in the 1950s) reached a climax in the 1980s with the

However, among the younger generation of Tibetans who grew up during the new Socialist times, only the descendants from rich families and those who had educated religious relatives could continue obtaining an education in Tibetan. The others were mainly educated in Chinese. Bilingual education was rare and some of the bilingual writers like Bstan 'dzin mgon po (1934–97) and Mgon po bkra shis (1938) chose to write in Chinese, because they were more comfortable in that language. Others—of very humble origin—were illiterate when, still adolescents, they joined the revolutionary ranks to participate in the 'construction of socialism'. Yi dam tshe ring (1933) is one of these (see also Nor rje pa sangs (1935), Skal bzang rdo rje (1936), Ngag dbang bstan 'dzin (1929), etc.). These writers from poor families were educated by the Chinese in the Chinese language, after their recruitment into the new political structures. Ever since the Long March, the Communist Party realised the potential of Tibetan recruits from poor families and some of these were sent to the party school: the Nationalities Institute founded in Yan'an in 1941. As Tsering Shakya pointed out, some of the first Tibetan Communists "were genuinely attracted to the promise of an egalitarian society. Others were young boys who drifted into the ranks of the PLA" (Tsering Shakya,1999:34).

Thus, since the 1950s (in spite of Beijing's official policy on literature and the arts), a Tibetan mother tongue literature and a Tibetan sinophone literature have undergone a parallel development. The expression of a certain 'continuity' with Tibetan literary tradition coexists with the expression of a major 'disjunction'. Tibetan 'post-Liberation' literature shows that—at the present time in Tibet—two cultures co-exist within a single social context. This shows that the relationships between the two are complex, sometimes antithetical, but that nevertheless they can bring about interesting results in terms of literary and linguistic hybridisation.[228]

---

collection of poems *Bsil dus gyi Bod ljongs* ("Tibet in Wintertime;" Lhasa, Bod ljongs mi dmangs dpe skrun khang, 1991).

[228] On 14 August 1978, *Beijing Information*'s announcement that "writers and artists were taking up once again their creative activity after 12 years of interruption" marked the beginning of a renewed poetic enthusiasm on the Tibetan plateau. At present, verse writers are astonishingly numerous in Tibet. This is especially true for poetry written in the Tibetan language. During a meeting in Xining with the staff members of *Sbrang char* (*Honey Rain*)'s editorial board, in October 1999, the publishers made a rough estimate of a printing of more than 5,000

2 Yi dam tshe ring's Awakening to the Question of National Identity

2.1 Son of the Revolution

> When I joined the revolution, I was just a 15/16-year old baby. At that time, all I knew was that old society meant suffering. Except for this, everything was obscure to me. In the revolutionary ranks, I was taught the Party principles and Mao's revolutionary philosophy. I became a member of the Party, and I really thought the Party was giving me wisdom and ideals.[229]

With the above words, Yi dam tshe ring acknowledges his initial enthusiasm for the ideals of socialism. To understand his particular development as a writer is to understand the change in his political and social commitment, particularly after the storm of the Cultural Revolution. Yi dam tshe ring was born in A mdo, in Tsong kha in 1933, into a poor family. His childhood as a shepherd, sometimes in the service of some local rich families, was simple but serene. Only as an adolescent—and in a very desultory way—did he attend classes in a primary school in Xining where he learned some rudimentary Tibetan. In August 1949, he was in school when rumour had it that the "red-hair green-eye PLA soldiers" (quoted in Yi dam tshe ring, 1999:245)[230] were coming. With great disappointment, Yi dam tshe ring ascertained that PLA soldiers were just "normal people," and, although a little irritated when the general called him *xiao gui* 小鬼 (little devil), he thought they were "good guys" because they distributed food and money for the villagers to buy sheep. Three months later, in November 1949, Yi dam tshe ring joined the revolutionary ranks. He was fifteen years old. With him were many other Tibetan youngsters who had joined.

From then to the mid 1960s he took part in all the political movements of the period: the land reform, the movement against the three

---

copies. This was for 1,000 authors and included both professional and amateur writers—constant and desultory ones—the great majority of whom are poetry writers. One should note that Tibetan sinophone poets are far less numerous than their tibetophone colleagues. This does not necessarily apply to prose writing.

[229] Opening sentence of the 1964 conclusion to Yi dam tshe ring's first collection of poems published in 1980; cf. Yi dam tshe ring (1980:181).

[230] Red-hair green-eye PLA: Hongfa luyan de jiefangjun. In *Lanzhou Daily*, Zhao Wen's interview to Yi dam tshe ring.

evils, the movement against the five evils, the rooting out of counter-revolutionaries, the anti-rightist struggle, the fight against local nationalisms, the socialist education movement,[231] etc. Meanwhile, in 1952, he entered the Dance and Music Department of the North-West Art Institute in Lanzhou. In 1954, he moved to the Song and Dance Troupe of the North-West Nationality Institute where he worked as a performer, lyricist, teacher of arts, choreographer-director of the dance troupe, and Director of the Creation and Research Centre. He became deputy director of the Preliminary Group of the Gansu Folk Art Research Committee. In 1955, due to the requirements of his work—and following the socialist theory of 'folk literature' as 'mass literature'—he started to collect, arrange and translate Tibetan folk songs into Chinese, and to compose new texts for ancient well-known tunes. Activities in the performing arts earned Yi dam tshe ring some popularity on the national level. In 1957, his dance choreography *Labuleng jieri* 拉卜楞節日 (Festival in Labrang) won the title of Programme of Excellence on the all-China level. In 1963 the text of his song for choir "Xueshan ba jianghe song chulai" 雪山把江河送出來 (Snowy Mountains Are the Sources of Rivers) was published in *Shanghai gesheng* 上海歌聲 (*Shanghai Singing Voices Magazine*)(Yi dam tshe ring, 1963:4).[232]

In the field of folk songs, Yi dam tshe ring's main achievement was the publication, in 1963, of *Hunli ge* 婚禮歌 (*Wedding Songs*)(Yi dam tshe ring,1963),[233] a collection of A mdo folk songs from the author's home country. The collection contains the Chinese translation of 14 long Tibetan folk songs. The Tibetan originals are not presented.[234] Yi dam tshe ring's interest in folk literature was more than incidental, and was not the mere consequence of the pro-folklore policy of the pre-Cultural Revolution years. Those "teachers

---

[231] In order: *Sanfan yundong*, 1951–52; *Wufan yundong*, started in 1952; *Suqing fangeming fenzi*, 1956; *Fan youpai douzheng*, 1957; *Fandui difang minzuzhuyi*, end 50s–beginning 60s; *Shehuizhuyi jiaoyu yundong*, 1963–66.

[232]"Xueshan ba jianghe song chulai" ("Snowy Mountains Are The Sources of Rivers"), in *Shanghai gesheng*.

[233] Regarded as an expression of the 'four olds' (old ideas, old culture, old customs, old habits), all the copies of the book were burnt during the Cultural Revolution. One volume has survived.

[234] The titles of the songs and some lines and expressions are presented in a Chinese phonetic homemade transcription of the original A mdo dialect. The translation is suggested in brackets and footnotes.

who initiated him into poetry" (Yi dam tshe ring, 1980:181–83)[235] (that is, folk songs and any genuine manifestation of popular culture) have been a permanent source of inspiration, and a field of constantly renewed investigation for our poet.[236]

In 1958, Yi dam tshe ring composed his first poem "Jinse de junma" 金色的駿馬 (The Golden Steed), a ten-quatrain hymn to the co-operative transformation of agriculture and to the efforts and determination of the people in constructing Socialism. In this period, his convictions in class struggle dynamics—as the deterministic force constituting societies—and his faith in the Socialist equalitarian utopia reached a climax. In September 1964, in the conclusion to his first collection of 35 poems, (Xueshan ji 雪山集 [Snowy Mountains Collection]) the poet explains to the reader the revolutionary mission of his poetic philosophy. Because "only those who climbed the Snowy Mountains can comprehend the smoothness of the road," (Yi dam tshe ring,1980:183), the revolutionary poet sings "for the workers, the people and the soldiers, for the socialist revolution and construction, for the revolution of all people in the world" (1980:183).[237] But History abruptly changed its course, and deeply affected Yi dam tshe ring's life and his philosophy. The Snowy Mountains Collection—ready for publication in 1965—was not published until 1980, after almost 15 years of 'witch hunting'.[238] It had to wait until the Cultural Revolution was over, and until the intellectuals (Yi dam tshe ring among his peers) were rehabilitated.

Regarding the excesses of the Cultural Revolution, we know from the Snowy Mountains Collection's "Conclusion to the Conclusion" (Yi dam tshe ring, 1980:184–87,written in 1979)[239] that the first accusations stigmatising Yi dam tshe ring as a "seventeen year

---

[235] "Minge shi wo xie shi de qimeng laoshi" ("Folk Songs are the Teachers who initiated me into Poetry").

[236] The paper "On A mdo Tibetan Folk Songs" bears witness to Yi dam tshe ring's uninterrupted activity in the field of folk literature. The draft, written in 1962, was brought up to date in 1998 and eventually published in 1999. See Yi dam tshe ring, "Guanyu Anmuduo zangzu minge" ("On A mdo Tibetan Folk Songs"), in Yi dam tshe ring (1999:120–37).

[237] Note that Yi dam tshe ring's evocation of the Maoist slogan is not precise. Gong min bing should be gong nong bing (the workers, the peasants [not the people!] and the soldiers).

[238] Witch hunting: hengsao yiqie niugui sheshen. Conversation with Yi dam tshe ring.

[239] "Houji de houji" ("Conclusion to the Conclusion").

literary black line's black specimen" and a "reactionary nationalist" became more virulent at the beginning of the 1970s. It was the time of the anti-Lin Biao and anti-Confucius campaign launched by the Chinese leaders following the 10th Party Congress of 1973. It was also the time of important introspection and coming of age for our poet. Strongly affected by the oppressive and stifling atmosphere of those days, Yi dam tshe ring, unable to contain himself any longer, wrote "The Sun and the River" (Yi dam tshe ring, 1980:186), a poem he exposed in *dazibao* 大字報 format. In it, using an easily decipherable metaphorical language, he denounced the corruption of the purity of initial political ideals, and affirmed the incorruptibility of those very ideals in people's hearts. Indeed, since the outburst of the Cultural Revolution and following the excesses it brought about, Yi dam tshe ring has been developing new and more mature political and philosophical reflections. As the poet often says: "so many sad events at least brought with them many opportunities of meditation." He did not keep silent during the years of the Cultural Revolution. "Having stopped up ears does not mean that silence reigns supreme," he wrote in "Truth is unfalsifiable" (Yi dam tshe ring, 1996:69),[240] the only poem to have survived a group of thirty composed in 1963 and subsequently burnt by the Red Guards. The poem is interesting because the tone shows well Yi dam tshe ring's true colours, his untameable disposition, his more sentimental than political thirst for Justice and Equality, his more humanistic than socialist meditations, all aspects which he would later largely develop in the poetry of his maturity.

2.2 MOTHER'S CALL: IDENTITY AND POETRY

During my first long conversation with Yi dam tshe ring in July 1996, he told me that it was only in his thirties (during the Cultural Revolution), while going through a period of self-searching, that he became aware of the true identity of his 'Mother' (Tibet) and of the immaturity of his previous view on life. He grew increasingly curious about the specificity of Tibetan culture, whose age-old traditions and splendour he knew nothing of up until then. For the first time, he realised that his Mother was getting weaker, that it

---

[240] "Zhende jiabuliao" ("Truth is unfalsifiable"), written in 1963, not published until 1996.

needed the support of her 'son' to survive: "if you don't even pour a drop of butter tea into your mother's bowl, what sort of son are you?" (conversation with Yi dam tshe ring).

Evaluating the capacity of Maoist philosophy to explain society and life, he began to understand that "equality could not be given to people as a gift. Teaching abstract principles was not enough; [equality is a kind of] people's awareness, of the self, first of all, and of the other" (conversation with Yi dam tshe ring). Culture, economics and politics are fundamental aspects in this process. Ever since, Yi dam tshe ring has been increasingly concerned with the development of Tibet and Tibetan language educational improvement. As far as his preoccupations with Tibetan language development are concerned, one should note that the poet himself, since the 1980s, has been learning and refining his skills in the Tibetan written language so that, at present, he can easily read Tibetan and personally review other people's translations of his poems into that language. In "Crystalline Seeds: Thon mi sam bho ta" (Yi dam tshe ring (1992:102),[241] a poem written in 1983, the author celebrates the richness of the Tibetan language. In spite of the recent "dismembering practices of an ice knife and a snow sword, [and after] the jade dragon's roar has calmed down," writes the poet, the "thirty crystalline seeds [a metaphor for the 30 letters of the Tibetan alphabet and for the Tibetan language] would fully bloom again." Moreover, Yi dam tshe ring is highly concerned with the development of Tibetan poetry written in the mother tongue. Some of his papers deal with this subject and focus on talented young Tibetan poets.[242] Poems such as "Faith on the Road Lies in [the Capability of] Surmounting the Warnings of one's own Sighs" (Yi dam tshe ring, 1991:39–41,

---

[241] "Jingliang de zhongzi: Tunmi Sangbozha" ("Crystalline Seeds: Thon mi sam bho ta").

[242] See Yi dam tshe ring, "Cong shiji « Liming tiannü de zhaohuan» kan zangzu dangdai muyu shige de fazhan" ("Considerations on the Tibetan Contemporary Mother-tongue Poetic Development. The Collection of Poems *Dawn Goddess' Call*"), in Yi dam tshe ring (1999:92–109). In this article, the poet describes the Tibetan 'poetic explosion' from both a quantitative and a qualitative point of view, and underlines that the development of Tibetan poetry lies in the development of mother tongue writing. "Dawn Goddess Call" is a collection of poems in Tibetan by the A mdo ba poet Lha rgyal tshe ring (1962). Original title: *Skya rengs lha mo'i 'bod brda'* (1998. Beijing: Minzu chubanshe).

written in 1986 in memory of Don grub rgyal, 1953–85),[243] are
indicative of Yi dam tshe ring's deep concerns with the future of the
new generation of Tibetan intellectuals. He has frequent contact with
them (especially with those coming from A mdo), and his communi-
cative temperament as well as his oratorical skills—greatly help him
to establish a lively human and intellectual dialogue with those
intellectuals. Still, he never denied his socialist *credo* and past, and
the conception of poetry and life of the two generations remain very
different. For the young, he is a symbol of moral integrity and human
dignity, a powerful literary spur, and a source of enthusiasm and
hope in a better future.[244]

It is only in the post-Cultural Revolution new age, following the
general revival of culture in the PRC (and relying on his reformu-
lated and more mature philosophy of life) that Yi dam tshe ring has
composed the bulk of his poetic work, and its best part. Leaving
aside *Xueshan ji* 雪山集 (*Snowy Mountains Collection*), which,
though published in 1980, contains poems written between 1958 and
1965, Yi dam tshe ring has published five volumes consisting
primarily of poems. There are also some essays. His anthologies are
the following:

1) *Xueshi ji* 雪獅集 (*Snow Lion Collection*, 1991): the book contains 76 long free-verse lyric poems composed from 1978 to 1990,
evoking ballads and folk songs in rhythm, music and structure. In
this collection, the poet meditates mainly on social issues. Two
poems should be singled out as landmark turning-points in Yi dam
tshe ring's career: "Wen ..." 問 ... (Questions ...) and "Muqin xinshou
de ge" 母親心授的歌 (The Songs Mother Taught Me). "Questions
...," composed in 1980, is an explicit questioning of existence in all
its dimensions, from the personal to the cosmological, putting special
allusive emphasis on the social and historical meaning of existence.
"The Songs Mother Taught Me," written in 1981, is a 49-quatrain
poem rich in political nuances, though far from the propagandistic
rhetoric of the past. Thanks to this poem, Yi dam tshe ring acquired

---

[243] "Lu de xinnian zaiyu chaoyue zishen kaitan de jingyu" ("Faith on the Road
Lies in [the Capability of] Surmounting the Warnings of one's own Sighs").

[244] During Yi dam tshe ring's Poetry Debate (Hezuo, 1996), small groups of
monks, with the poet's Chinese anthology in their hands, came from the nearby
monasteries to ask for his autograph.

the official literary recognition of the Chinese intelligentsia on the all-China level.[245]

2) *Xueyu ji* 雪域集 (*Snow Land Collection*, 1992): this is an anthology of 179 poems composed between 1974 and 1991 in a new poetic pattern experimented by Yi dam tshe ring since the 1960s, a pattern which has not been abandoned to this day. This new pattern is called *si yi er shi qi hang shi* 四一二式七行詩 (seven-line poem in four-, one-, and two-line stanzas), which means that one poem has seven lines divided in three stanzas of 4, 1 and 2 lines each. Each of the three sections of the poem corresponds to different categories of meaning, and to different linguistic registers and rhetorical devices.[246] In this collection, the poet's voice shows an increased detachment and wisdom. Yi dam tshe ring's social view on life turns into a cosmological awareness, into a meditation on ultimate truths. The evolution of the poet's philosophy reaches full maturity (from meditations on the "sufferings of the old society" to reflections on the sufferings of all societies, until the realisation that existence itself is suffering).

3) *Xueyun ji* 雪韻集 (*Snow Rhymes Collection*, 1996): this collection of 114 scattered poems written from 1963 to 1996 was compiled specifically to be distributed during the conference on Yi dam tshe ring poetry in Hezuo, on 10th–11th July 1996.

4) *Xueyu de taiyang* 雪域的太陽 (*The Snow Land Sun*, 1997): published in 1997, is a selection of Yi dam tshe ring's best poems chosen from the previous anthologies.

5) *Xueshan shizi hou* 雪山獅子吼 (*The Lion of the Snowy Mountains Roars*, 1999): published in 1999, it is an anthology of essays by the poet and on the poet, arranged in thematic order.

---

[245] The Tibetan grapevine suggests that the author was requested to change some parts of "Questions ..." which he did not. But he negotiated, in exchange, the composition of a 'politically correct' poem: "The Songs Mother Taught Me."

[246] The three sections are arranged as follows: 1) In the opening quatrain, the skilful use of the metaphorical language, rich in evocations and allusions, produces images and shocks of emotions in the mind of the reader in a gradual crescendo of lyrical tension. 2) In the mono-line verse, the poem reaches a climax. The voice of the poet suggests the key to interpret the four previous lines, to decode the allusive message behind them, and to give coherence to the reader's images and emotions. This line revels the deep meaning of the poem and denounces the implications of that same meaning. The tone is emphatic. The line often ends with an exclamation mark. 3) In the last couplet, the poetic tension calms down, emotions are diluted. This is the conclusion of the poem, an admonition moment often formulated as a rhetorical question.

Moreover, in December 1999, Yi dam tshe ring edited *Xueyu zheren de sibian zhi hua* 雪域哲人的思辯之花 (*The Flowers of the Thoughts by a Snow Land Sage*), a collection of essays (and a few poems) by different authors, on Phun tshog dbang rgyal's scientific activity. Phun dbang's theory proposing that there is water on the other side of the moon has attracted worldwide attention and has gained universal recognition (Phun tshog dbang rgyal, 1994).[247] *The Flowers* is not only Yi dam tshe ring's homage to an old friend and to a Tibetan historical and scientific epoch-making figure. It is first and foremost the poet's assertion that Tibetan culture can reach a high level of scientific development and can compete in the modern and scientific world in a dignified manner. *The Flowers* shows well Yi dam tshe ring's constant attention to worldwide events and his interest in science and the modern world. When looking for a reference in Tibetan tradition to legitimise his views on life, on progress and on Tibetan issues, he likes to evoke the brilliant and iconoclast figure of Dge 'dun chos 'phel (1905–51).

3 RE-CONSTRUCTING TIBETAN NATIONAL IDENTITY

3.1 SNOW LION: THE POWER OF SYMBOLS AGAINST THE SYMBOLS OF POWER

The control of the means of communication is the empowering factor in any hegemonic enterprise. Then the writer's very practice of writing becomes an attempt to resist the control of the processes of communication. By proposing his specific literary language, by using symbols rich in cultural connotations that differentiate his works from the official discourse, the writer expresses his own sense of 'otherness' against the establishment in a creative way.

As we have seen, in Yi dam tshe ring's artistic and humanistic project, communication holds a privileged position: "Poetry is a dialogue between souls" and "Poetry which does not strike a sympathetic chord with its audience is like a stillborn foetus" (Yi dam tshe ring, 1992:191-2). writes the poet in *Snow Land Collection*. In his view, the poet has a social and a humanistic mission. He is a bard, a prophetic and admonishing voice who invites his audience to meditation and action. According to Yi dam tshe ring, poetry means

---

[247] *Yueqiu cunyou yetai* (*There is Liquid on the Moon*).

first and foremost national poetry (1992:191-2). As he wrote in one of his essays, poetry is the expression of "a nation's heartfelt aspirations" (1992:189).

Poetry allows Yi dam tshe ring to communicate on an emotional level. His highly figurative style is consonant with his exuberant temperament, and makes his discourse supple enough to adjust to the changing weather of the society in which he lives. His poetry, deeply nourished by Tibetan oral tradition, is permeated by a recurrent set of images widely known to the Tibetan reader. Skilfully used, these images are discreetly allusive. They evoke ancient meanings and suggest new meanings.

'Snow Lion', one of most ancient Tibetan literary images documented since the Dunhuang manuscripts,[248] is possibly the most powerful pervasive metaphor recurring in Yi dam tshe ring's *repertoire* and, surely, the one he cherishes the most. On its first level of meaning, Snow Lion is the poet's nickname. It was firstly attributed to him in 1982, in Beijing, after his speech to the first conference at the Chinese Institute for National Minority Literature. There, Yi dam tshe ring introduced himself as the "little lion descending from the Turquoise-mane White Lioness living on the mountains of Tibet since ancient times" (Yi dam tshe ring, 1991:267).[249] Moreover, in Yi dam tshe ring's poems, Tibetans are often portrayed as "little lions nourished by the milk of their Mother, the Lioness," or as "Snow Lions towering" on "the high peaks and pure earth" of Tibet. In *Snow Lion Collection*, Yi dam tshe ring explains:

> The image of Snow Lion, has permeated the geography, the history, the culture, the art, the religion and every aspect of life in the Land of Snow, that is, our spiritual and material world. It naturally stands for the solidarity spirit of Tibetans. (1991:270)

He then gives a four-page list of examples taken from Tibetan geography, language, literature, art, etc. to prove the 'real existence' of Snow Lion in Tibet. To him, Snow Lion not only vividly exists in

---

[248] In the Tibetan tradition 'Snow Lion' is an epithet of Buddha, but also of Gshen rab mi bo che ('Smra ba'i seng ge', 'Lion of Speech'), Mi la ras pa ('Seng chen rje', 'Lord, Great Lion'), Gesar ("Jam gling seng chen rgyal po', 'King, Great Lion of of the World'), etc. See R. Stein, *La civilisation tibetaine*, Paris, L'Asiatheque (1996:18,130).

[249] On Snow Lion in Yi dam tshe ring's conceptual world, see *Bod kyi dus bab* (Dharamsala 28/2/1998).

the Tibetan imagery, its existence has a value "very similar to the symbolism of the dragon in Chinese culture" (Yi dam tshe ring,1991:270).[250]

One can assume that this *cortege* of Turquoise-mane Snow Lions permeating the Tibetan conceptual world, and so many lines of Yi dam tshe ring's poetry, has, in the poet's universe, a richer meaning than a mere parade of native cultural metaphors. Each time Yi dam tshe ring recalls tradition, he invites Tibetan readers to confirm (to say it in Ernest Renan's words) his recognition of a common "rich legacy of memories," and his "consent," that is "his expressed desire to continue living together." Such recognition and consent are the two aspects of a "spiritual principle," that "huge solidarity" which is the nation.[251]

3.2 EXPLORATIONS IN SPACE AND TIME

Yi dam tshe ring's poetic universe is deeply linked with the concept and practice of 'going'. As Robert B. Ekvall points out, the ontological importance of 'mobility' in the conceptual and practical world of Tibetans is reflected in their vocabulary: "A living being is a *'gro ba* ("go one"), Buddha is called *'Gro ba'i bla ma* ("high one of the goers"), [...] man is variously called *'gro ba rin chen* ("great value goer"), *'gro mchog* ("perfect goer"), or *langs 'gro* ("erect goer"), etc.," a long list of examples to show that "in the conceptual world of the Tibetan, *being* is evidenced by *going*" (Ekvall, 1964:228). Tibetan nomadic lifestyle, circumambulations and pilgrimages are just some of the everyday practices that bear witness to Ekvall's thesis.

Yi dam tshe ring has travelled a lot throughout the Tibetan plateau, especially during the early 1980s, after the Cultural Revolution years, when the feeling of disjunction with his culture had reached its height. Thus, every journey became a stage in the process of recovering an identifying relationship between self and place, and a source of poetic inspiration and composition: "My aspirations

---

[250] It is interesting to note that Yi dam tshe ring discourse on Snow Lion reminds us of Dge 'dun chos 'phel's discourse on the same subject in *Hi ma la ya'i bstan bcos* (*Treaty on Himalaya*) (Lhasa, xylographic edition, Hor khang bsod nams dpal 'bar ed., undated; Leh, 1979, *Smanrtsis shesrig spendzod series*, XCVIII :93-101). See also Stoddard (1985:331).

[251] See Ernest Renan's *Discours et Conferences*, quoted in Stoddard (1994:122).

drawn by the golden chariot of the sun," writes the poet, "[when travelling] I start building the golden bridges of my deepest ideals" (Yi dam tshe ring, 1991:264). In Yi dam tshe ring's 'going' dimension, the experience of recovering the past, exploring and regaining contact with one's own territory and culture is not only an archaeological moment. It is first and foremost a moment of '(re-)construction', that is, an attempt to "re-member the dismembered body"[252] of one's own cultural and emotional geography, of one's intimate Tibetan world and, finally, of one's Tibetan self.

We can find the bulk of Yi dam tshe ring's 'travel poems' in *Snow Land Collection*. In this volume, the section called "Xueyu yao" 雪域謠 (Snow Land Ballads)(1992:87-149) contains 62 poems, 57 of which record one specific stage of the poet's travels and of his meditative journey. These poems can roughly be grouped into three different ways of commemorating Tibet: 1) the natural beauty of a site (one poem is on Yang pa can geothermal station, one on Mtsho bar rgya rtse, one on Gangs dkar, one on Mount Kailas, two on Yar brog g-yu mtsho, etc.); 2) the cultural value of a monument or a place (three poems are on the Potala Palace, two on the stele inscription of the Tibeto-Chinese peace treaty, one on Yum bu bla sgang, one on Sde dge par khang, etc.); 3) the greatness of an outstanding personality (four poems are in memory of the Tenth Panchen Lama [1938–89], two in honour of Thang stong rgyal po, one for Thon mi sam bho ta, one for Bu ston, one for Tsong kha pa, one for the Venerable Atisa, etc.).[253]

As in a system of correspondences, the genesis of the 'travel poem', its content and the structural arrangement of the text reflect the logic of 'moving' in different dimensions at once, that is in space (the real travel of the poet in the present); in time (the past history of the site recalled in the poem); in poetry (the travel experience becomes a source of meditation and creativity). The 'travel poem' is usually composed during the journey, at the very place and time of

---

[252] Expression borrowed from D. Germano, "Re-membering the Dismembered Body of Tibet", in M.C. Goldstein and M.T. Kapstein eds., *Buddhism in Contemporary Tibet*. Berkeley: University of California Press. (1998, 53-94).

[253] For the references of the examples of the three categories (sites, monuments, personalities) quoted above, see in the given order: 1) sites, Yi dam tshe ring (1992), 116, 118, 125, 143, 114, and 115; 2) monuments, Yi dam tshe ring (1992), 89, 92, 93, 90, 91, 95, and 126; 3) personalities, Yi dam tshe ring (1992), 110, 111, 112, 113, 103, 104, 102, 108, 106, and 109.

the poet's visit. The date and the name of the place visited are annotated at the end of the poem (that is 'outside' of the lyric moment). They record the poet's 'present' experience of the journey. The toponym used in the annotation of the poet's visit is often the official Chinese toponym. This is not the case when the toponym appears 'in' the poem, where the place is designated by its traditional name or alluded to by a metaphor related to traditional culture. The lyric moment of the poem is intimately related to the past. Only the poet's meditation in the last couplet leads the poem back to the present.

In Yi dam tshe ring's poems, the presence of the semantic interaction between present and past corresponds to a specific organisation of the literary page. While the poem is the centre of the literary page, additional explanatory information surrounds it, and shares with it the same page. Besides the annotation of the date of the poet's visit, a title and a long subtitle directly lead the reader to the core of the poem. Moreover, the great majority of Yi dam tshe ring's poems (the 'travel poems' in particular, because they are rich in cultural references) are followed by postscripts and footnotes outlining the history of the visited place, elucidating difficult cultural references and tropes which are too dense. Footnotes are written in prose. They are not a part of the poem but they are fundamental to understand its alluded meaning. Thus, on Yi dam tshe ring's literary page, past and present, verse and prose, evocations (of the past culture) and explications (to the present reader) often share one same space and cohabit in a text where tradition needs to be explained.

The diagram below illustrates the two sets of related correspondence that construct the texture of Yi dam tshe ring's 'travel poems'. The poet is the link between these two sets of correspondence:

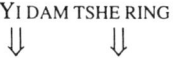

YI DAM TSHE RING

⇓   ⇓

I Semantic Group	*II Semantic Group*
PRESENT TIME → JOURNEY IN THE PRESENT → PRESENT TOPONYM (CHINESE TOPONYM) → PROSE/EXPLANATORY NOTES → ACTUAL DIMENSION →	PAST TIME → JOURNEY IN THE PAST → PAST TOPONYM (TIBETAN TOPONYM) → POETRY/ARTISTIC CREATION → EMOTIONAL DIMENSION →
=	=
PRESENT / CHINA / ACTUALITY	PAST / TIBET / EMOTIONALITY

3.3 THE 'TIBETANISATION' OF THE CHINESE LANGUAGE[254]

Writers working within a diglossic context often practice intentional and unintentional translations from the mother tongue of the spoken word into the adopted language of the written word. I have chosen to name this particular conceptual phenomenon the 'translation dimension'. It is with this notion in mind that we can now take into account what I have referred to as the 'Tibetanisation' of the Chinese language.[255]

To Tibetan sinophone writers like Yi dam tshe ring (illiterate in Tibetan and educated in Chinese only in his late teens), the core of the problem lies in the question of how to "convey in a language that is not one's own the spirit that is one's own" (Rao, 1938).[256] In fact, Chinese is not really an alien language to the majority of post-Liberation Tibetan intellectuals. Yet, it is the language of their intellectual make-up but not of their emotional make-up. The way in which Tibetan writers like Yi dam tshe ring use the Chinese language often shows their effort to negotiate a gap between two 'worlds', a gap in which two simultaneous processes continually strive to define their practices.[257] On the one hand, there is an 'abrogational' moment, which is a sort of cultural and sentimental resistance against the use of the 'imported' language, a refusal of its categories and connotations. On the other hand, there is a moment of

---

[254] Note that, in this section, when I speak of 'original' or 'first' language, I do not mean 'original' or 'first' in the historical and cultural evolution of the language considered. I simply refer to the linguistic/psychological process from 'original' Tibetan to 'adopted' Chinese in the specific case of Yi dam tshe ring and some other Tibetan sinophone writers.

[255] The Tibetanisation of the Chinese language and the translation dimension are two important aspects of my research. I introduced them in my Master's thesis, and I intend to fully develop them in my Ph.D. thesis. In this paper, I briefly introduce the question in relation to Yi dam tshe ring's use of the Chinese language, which is not representative of the diverse ways in which different Tibetan writers can use Chinese. See Lara Maconi, *Lhasa-Pekin: l'example de Yang Zhen (Dbyangs can), jeune femme ecrivain tibetaine*, Memoire de DEA de Tibetain, discussed on 18/9/1998, Langues 'O INALCO, Paris, unpublished. See also Lara Maconi, "One Nation, Two Discourses. 'Post-Liberation' Literature in the Diglossic Context of China's Tibet: The Language Debate," paper given at 2001 AAS Annual Meeting, Chicago, March 22–25, 2001

[256] Raja Rao, *Kanthapura*, New York: New Directions (1938:vii), quoted in B. Ashcroft, G. Griffiths and H. Tiffin (1991:39).

[257] For the terms I use here to designate the two processes (abrogation and appropriation), see B. Ashcroft, G. Griffiths and H. Tiffin.

'appropriation', that is the final adoption of the 'imported' language that is taken and made to express one's own Tibetan experience of life.

Yi dam tshe ring's poems are always written out from the tension between these two moments. It is a tension in which the objective difficulty of 'translating' into Chinese a 'world' supposedly experienced, conceived and felt in Tibetan (this original purity being strongly maintained by the poet himself), coexists with the conscious and unconscious will not to completely abandon the mother language. This cultural and linguistic tension, rather than being the mere psychological strain experienced by the poet at the moment of composition, becomes a literary reality inscribed into the text by means of linguistic devices.

Rather than describing this tension, Yi dam tshe ring's poems diffusely objectivise it by playing with characters. One can 'read' the tension, not because it is the subject of any given poem, but because it is the latent theme evoked by the linguistic style: incommensurable voids of meaning suggesting the psychological abyss between cultures. And when 'editorial intrusions' made by the poet (glosses, footnotes, explanatory postscript, prefaces) try to fill in those voids, the cultural distances in the cross-cultural text come to the foreground. In so doing, Yi dam tshe ring reveals his self-consciousness at constructing a linguistic variation on Chinese. He is the first interpreter of his own texts. Through the 'Tibetanisation' of Chinese, the reader is made to experience a linguistic hybridity where Chinese is not Chinese any longer, and where Tibetan becomes the necessary referential body to understand this brand of Chinese. In fact, to fully voice that cross-cultural world which is Yi dam tshe ring's experience of Tibet, neither Tibetan nor Chinese are enough any longer.

The expression 'Tibetanisation' (of the Chinese language) designates here all the linguistic strategies that Yi dam tshe ring adopts to convey his sense of cultural distinctiveness with regards to Chinese, by keeping a certain degree of 'fidelity' to the Tibetan. Yi dam tshe ring 'Tibetanises' the Chinese language in a selective way. That is, only certain specific linguistic parts of his poetic discourse are consciously worked into a Chinese capable of evoking Tibetan. The frame of reference for his poetic language remains faithful to Chinese morphology, and the basic rules of Chinese grammar and syntax are generally observed. Nevertheless, some components of his poetic language patently correspond to a Tibetan linguistic reference. In such cases, to know Tibetan is necessary, if not indispensable. 'Tibetanisation' mainly concerns characters who are relevantly chosen because of their phonetic and/or semantic value to the detriment of their original Chinese semantic, grammatical and syntactical value in a given sentence. The most recurrent 'Tibetanising' practices can be categorised in terms of the following three concepts:

A) *Translation*: this practice consists in translating into fluent Chinese (that is observing its semantics, grammar and syntax) the meaning of established Tibetan expressions (metaphors, proverbs, sayings, proper names, toponyms, etc.), and embedding them in a poem as a coherent part of the main poetic framework. The result is a poem in fluent Chinese but with no (or little) Chinese meaning. No linguistic evidence in the translated elements suggests the Tibetan references behind those expressions. The reader can understand the Chinese version at a first level of meaning without recollecting the Tibetan original references, missing the richness of the allusive message, and possibly having a sensation of 'unfamiliarity' with the text. Examples belonging to this category include:

1. Lingyang cheng 羚樣城 (Antelope city) refers to Hezuo 合作 (county in Gannan Tibetan Autonomous prefecture) whose traditional Tibetan name is Gtsod (Antelope) (Yi dam tshe ring, 1992:120);[258]

2. Jijiao cheng 犄角城 (Horn citadel, tib. Rwa mkhar) refers to "the citadel built with animal horns by 'Brug mo, the wife of Gesar, to store provisions for the army of Gling at war with the enemies. The citadel was located in Mgo log Dar ri county" (Yi dam tshe ring, 1992:119);[259]

3. Ru hai 乳海 (Milk sea) refers to 'O mtsho, "the milk sea on which Jo khang was built" (Yi dam tshe ring,1992:106);[260]

4. *Ma la jin nian* 馬拉金輦 (the golden chariot drawn by horses). This is a Tibetan metaphor from Indian classical poetry, for the sun

---

[258] "Yelai de yanshen. Zhi Lingyang cheng" ("A Nightfall Sight. On Antelope City").

[259] Footnote by the author, in "Sikao de jiegou. Zhumu Jijiao cheng bei hui suogan" ("The Structure of Thought. Meditating on the Demolition of 'Brug mo's Horn Citadel").

[260] Footnote 4 by the author, in "Gunben Fouyan. Zonggaba qiangu yimeng." ("Sku 'bum Buddha Countenance. Tsong kha pa's Eternal and Only Dream").

whose "golden chariot is said to be drawn by seven horses" (Yi dam tshe ring,1992:122). [261]

5. *San sui maju de hanshui* 三歲馬駒的汗水 (the sweat of a three-year old colt). This is a metaphor for Rgyal mo rngul chu river (the sweat from Rgyal mo) in Rgyal rong. "According to the legend, the river is nourished by the sweating stream of a three-year old runaway colt" (Yi dam tshe ring, 1992:121).[262] The actual Chinese name is Dadu he 大渡河 (Dadu river).

Possibly one of the most pervasive examples of this 'translation' device occurs in the poem "The Songs Mother Taught Me"(Yi dam tshe ring, 1991:11–21).[263] Here, the poet constructs his poetic discourse like a true patchwork where lines composed by the author rhythmically alternate with translated lines from Tibetan folk stories, aphorisms, proverbs and A mdo folk songs. These lines serve as a refrain to the poem.[264]

B) *Phonetic transposition*: this widely used practice consists in reproducing in Chinese the phonetics of Tibetan proper names, toponyms and culturally specific expressions which do not have a satisfying Chinese translation or whose Chinese version would result in a prolix locution. Neither the original Tibetan meaning nor the meaning of the character chosen to reproduce the Tibetan text is taken into account. The intelligibility of the phonetic transposed versions is often very problematic, mainly for two reasons:

---

[261] Footnote 5 by the author, in "Ma la jin nian de zheji. Duo Kang diming de qishi" ("The Ruts of the Golden Carriage Drawn by Horses. Clarifications on A mdo and Khams Toponimy"). For Tibetan epithets for the sun, see: *sna tshogs shing rta* "the multicoloured carriage", *rta bdun pa* "the having seven horses one," etc.

[262] Footnote 1 by the author, in "San sui maju de hanshui. Daduhe de chuanshuo" ("The Sweating Stream of the Three Year Old Colt. Dadu River Legend").

[263] "Muqin xinshou de ge" ("The Songs Mother Taught Me").

[264] In particular, translated strophes from two folk songs constantly recur in the poem occupying, in an alternative way, the entire last quatrain of the 7 main sections that make up the 49-quatrain composition. Thus, quatrains no.5, 17, 31, 42 and 49 are from "Wo changzhe tiaozhe dao ... qu" ("Singing and dancing I go ...") folk song pattern. Quatrains no.10, 24 and 38 are from the "Hao a! Hao a! Jinzhao hao ..." ("Good, good, today is a good day ...") folk song pattern. I have no access to the original Tibetan version of the first song. Regarding the second one, here are the three couplets from the refrain handwritten by Yi dam tshe ring's on the front cover of Yi dam tshe ring (1997): "Rten 'brel gyi smon tshig" (*glu*): *yag ga yag ga da nangs yag / dgung a sngon nyi ma 'char srol yag // yag ga yag ga da nangs yag / Seng dkar mo gangs nas 'gying srol yag // yag ga yag ga da nangs yag / stag shar ra'i dpa' rtsal ngom srol yag //*.

1. The Chinese language is structurally different from Tibetan, and Chinese characters' phonetics can hardly guarantee a minimum of fidelity to Tibetan phonetics. Phonetic transpositions of Tibetan words into Chinese are often very far from the original expression. To the bilingual reader it is often difficult to retrace the source. To the sinophone monolingual reader it is practically impossible as the following examples show: Yangzhuo Yongcuo 羊卓雍措 refers to Yar 'brog g-yu mtsho; Sanmuchu 散姆楚 stands for Bsam 'grub; Jianzi Baguo'er 江孜巴郭爾 or Baiju 白居 for Rgyal rtse dpal skor; Cuowa'er Jiazi 措哇爾戛孜 for Mtsho bar rgya rtse; *wu'erduo* 烏爾多 for *'ur rdo*; Gunben 袞奔 for Sku 'bum, etc. (Yi dam tshe ring, 1992):114, 141, 99, 118, 160, 106).

2. The characters chosen to give the Tibetan phonetics appear in the text with no coherent connection to the meaning of the text. It is their phonetic value that justifies their choice. However, because of the strong image-evoking potentiality of Chinese characters, it is very difficult to the sinophone reader to completely ignore their Chinese meaning when they appear in a text as mere phonetic transpositions. Shifts in meaning, contradictions in terms, distortions, nonsense, misunder-standings are the consequent results. Here are some examples: *tun mi* 吞米 (swallow rice) to say Thon mi (the Man from Thon, cf. Thon mi sam bho ta); Qiongjie [wangling] 瓊杰〔王陵〕 (Fine jade outstanding [Royal Tombs]) to say 'Phyong rgyas [Imperial Tombs]; *bai ma* 白馬 (white horse) to say *pad ma* (lotus flower); etc. (Yi dam tshe ring, 1992:102, 96,148).

C) *Compound solutions*: this linguistic device consists in combining the two previous practices, that is, when choosing the characters to refer to the Tibetan expression, both the phonetics and the semantics of the two languages are to a certain degree taken into account. For instance, to say Zho ston (Yogurt festival), Yi dam tshe ring writes *xue dun* 雪頓 where *xue* [3.] (snow) is intended to recall the Tibetan pronunciation of *zho* (yogurt), and evokes the important symbolism of the white colour; and *dun* 頓 (break, interval, pause, but also a classifier for meals) has some phonetic similarities with *ston* (festival), and possibly suggests the restful atmosphere of a festival where food delicacies (yogurt?) play an important part. Another example is *kadian* 卡墊 to refer to *kha gdan* (Tibetan style carpet). *Ka* 卡 (to block) is chosen merely for phonetic reasons, but *dian* 墊 (pad, cushion, mad) evokes, both phonetically and semantically, the Tibetan *gdan* (carpet). In Luobu linka 羅布林卡 (Nor bu gling ka), the characters *luo* 羅 (net for birds) and *bu* 布 (cloth) have no semantic relationships with *nor bu* (jewels). *Lin* 林 (forest), however, corresponds well *gling (ka)* (garden, park), both semantically and phonetically (Yi dam tshe ring, 1992:132, 148-9).

Yi dam tshe ring's use of cross-linguistic devices is much larger. My purpose here is to show that the Chinese language, if skilfully used, can be an important source of creativity and expressiveness in the hands of the Tibetan sinophone writer. This creative potentiality, because it derives from the writer's illiteracy in Tibetan and requires a concentration of poetic work on the Chinese version, is detrimental to the evolution of the Tibetan language and to Tibetan literature. Nevertheless, this practice potentially enriches the Chinese version while it destructures it at the same time. Providing Chinese with neologisms, new images and new linguistic solutions also challenges the established structures and the authoritative exclusivity of Chinese expressions.

The 'Tibetanisation' of sinophone literature, both in its contents and in its language—which is at first the poet's demonstration of his own sentimental attachment to his mother culture—can open further possibility of meditation to the writer and to the reader. By reading in a cross-cultural perspective, one experiences a sort of 'revitalising explosion' of canons: the canon of Tibetan tradition and its established values; the canon of Chinese standards and their civilising discourse; of the centre and the margin, of the native and the imported, of the writer and the reader, of the interpreter and the interpreted. The very axioms upon which canons are based are undermined, and the ensuing dualism makes room for other-ness, variety, and complexity.

CRYSTALLINE SEEDS

Thon mi Sam bho ta[265]
by Yi dam tshe ring

Since the man of Thon sowed
The thirty crystalline seeds
The annals of civilisation
Have recorded the splendid vestige
Of the three *skor*, the four *ru* and the six *sgang*[266]
Afterwards, an ice knife and a snow sword
Dismembered the body of *Dbus*, *Gtsang*, *A mdo* and *Khams*
But the fertile seeds still lie
Buried deep in the Bod pa's pure heart! [267]

Even the cold of a doubly severe winter
Can no longer lock up the sowing season!

Today the jade dragon has already roared
The seeds are ready to sprout
Barefoot I reclaim the land of my heart
To cultivate a brand-new century!

---

[265] "Thon mi Sam bho ta is the creator of the Tibetan alphabet. Thon mi (that is, a person from Thon or a person whose surname is Thon) and Sam bho ta (a man's first name) together produce the full name Sam bho ta from Thon. The thirty seeds are the thirty letters of the Tibetan alphabet" (note by Yi dam tshe ring).

[266] "These are Tibetan ancient territorial divisions: above the three *skor* of Mga' ris; at the centre the four *ru* of Dbus Gtsang; below the six *sgang* of Mdo Khams (*skor*, *ru*, *sgang* are all territorial units" (note by Yi dam tshe ring)

[267] "Bod: This is the name Tibetans use to refer to themselves (the name of the nationality). 吐蕃 (Tubo) is the phonetic transcription of the name that we use to refer to ourselves. 西藏 (Xizang) in Tibetan is "Bod." The use of the term 藏 (Zang) originated during the Qing dynasty and is derived from the name of the region of Gtsang, one of the three regions in the designation 'Mdo, Dbus, Gtsang' " (note by Yi dam tshe ring, 6 January 1983).

BIBLIOGRAPHY

Ashcroft Bill, Griffiths Gareth, Tiffin Helen. 1991. *The Empire Writes Back. Theory and Practice in Post-colonial Literatures*. London & New York: Routledge.

Gson tshe. 1998. "Snyan rtsom zhib dpyad tshogs chen zhig A mdor 'tshogs pa" (Debate on Poetry in A mdo), *Bod kyi dus bab*, 28/2: 3.

'Gyur med (ed). 1990-93. *Bod kyi deng rabs rtsom rig dpe tshogs* (*Tibetan Contemporary Literature. A Collection*), 10 vol. Xining: Mtsho sngon mi rigs dpe skrun khang.

Hong Zicheng. 1996. "Dangdai wenxue de gainian," 當代文學的概念 ("The Concept of Contemporary Literature"), *Wenxue pinglun*, (6):38–49.

Hsuan Mo. 1981. "Mainland China's Autocratic Policy Toward Literature and Art: Its Practice and Stratagem," *Issues & Studies*, XVII(12):33–46.

Li Jiajun. 1989. *Wenxue minzu de xingxiang* 文學, 民族得形象 (*Literature, The Image of a Nationality*). Lhasa: Xizang Renmin chubanshe.

Ma Lan (Maconi Lara). 1996. "Dui dangdai zangzu wenxue de yidian kanfa. Chaoyue. Benyuan. Zheli" 對當代藏族文學的一點看法. 超越. 本源. 哲理 ("On Tibetan Contemporary Literature: Transcending, Origins, Wisdom"), *Gesanhua*, 1996(1):61f.

Rabut Isabelle. 2000. "A propos de quelques problematiques nouvelles dans la critique litteraire chinoise," in J.J. Gandini (ed.), *Où va la Chine*. Paris: Ed. du Felin, 140–62.

Shakya Tsering. 1999. *The Dragon in the Land of Snows*. London: Pimlico.

Stoddard Heather.1985. *Le Mendiant de l'A mdo*. Paris: Societé d'Ethnographie.

—— 1994. "Tibetan Publication and National Identity," in R. Barnett and S. Akiner (eds.), *Resistance and Reform in Tibet*. Bloomington: Indiana University Press, 121–56.

—— 1994. "Don grub rgyal (1953–1985): Suicide of a Modern Tibetan Writer and Scholar," in Per Kvaerne (ed.), *Tibetan Studies: Proceedings of the 6th Seminar of the IATS, Fagernes 1992*. Vol.2. Oslo: The Institute for Comparative Research in Human Culture, 825–34.

Yi dam tshe ring. 1963. *Hunli ge* 婚禮歌 (*Wedding Songs*). Shanghai: Shanghai Wenyi Chubanshe, 96f.

—— 1980. *Xueshan ji* 雪山集 (*Snowy Mountains Collection*). Lanzhou: Gansu Renmin Chubanshe,187f.

—— 1991. *Xueshi ji* 雪獅集 (*Snow Lion Collection*). Xining: Qinghai Renmin Chubanshe, 271f.

—— 1992. *Xueyu ji* 雪域集 (*Snow Land Collection*). Chengdu: Sichuan Minzu Chubanshe,198f.

—— 1996. *Xueyun ji* 雪韻集 (*Snow Rhymes Collection*). Restricted Publication, Internal distribution. Lanzhou: Gannan Tibetan Autonomous Prefecture's Federation of Writers & *Zla gsal* (*Clear Moon*) magazine (eds)., 120f.

—— 1997. *Xueyu de taiyang* 雪域的太陽 (*The Snow Land Sun*). Beijing: Zuojia Chubanshe, 400f.

—— 1999. *Xueshan shizi hou* 雪山獅子吼 (*The Lion of the Snowy Mountains roars*). Lanzhou: Gansu Renmin Chubanshe, 250f.

—— 1999. *Xueyu zheren de sibian zhi hua. Jushi shouci dechu yueqiu you shui de kexue jielun* 雪域哲人的思辨之花. 舉世首次得出月球有水的科學結論 (*The Flowers of the Thoughts by a Snow Land Sage. Scientific Conclusions on the First International Results Proving that there is Water on the Moon*). Beijing: Dangdai Zhongguo chubanshe, 316f.

Yidam Tsering. 2000. "Two Poems," in F. Stewart, H. J. Batt, and T. Shakya eds., *Songs of the Snow Lion*. Herbert J Batt (tr.). Honolulu: University of Hawai`i Press, 12.2.

晶亮的種子
—— *吞米桑博扎*[268]

打從吞域人播下三十顆晶亮的種子，
文明的歷册收攬了三部四茹六岡[269]的勝跡，
後來冰刀雪劍割裂了衛藏多康的肌膚，
萌芽的種子還深埋在蕃域人[270]的完美的心里！

再冷的嚴冬也鎖不住播種的季節！

今朝玉龍已經詠嘯，種子就要發芽，
我赤腳墾拓心田，耕植嶄新的世紀！
1983。1。6

---

[268] 吞米森博扎：藏族文字的創制者。吞米：即‧吞，地方的人（或吞姓人）森博扎：即名字，就是：吞地人森博扎。30顆種子：指藏文30字母。

[269] 指藏族古代區劃：即上阿里三部，中衛藏四茹，下多康六岡（部，茹，岡均爲區劃單位）。

[270] 指藏族的自稱（即族名），如吐蕃就是自稱的譯音。‧西藏‧在藏語里稱‧蕃‧。‧藏‧源于清時朵衛藏的省稱。

CHAPTER EIGHT

A MYTH OF TIBET: REVERSE ORIENTALISM AND SOFT POWER

JAN MAGNUSSON (LUND UNIVERSITY)

INTRODUCTION

With the increasing reflexivity in notions of the Other, Tibetan studies have turned more towards deconstructing the Western myth of Tibet. Mythic elements have been exposed in the exile community's image management, modern travel journalism and in the contemporary New Age movement but not so much has been said about its political context. Lopez (1998) describes the myth as a prison that the Tibetans seem to be unable to escape from in dealing with the West. But the myth can also be a useful resource in world politics. In this short paper I want to discuss how Tibetans have politicised the myth of Tibet as a soft power resource in world politics, how this power draws on reverse orientalism and how it is manipulated in the issue of Tibet. With the term manipulate I mean the dictionary definition: negotiate, control and influence actors (*Collins English Dictionary*, 1994).

A WESTERN MYTH OF TIBET

Myths surrounding Tibet and its culture have increasingly become objects of study in Tibetan studies. A generic term for these myths has been Shangri-La, which is the name of a hidden Himalayan valley in James Hilton's 1933 novel *Lost Horizon*. The story is about four Westerners who are brought to the valley and gradually discover its secret: an extreme prolongevity as the result of a serene, tranquil, peaceful, and dispassionate lifestyle. The valley is rich in gold and many newcomers are initially overwhelmed by greed. But as they are subjected to the valley's power they change their minds and settle there for good. The inhabitants have devoted their lives to preserve a disappearing human refinement and wisdom while the modern world outside is rapidly approaching self-destruction. Then, it is predicted, the Christian faith will return and prevail on earth. At the center of Shangri-La is the Grand Lama, a man who turns out to be Father Perrault, a more than 200 year-old former Capuchine friar missionary from Luxembourg who has found inspiration in Buddhism. In the early 1800s Perrault was joined by Henschell, an Austrian nobleman and soldier with exceptional organisational skills. Then, one after the other, more Westerners drop in: two English missionaries, a Greek merchant, three Spanish gold diggers, two German, a Russian and a Swedish explorer. They form the core of Shangri-La's brotherhood, and local Tibetans do the labor and farm work. But none of the Tibetans enjoy the same prolongevity as the newcomers. Why? As the Grand Lama explains, the power of the valley does not work as well on Tibetans as it does on Nordic and Latin races. It is obvious how the elements of the novel have been borrowed from Tibetan Buddhism, even more so from theosophy, and perhaps also from the science of eugenics that was popular at the time. When the secret of Shangri-La is revealed it is strikingly colonial and Christian in structure and organisation. As it turns out, utopia does not really belong to the 'Other' but is merely a reflection of the Western Self.

The term Shangri-La was established as a concept in Tibetan studies by the Australian researcher Peter Bishop's publication of *The Myth of Shangri-La* (1989). In his book Bishop deals with the myth as expressed in travel accounts written by explorers and travelers from the West. Working with concepts from archetypal psychology, humanistic geography, and French deconstructivism he explores the 'inner meaning' of Tibet to Western societies and maps a process of change from Tibet as a geographically grounded place to a placeless utopia, an alternative society and as a criticism directed at modern society.

Writing about the myth, American anthropologist P. Christiaan Klieger (1997) traces its creation back to Greek writers such as the 5th century B.C. historian Herodotus. Also, romanticisations of Alexander the Great's Asian campaign, the publication of the accounts of Marco Polo's travels as well as invasions by Huns and Mongols combined to pave the way for the creation of an Asian Other including Tibet in the Western world, Klieger argues. The imperialistic expansion of Western powers in Asia was followed by a "transformation of the Other from an object of fear into an object of desire" (Klieger, 1997:63) and, as seems to have been clear already to Herodotus, "the most distant parts of the world, as they enclose and wholly surround all other lands, should have those things which we deem best and rarest" (Herodotus, cited by Hodgen in Klieger, 1997). Another expression of the same transformation was the Western 19th century conception of the *noble savage*, Klieger continues. On the one hand, he belonged to a materially underdeveloped part of humanity but on the other hand, he possessed important ancient knowledge that had been lost to the modern Western mind. Towards the end of the 19th century a separation of images of Tibet into comparative, although positivist and ethnocentric ethnography, and a "utopia of never acquired hopes and transcendental aspirations" (Klieger, 1997:64) occurred. A commercial as well as a New Age-created fantasy land started to emerge. For instance, according to McKay (1997:206) accounts of Tibet written by British civil servants and military officers in the front cadre were made more interesting to readers by incorporating (often under pressure from the publisher) more 'thrilling' and 'colourful' descriptions in concordance with the contemporary common image of Tibet in the West. On the utopian side of Tibet myths one finds Helena Blavatsky's *Secret Doctrine* and the Theosophical society's construction of an esoteric system of a Hindu-Buddhist inspired religious cult, as well as Alexandra David-Neel's vivid accounts of the more mystical and magical sides of Tibetan Buddhism. The utopian image continued to have a strong hold over the popular conception of Tibet. For instance, in the mid 1950s, a book called *The Third Eye* and claimed to be written by a Tibetan lama called T. Lobsang Rampa was published. It is supposedly Rampa's autobiography and describes how he is initiated into an occult and mystical Himalayan based incarnate brotherhood. But after a while Rampa was disclosed as C. J. Hoskins, an Irish plumber's son who had found the material for his book browsing in London libraries. The exposure of Hoskins did not discourage Western publishing companies and in the eyes of many people Rampa's account was still held to be authentic. In fact, Hoskins could later move to Canada and set up an ashram in Toronto (Bharati, 1974). *The Third Eye* as well as its sequels became immensely popular and for many people in the West, including some of the most distinguished Tibet researchers today, it came to spur a renewed interest in Tibet.

The myth of Tibet continues today, in travel accounts as well as in New Age literature, both that can be described as literary genres. The first genre emerged from travel accounts written by missionaries, soldiers, civil servants, and explorers (see above). Besides being mystic, Tibet was also imagined as closed and inaccessible to outsiders. These particular elements gave the accounts a heroic and adventurous quality, something that is carried on in many of today's travel stories where Tibet continues to be 'discovered' by Western journalists, writers and tourists. As exile-Tibetan historian Tsering Shakya (1994) argues, Tibetan refugees and Chinese destruction and repression in Tibet has been integrated in the myth. Recent accounts are thus often dramatised as a life and death drama populated with Tibetan partisans and Chinese security forces, where the Westerner, at the risk of his or her life, is in secret collusion with the Tibetans. As a case in point I want to relate an article written by a Swedish visitor to Tibet and published 1994 in a Swedish newspaper in connection with the commemoration of the Lhasa Uprising Day, March 10, 1959. In the article the author uses a poetical and impressionistic language to describe a Tibet that has been inaccessible to foreigners, that is every travel writers' dream, and synonymous with the institutions of Tibetan Buddhism. He ends by relating an incident that occurred during his visit to the Potala palace in Lhasa:

> I don't like this job ... a monk in the souvenir shop confides to us. What he can't see is that a police officer suspiciously comes up behind him. Quickly we interrupt him by asking an irrelevant question about the postcards on display. The heart beats agitated and frightened. Gagged monks. In the hawkers' Potala (Sydsvenskan, 1994:3-9).

The quotation has several mythological implications: The innocence of the monk, a helpless victim saved in the last second by the tourist, the visit to the Potala as a life and death adventure with the tourist as the hero, the collusion between the tourist and the monk, and the Chinese profanation of the spiritual side of Tibet.

The second genre is part of the Western re-interpretation of Asian religions (and it is this re-interpretive quality that makes it New Age). As is the case with the travel accounts, this genre also started with reports about exotic religious traditions written by missionaries, soldiers, civil servants, and explorers. Later, pioneering individual

Western converts started to publish books about their experiences and gradually groups of Western followers began to form. It is in the last stage of this movement that the second genre emerged. Taken to the West, the traditions are adapted and presented as a pure core of wisdom and mysticism deprived of sociocultural historic circumstances (cf. Hammer, 1997:85). They are often presented as "accessible without any intellectual effort, without any discursive input" (Bharati, 1974:1). When it comes to the spread of Tibetan Buddhism in the West it is often channeled through either Tibetan exile lamas teaching Western students or Western converts writing and teaching. A good example is the Tibetan Nepal-based lama Chökyi Nyima Rinpoche. He is popular with Western students and has said that it is often easier for the Western than the Tibetan mind to understand the more advanced teachings of Tibetan Buddhism. His book, *The Bardo Guidebook* (1991), is a typical product for the Western market. As with many works in this genre it is based on lectures held by the teacher (in this case in Nepal, 1987). Another similar example with the same theme that also adapts Tibetan Buddhist concepts and rituals to a Western secular context (such as suicide and care of the dying) is Western based lama Sogyal Rinpoche's bestselling *Tibetan Book of Living and Dying*. Chökyi Nyima Rinpoche's and Sogyal Rinpoche's lectures are commentaries to root texts that have been recorded, transcribed, collaborated with its sources, and handed back to the teacher for approval, corrections, and additions. Westerners who belong to the teacher's inner circle of students usually do the editorial work. The final product becomes a very condensed version and it is difficult to know how well it corresponds to the original lectures and talks. When the books are marketed there is also a tendency to mix up these commentaries with the root texts. Teachings that are spread in this fashion have constructed a modernised and adapted version of Tibetan Buddhism where its doctrines are coupled to modern Western problems.

The term Shangri-La reappears in the title of what is probably the most important book about the myth of Tibet so far, Donald Lopez's *Prisoners of Shangri-La: Tibetan Buddhism and the West* published in 1998. Lopez examines several colonial traits in the construction of a Western myth of Tibet and questions their authencity. On point after point Lopez refutes the myth and shows how Tibet and its culture have been understood both as superior and inferior to the

West depending on who has been representing it. It is only as recent as after the Chinese occupation in the 1950s and the exile of many Tibetans that a modern post-colonial image has emerged. But, as Lopez (1999:184), points out "agency, whether Tibetan or Western is not a fixed point or an innate ability but rather a process of circulation and exchange." Today, the Tibetans have to make use of the myth as a means in the struggle with China. For Lopez this strategy has created a 'prison' from which the Tibetans seem unable to escape. To win our sympathy the Tibetans have to deliver what we expect from them. Lopez (1999:202) writes:

> Tibet operates as a constituent of a romanticism in which the Orient is not debased but exalted as a surrogate self endowed with all that the West wants. It is Tibet that will regenerate the West by showing us, prophetically, what we can be by showing us what it had been. It is Tibet that can save the West, cynical and materialist, from itself. Tibet is seen as a cure for an ever-dissolving Western civilisation, restoring its spirit. An internal absence is thus perceived as existing outside, and if it be outside, let it be found in the most remote, the most inaccessible, the most mysterious part of the world.

In a sense, what Lopez is talking about is eloquently captured by the book's cover photograph: A Tibetan monk wearing robes and a pair of big sunglasses. The power of the myth is disclosed by the Western reader's immediate feeling that this is somehow unfitting. The monk should not be wearing sunglasses and they should definitely not be Western in origin, a spinal reaction that is indicative of Western images of authentic Tibetans.

Following an international Tibet symposium held in Bonn 1996, the term Shangri-La has been challenged by the term *Mythos Tibet*. At the symposium a select group of 18 well-known Tibet researchers, including some Tibetan scholars and intellectuals, talked about different aspects of the myth of Tibet. This was quite unprecedented. At the International Seminar for Tibetan Studies held in Graz, Austria, only a year before, attempts of deconstruction was met by a hostile attitude from several of the participants. For instance, Andrea Loseries-Leick's showing of video footage of Tibetan Buddhism's 'secret' so called *tumo* practice in the correct sequence of the moves was criticised on the ground that she, by showing the video, in fact initiated the viewers without being empowered do so. Similarly, Heinz Räther, after describing a controversy within the Karma

Kagyu school of Tibetan Buddhism over the 17th reincarnation of Karmapa was asked by several participants to drop this subject since they thought that common knowledge about it would destroy the current benign Western image of Tibet. At the *Mythos Tibet* symposium a number of different sub-myths were brought up and examined, such as, for instance, Tibetan culture as green, feminist, and non-violent. Some other subjects were Tibet in the New Age movement, in Western literature, in Chinese art and propaganda, in the cinema, in Nazism, the impact of the myth on the Tibetan self-identity and on the Tibet researchers themselves. Interestingly enough, the auditorium was split down the middle with a group of academics and students on one side and a group of Western followers/supporters of Tibetan Buddhism on the other side. The discussions that followed the different lectures indicated that the academic side seemed to be quite pleased that a de-construction of *Mythos Tibet* was out in the open, while the group on the other side seemed to resist it.

A problem with using a concept like 'the myth of Tibet' is that it implies an essentialist understanding of culture and a cultural Golden Age somewhere in the past. But as Korom (1997) has noted, the increasing reflexivity over the myth owes a lot to the exile of more than a hundred thousand Tibetans following the Chinese occupation of Tibet in the 1950s. A re-interpretation of the Tibetan exile as a diaspora and a globalisation of Tibetan culture meant that the West "could no longer construct Tibet in relative isolation from the people of that nation, for now a significant number of Tibetans were in their midst, rallying for the cause of regaining their homeland" (Korom, 1997:2). The use of diaspora discourse has led several Tibet researchers to look more critically at Tibetan culture as a multiplicity that is continuously re-negotiated across the global arena. A number of Tibet researchers were brought together on this subject for the first time in the 1997 symposium "Tibetan Material Culture in Exile" held in Santa Fe, USA. The different papers presented at the symposium trace the origins and development of the Western construction of Tibet as well as investigate some of its current expressions (see Korom, 1997).

THE SOCIAL MECHANISM OF REVERSE ORIENTALISM

Having discussed the myth of Tibet and how it has been understood
and dealt with in Tibetan studies I will now move on to discuss its
social meaning in Western societies by introducing a second important concept in this paper- *reverse orientalism*.

It is perhaps true that the use of diaspora discourse softens the
inherent language of difference in *culture* as a concept and combats
essentialist tendencies in the understanding of a concept like Tibetan
culture in particular. Nevertheless, to a certain extent even critical
studies and deconstructions contribute to a reproduction of the myth.
All along there has been a Western willingness to idealise and
romanticise Tibetan culture as a source of remedy for shortcomings
in modern society. With some exceptions, Tibetan culture has
usually not been subordinated as inferior as would have been the
case in an *orientalist* discourse. On the contrary, the myth has
commonly represented Tibetan culture as superior in many aspects —
predominantly on the spiritual side of human existence. The myth is
a positive model in polarity with what is seen as negative aspects of
Western societies, e.g., materialism, environmental pollution,
violence, etc. (cf. Inden, 1990). Tibetan culture is seen as the last
vessel of a human wisdom lost by the peoples of the material West.
Lopez (1994) even speaks of Tibet as a surrogate for *everything*
Western societies find themselves lacking. The Tibetans are thought
to possess a power to regenerate Western man by showing him what
he once was.

It is this perceived essence and power that is pivotal to the politicisation of the myth. It is open to manipulation in order to find a
power to influence the agenda of the global political arena. It is a
source of power that has been recognised by anti-colonial movements and struggles before, for instance by Gandhi and the Indian
independence movement. Lila Abu-Lughod has coined the concept
reverse orientalism: "seeking to valorise for the self what in the
former system had been devaluated as other" (Abu-Lughod,
1991:144), or to put it in plain language, turning contempt into
admiration. It can be understood as a counter reaction to orientalism
but in this case, as argued above, Western societies have a long
nursed romantic image of Tibet as a symbol of the 'good' sides of
humanness. Reverse orientalism can be understood as a social

mechanism helping the Tibetans in their attempts to manipulate certain aspects of Tibetan culture that the West admires, wants and values to influence the issue of Tibet.

A good case in point is Huber's (1997) analysis of how the image of a Tibetan 'green' essence of ecological awareness, environmentalism, and the protection and preservation of nature has been formed quite recently. An important factor in this process was reports about environmental destruction in Tibet in the late 1970s and early 1980s. The backdrop is the 1960s environmentalist representation of materially simple cultures as ecological and the view that ecological crisis could be deduced from an idea that Christianity was a religion that allowed exploitation of nature whereas Asian religions fostered a more ecological approach. Huber shows how Tibetan intellectuals and Western scholars, when the reports about environmental destruction in Tibet started to come in, suggested to the Tibetan government-in-exile that Tibetan culture should become 'green' to increase international sympathy for the free Tibet project. Representatives of the Tibetan exile society's political elite then started to participate in various institutions promoting the religious environmentalist paradigm. Several projects were established and funded by large NGOs. In this way the exile government could connect to global networks and link Tibetan culture, especially its more Buddhist side, to the global discourse of environmentalism. With a 'green' image established the exile government started to systematically produce and distribute promotional material, predominantly in the English language. The image was politicised so as to construct

> a negative ecologically destructive Chinese 'Other' [...] The political context here is that Green Tibetans should gain their independence because they would 'obviously' do a better job of maintaining the environment than the Chinese have in the past (Huber, 1997:112).

As Huber concludes, the image of Tibetan culture as 'green' and its dissemination is largely a product of a small circle of the exile-Tibetan elite. Also, the formation of the image has been a process driven by forces outside the Tibetan exile community. My own point here is that the image of 'Tibetan culture' as 'green' also fits well into the Western image of the pre-Chinese occupation Shangri-La. Since Tibetan culture is the West's symbol of 'good', the Westerners want to believe that it is being destroyed by the evil modern and secular Chinese exploitation. It is not just the physical geography of Tibet but also the last remnant of a good human essence that is under destruction.

SOFT POWER AND SOFT ISSUES

In this section I want to provide a framework for the politicisation of the myth by applying the concept *soft power*, as coined by American political scientist Joseph S. Nye in 1990. When we are discussing power in world politics we usually mean the ability of actors to control others, Nye argues. This ability to control is also associated to certain resources like possession of population, territory, natural resources, economic size, military force and political stability. In the post Cold War world, however, power is being defined less in resources and more in the actual *ability* to change the behaviour of states, to make the others voluntarily *want* what you want. The emphasis is on power over outcome of issues rather than power over states, an ability, if not to set, at least to influence the agenda. Today, complex coalitions of actors affect the outcome of issues in world politics. Even though military force remains as the ultimate power, communications, organisational and institutional skills, and the manipulation of interdependencies are also important. World politics is split up in multiple arenas that include different combinations of state and non-state actors. Nye argues that this power shift has made smaller non-state actors more powerful than in the past and that "new power resources, such as the capacity for effective communication and for developing and using multilateral institutions, may prove more relevant" (Nye, 1990:164).

Nye speaks of two dimensions of this new soft power in world politics. There is a *co-optive power* to get others to want what you want, and there are *soft power resources*, resources like cultural attraction, ideology and international institutions. If the culture and ideology are attractive, others will more willingly follow, Nye argues. If an actor, by supporting an institution, can make others shape their activities in line with its preferences it can avoid the exercise and costs of hard power.

If Nye is correct in his assumptions, the attractiveness of Shangri-La version can be a useful power resource in influencing the global agenda of the Tibet issue. The power becomes even stronger as

Tibetan cultural and ideological expressions, promoted by supporters among celebrities from the cinema and music scene, catch on and become icons of globalised popular culture.

How does this particular soft power work? During the exile, especially since the mid-1980's, a lot of effort has been put into a build-up of Tibet as a transnational symbol of *soft issues* (e.g. human rights, peace, ethics an environmental protection) in world politics. Once associated with solutions to durable problems in the modern world, Tibet becomes a source of soft power and conferred with a certain legitimacy in the global community. As already indicated by Huber's study there is presently a global marketing of Tibetan culture as inherently good and as a protector of a wisdom needed to solve global soft issues that goes back to the 1980s. Another indicator can be found in the promotional world tours of the Tibetan leader, the Dalai Lama. After his 1959 exile to India it was not until 1967 that he could travel further abroad. The first countries he visited were Japan and Thailand. On most of these early tours he met mainly with people interested in Tibetan Buddhism and with Tibet supporters. There was no official interaction with governments and he avoided bringing up political matters. In 1973 the Dalai Lama visited the Pope in Rome and went on to Switzerland and the Netherlands. He continued to Iceland and Norway, went through Sweden and Denmark, and to the UK. In 1974 and 1978 he went briefly abroad but it was not until the extensive 1979 tour covering Mongolia, Switzerland, Greece, and the USA that he accessed non-religious forums. In 1980 he once again visited the pope on his way to Canada. In 1981 he led the first so-called Kalacakra initiation in Tibetan Buddhism outside Tibet and India. In 1982 he visited South East Asia, Australia, Mongolia, the Soviet Union and Europe. In the years that followed his touring intensified and a more systematic interaction with actors in world politics developed. An indicator of his global prominence was when he was awarded the Nobel peace prize in 1989.

Looking at the topics of his public lectures the large majority of them dealt with global soft issues, often linking problems of the modern world with perspectives taken from Tibetan Buddhism and to the issue of Tibet's future. For instance, on his tours in 1993/94 the titles of the lectures were typically "Culture Overlapping Ethics Today," "Human Rights and Non-Violence," "Reflections on Society and the Future of the World," "Global Community and the Need for Universal Responsibility."

The lectures fell roughly into four categories: 1. Human Ethics, 2. Global Peace, 3. Environmental Issues, 4. Tibet (if topics overlap in a single lecture they appear in more than one category). The first two categories amounted to about 75 percent of the lectures and environmental issues to about 17 percent. Only three out of a total 22 lectures had the issue of Tibet as its main topic (Magnusson, 1994, [sources: Hicks & Chogyam, 1990, *Tibetan Bulletin*, the official bulletin of the Tibetan exile government, July–August 1993, September–October 1993, November–December 1993, January–February 1994]). To get a better idea of the language used in this context I want to take a closer look at a talk given by the Dalai Lama at Los Angeles World Affairs Council (LAWAC, Dalai Lama, 1988:58ff., see also www.lawac.org) and his book *Ethics for A New Millennium* [1999] published a decade later. LAWAC is a forum for discussion of global affairs. The Dalai Lama's talk there has been published and provides an example of a rather straightforward manipulation of some of the mythical elements to political ends. In his talk the Dalai Lama links ideas about global interdependence with Tibetan Buddhism and the issue of Tibet.

In the first part of the talk he elaborates on a basic sameness of human beings and a human capacity for co-operation and mutual understanding. The discourse is drawn from the concept of compassion in Hinayana Buddhism. Then he moves on to talk about global interdependence:

> For instance, thousands upon thousands of new cars are moving in the streets of New York, Washington, or here in Los Angeles, but without oil they cannot move. Though at the moment human beings are carried by cars, if that fuel is finished, the humans will have to carry these big cars. Prosperity depends on other factors in other places. Whether we like it or not, this shows that we are interdependent [...] Unless we have real cooperation, harmony and common effort, difficulties will be created. Since we must live together, why not do so with a positive attitude, a good mind? Why is it instead we feel hatred for each other and bring more trouble to the world? (Dalai Lama, 1988:61)

As a model for managing the problematic processes of global interdependence, the Dalai Lama suggests a Tibetan Buddhist approach. He conjures up the materialistic West versus the spiritual

East stereotype to imply that the problems cannot be solved by Western materialism:

> From my viewpoint all things first originate in the mind. Things and events depend heavily on motivation. A real sense of appreciation of humanity, compassion and love are the key points [...] A good heart is both important and effective in daily life. If in a small family, even without children, the members have a warm heart to each other, a peaceful atmosphere will be created. However, if any of the persons feel angry, immediately the atmosphere in the house becomes tense. Despite good food or a nice television set, you will loose peace and calm. Thus, things depend more on the mind than on matter. Matter is important, we must have it, we must use it properly, but this century must combine a good brain- intelligence- with a good heart. (Dalai Lama, 1988:61)

At the end of the talk he takes the logic of this more general approach to global interdependence and applies it directly to the Tibetan issue. For reasons logically deduced from the state of global interdependence Tibetan culture must be allowed to flourish freely:

> I am serving our cause with the motivation of service to humankind, not for reasons of power, not out of hatred. Not just as a Tibetan but as a human being. I think it is worthwhile to preserve that culture, that nation, to contribute to world society. (Dalai Lama, 1988:63)

The Dalai Lama thus links the issue of Tibet's independence from China to the future of humankind. Tibet is implied as hosting a wisdom—predominantly of Tibetan Buddhist origin that needs to be protected and have the power to make a better world (and a worse one as well, if this contribution is denied).

With his recent bestseller *Ethics for the New Millenium* (1999) the Dalai Lama continues to address a Western audience using the same approach. Again he makes himself a spokesperson for a global soft issue, in this case ethics. In the book the particular elements of Tibetan wisdom are spelled out more explicitly and referred to Tibetan concepts. Although most of these concepts originate from Tibetan Buddhism they are expressed in secular language.

Already in the preface the Dalai Lama states that what he is dealing with are universal principles (1999:xiii) logically based on the simple fact that all humans strive to be happy and to avoid suffering. Mankind needs to develop its spiritual side to survive. As in his talk at LAWAC his message is that material development and modern science cannot make people happier and will not solve any problems in the world:

> Yet strangely, my impression is that those living in materially developed countries, for all their industry, are in some ways less satisfied, are less happy, and to some extent suffer more than those living in the least developed countries [...] This is suggested both by the high degree and by the disturbing prevalence among the populations of the materially developed countries of anxiety, discontent, frustration, uncertainty, and depression. (1999:5)

As an example of "the link between our disproportionate emphasis on external progress and the unhappiness, the anxiety, and the lack of contentment of modern society" (1999:9) the Dalai Lama, tells the reader what happened to the exile-Tibetans when they were exposed to modern society:

> Whereas, for example, suicide was almost unheard of in Tibetan society, lately there have been one or two tragic incidents of this kind, even within our exile community. Likewise, whereas drug addiction among young Tibetans certainly did not exist a generation ago, we now have a few cases—mostly, it must be said, in those places where they are exposed to the modern, urban lifestyle. (1999:15)

The foundation for a human set of ethics for the new millennium as discussed by the Dalai Lama is individual development of inner, spiritual qualities. These qualities, he continues, might not have a ready equivalent in other languages, but are in fact universal and contained in a number of Tibetan concepts like, for instance, *kun long* (motivation, 1999:30), *ten del* (dependent origination, 1999:36), *de wa* (happiness, 1999:53), *shen dug ngal wa la mi sö pa* (empathy), *nyong mong* (afflictive emotion, 1999:90), karma (action, 1999:136), and *chi sem* (universal consciousness, 1999:162). Within the text one also finds different discourses from Buddhist teaching such as those about impermanence, emptiness, attachment and meditation, although described in modern secular language. The concepts are translated and explained by the Dalai Lama. For example, in a rather Geluk fashion he distinguishes *de wa* (happiness) in ephemeral and genuine happiness. The former is a temporary and impulsive kind of happiness while the latter is characterised by inner peace. In the long run only genuine happiness will do, Dalai Lama argues. To achieve it we must define its causes and conditions, guard against factors obstructing it, and cultivate factors that are conducive to it. Inner peace has two sources: our basic attitude (how we relate to external circumstances), and the actions we undertake in our pursuit of happiness (1999:57).

The Dalai Lama holds a strong essentialist view of humans and all through the book he often refers to "basic human nature." *Snying rje* (compassion) is the foremost of the human, spiritual qualities of our basic nature. As with several other qualities s*nying rje* is an emotion, although an emotion with "a more developed cognitive component" (1999:74). The Dalai Lama describes the feeling as a combination of empathy and reason. The development of *snying rje* "breaks down the very barrier which inhibits healthy interaction with others." And "to the extent that we are able to open this inner door, we experience a sense of liberation from our habitual preoccupation with self" (1999:75). Short of compassion, *sö pa* (patience) is the most basic of the human qualities:

> denotes a deliberate response (as opposed to an unreasoned reaction) to the strong negative thoughts and emotions that tends to arise when we encounter harm. As such sö pa provides us with the strength to resist suffering and protects us from losing compassion even for those who would harm us. (1999:102)

Although we might not be familiar with our basic spiritual qualities they are in our nature and can be retrieved and developed if we only go systematically about it. The practice of inner discipline is the key, and we need to learn how to control the mind's (*lo*) response to negative thoughts and emotions. Thus emotion and consciousness are distinguished which logically means that we do not have to be controlled by the former if we are masters of the latter.

From this discourse of ethics founded in spiritual qualities of a basic human nature, the Dalai Lama moves on to deal with ethics on the level of society. In comparison with the elaborate reasoning about ethics on the individual level he does not have very much to say except for a rather programmatic count of advise to the world: We have to teach our children to lead ethical lives, the media must be responsible and not focus too closely on the negative aspects of human nature, we have to find ways of manufacture, etc. that do not destroy nature, family planning is important, the market should be based on "constructive competition" putting "people before profits," the only valid peace is world peace, and we should begin to dismantle the military establishments because global interdependence is bringing us together into a single human community (1999:161). He even suggests the establishment of a global police force under the United Nations, and a global moral institution with "the task to monitor human affairs from the perspective of ethics" manned by

> artists, bankers, environmentalists, lawyers, poets, academics, religious thinkers, and writers as well as ordinary men and women with a common reputation for integrity and dedication to fundamental ethical and human values. (1999:216)

I will leave it up to others to discuss to what extent the modern world suffers from an ethical deficit and the validity of the Dalai Lama's approach to this issue. What interests me here is how his message is underpinned by myths about Tibet, and how the West is predisposed to accept a Tibetan definition of basic human nature, and how to develop its spiritual qualities. Since the publication of *Ethics for the New Millenium* the Dalai Lama has toured the world, giving lectures on this subject. A public lecture before a large crowd in Lund, Sweden in 2000 that I attended can serve as an example. The Dalai Lama knew what the crowd expected from Tibet and did not disappoint it and I think it is this is what Lopez (1998) means when he says that the myth has created a prison for the Tibetans. To recruit supporters in the struggle with China over Tibet's future the Dalai Lama is forced to play his part in the myth, and reinforce the crowd's demand for universal truths. That he is reflexive over this fact was clear when he opened his lecture by saying that those who had come to find universal truths would leave disappointed. But his reflexivity did not diminish the crowd's inclination to imagine him as holder of a wisdom lost by Western man in his endeavour for material development. The Dalai Lama is trapped in this prison and his book as well as most of his encounters with a Western audience finds its meaning within it.

Political leaders in Western countries and other powerful potential supporters of the Tibetan cause in the West are little different from the crowd in Lund when it comes to their receptiveness for global ethics presented by the Dalai Lama. Coming from him, a set of ethics and methods to achieve them is more attractive than a document published by a UN committee or a human rights NGO. From a more pragmatic political perspective, the moral ground is probably the only battlefield where the Chinese counterpart is not stronger.

In conclusion, one can perhaps say that the myth of Tibet is both a prison and a power for Tibet. The Western context for everything Tibetan is the myth of Tibet and a reverse orientalist admiration for Tibet and the Dalai Lama. It is our expectations on the Tibetans as holders of a wisdom that we search as a remedy four our own and our societies shortcomings that makes us so receptive to what the Dalai Lama has to offer. But in the service of the Tibetans the myth and Tibet's enchantment of the Western mind is also a soft power resource that can be manipulated to get attention and to get some access to the stages of world politics.

BIBLIOGRAPHY

Abu-Lughod, Lila. 1991. "Writing Against Culture," in Richard G. Fox (ed.), *Recapturing Anthropology: Working in the Present*. Santa Fe: School of American Research Press.
Bharati, Agehananda. 1974. "Fictious Tibet: The Origin and Persistance of Rampaism," *Tibet Society Bulletin*, (7).
Bishop, Peter. 1989. *The Myth of Shangri-La: Tibet, Travel Writing and the Western Creation of Sacred Landscape*. London: The Athlone Press.
Chökyi Nyima Rinpoche. 1991. *The Bardo Guidebook*. Hong Kong: RangjungYeshe Publications.
Dalai Lama. 1988. *Kindness, Clarity and Insight*. Ithaca: Snow Lion.
—— 1999. *Ethics for the New Millennium*. New York: Riverhead Books.
Hammer, Olav. 1997. På spaning efter helheten. *New Age: en ny folktro?* Wahlström & Widstrand.
Harper Collins. 1994. *Collins English Dictionary*. New York: Harper Collins.
Hicks, Roger and Ngakpa Chogyam. 1990. *Great Ocean: An Authorized Biography of the Dalai Lama*. London: Penguin.
Hilton, James. 1936. *Lost Horizons*. London: MacMillan & Co.
Huber, Tony. 1997. "Green Tibetans: A Brief Social History," in Frank Korom (ed.), *Tibetan Culture in the Diaspora*. Papers presented at a panel of the 7th International Seminar of Tibetan Studies, Graz, 1995.
Inden, Ronald. 1990. *Imagining India*. Oxford: Basil Blackwell.
Klieger, P. Christiaan. 1997. "Shangri-La and Hyperreality: A Collision in Tibetan Refugee Expressions," in Frank Korom (ed.), *Tibetan Culture in the Diaspora*. Papers presented at a panel of the 7th International Seminar of Tibetan Studies, Graz, 1995.
Korom, Frank. 1997. "Introduction," in Frank Korom (ed.), *Constructing Tibetan Culture. Contemporary Perspectives*. Quebec: World Heritage Press.

Lopez, Donald S, Jr. 1994. "New Age Orientalism: The Case of Tibet," *Tibetan Review*, 29:16–20.

—— 1998. *Prisoners of Shangri-La: Tibetan Buddhism and the West.* Chicago: University of Chicago Press.

Magnusson, Jan. 1994. "The Dalai Lama in the Interorganizational Field." Unpublished paper. School of Social Work, Lund University.

McKay, Alex. 1997. *Tibet and the British Raj: The Frontier Cadre 1904–1907.* Surrey: Curzon.

Nye, Joseph. 1990. "Soft Power," *Foreign Policy*, 80:153–71.

Shakya, Tsering. 1991. "Tibet and the Occident: The Myth of Shangri-La," *Lungta*, 5:21–23.

Sogyal Rinpoche. 1994. *The Tibetan Book of Living and Dying.* San Francisco: Harper San Francisco.

Sydsvenskan. 1994. "Potala- frånvarons museum," *Sydsvenskan,* 3(9):4.

Tibetan Bulletin. 1993. July–August; September–October; November–December. Official Publication of the Tibetan government-in-exile.

——1994 January–February.

CHAPTER NINE

VISIONS, ARCANE CLAIMS, AND HIDDEN TREASURES: CHARISMA AND AUTHORITY IN A PRESENT-DAY GTER STON

ANTONIO TERRONE (CNWS RESEARCH SCHOOL, LEIDEN)

INTRODUCTION

This article is a preliminary exploration of some of the features that characterise the charismatic personality of a visionary tantric layman at the heart of the phenomenon of 'treasure discovery' operating nowadays in Tibet itself. While outlining this process, I will also venture some tentative hypotheses as to how treasure discovery may be considered as an active force in the process of revitalisation of religious practices in Tibet.[271]

The phenomenon of the discovery of treasure teachings (*gter chos*) and of its proponents (*gter ston*) is one of those fascinating, yet controversial activities that characterises the religious world of Tibet. The institution of *gter ma* is still active in today's Tibetan cultural and ethnic areas. Recent studies[272] have shown an increasing interest

---

[271] This paper is a preliminary study on a topic I am more widely exploring for my actual Ph.D. research project supported by the Research School CNWS of the University of Leiden, The Netherlands. In my current study I am investigating visionary movements in contemporary Tibet in general, and studying the life and a selection of revealed works of a present-day *Gter ston*. My comments are based on observations made during extended stays between 1997–2000 in Khams and Dbus Gtsang (Central Tibet) specifically, now politically classified as Qinghai/Sichuan Provinces and Tibetan Autonomous Region (TAR) of the People's Republic of China (PRC), respectively. During that period I visited a small religious community belonging to the Rnying ma school of Tibetan Buddhism led by Gter chen Bde chen 'Od gsal Rdo rje. Most of the data reported herein are gathered from personal interviews with Gter chen Bde chen 'Od gsal Rdo rje, and from his autobiography.

[272] Dargyay (1977), Prats (1982), Thondup (1986), Gyatso (1992 & 1998), Butters (1995), and Rgya ye Bkra shis Phun tshogs (1997). See Aris (1988) for Treasure Tradition in general and Padma gling pa in particular. See also Mayer (1996) for the issue of *gter ma* literature in the Tibetan Buddhist Canon.

in this phenomenon within its historical and textual contexts, but only few attempts have been made to study it in the radically contemporary world.[273] One of the advantages of studying Treasure cults as contemporary, viable, and generative symbolic religious movements is that this enables us to explore the connections between Buddhist cosmologies, ethical ideas, bodily ritual practices, and organisation forms, which have been lost in earlier historical and anthropological studies.

The phenomenon of treasure discovery is interpreted by many observers as part of Tibetans' general attitude, which is characterised by a strong desire to remember and revive Tibet's glorious past.[274] The extensive and dense network of functioning monasteries, nunneries, retreat centers, and mountain hermitages, pilgrimage sites, and sacred places are at least a sign of the tremendous efforts that Tibetan religious communities make in order not only to continue the practice of their religion, but also to oppose the possible decline and overshadowing of their cultural legacy. In this context and framework *gter ma* still find their own way to express their high potentiality. As I see it, *gter ma* teachings are still dynamic and efficient in their capacity in keeping their greatest strength, their innate psychological impact and freshness.[275]

In Tibet living *gter ston* emerge periodically to shape and reshape a sacred landscape and holy places. In embodying the sacred as lived reality they thus create and extend new religious groups, focused regional cults, pilgrimage centers, a vast network of individual supplicants and devotional communities generated through loyalties that extend beyond local and regional boundaries. Throughout Tibet, treasure places (*gter gnas*), mountain hermitages (*ri khrod*), and treasure discoverers (*gter ston*) appear juxtaposed upon other complex, modern, and post-modern realities. They exist alongside the majority of monastic-based Buddhist institutions. Though nowadays *gter ston* are in few cases to be found amongst the ranks of *bla ma* and sages whose high spiritual and educational standing is

---

[273] For accounts of contemporary treasure finders' activities in Tibet see Hanna (1994), Germano (1998). See also Norbu (1986) for a personal account of a modern treasure finder's life, Rig 'dzin Byang chub Rdo rje. The lack of this sort of studies is also due to the difficulties in obtaining permits to conduct scientific researches in the PRC.

[274] In this I agree with the interesting comments made by Germano (1998).

[275] See Chris Butters (1995:16)

already established, most of them are still laymen and non-monastically trained tantric practitioners.

Throughout the entire process of concealment (*sbed pa*, *sba ba*) and discovery (*'don pa* or *bzhes pa*) of *gter* items the main role is attributed to a human being. On the one hand is the legendary figure of Padmasambhava, or his close disciples. On the other is the pre-determined emissary who will then receive the order through a mind-mandate transmission. Also relevant is the union between human beings, in this case a Tibetan Buddhist devotee,[276] and the soil and the landscape of Tibet.[277] This relationship should also be understood as central in the experience of Treasure Discovery and in the perception of self-identification, and successive self-presentation, of the human being as Treasure Discoverer.[278] Due to its characteristics *gter ma* reception, or discovery, includes certain kinds of claims related to Tibet's past personages and their lives. These claims are the real structure, which constitutes the basis for the building of a specific legitimacy style conveying charisma[279] and authority to the person who invokes them. But the *gter* theory of charisma and the elaborate cosmology it has generated are not necessarily articulated explicitly either by *gter ston* nor their devotees. On the one hand we have the socially constructed world sorrounding the *gter ston*, and on the

---

[276] The ritual concealement, retrieval, and use or re-use of religious texts and artifacts is not confined to Buddhism in Tibet, but is also accepted and practiced by representatives of Bon. In this study I will confine myself only to *gter ma* Tradition as it appears in the Rnying ma school of Tibetan Buddhism. Moreover I use here the general term 'Buddhist devotee' since it is still more common, if not a rule, to find *gter ston* among lay tantric practitioners than among monastically vowed monks.

[277] As for the peculiarity of the 'soil' or 'landscape' element in the analysis of *gter ma* in Tibet see Germano (1998).

[278] Self, the presence of self in human activities, and the concept of identity have been central issues of various sociological, socio-psychological, and of many socio-scientific studies. For my analysis I have taken as a model the definition offered by Perinbanayagam (2000:83): "Self is reflexive objectification of one's presence in a world of other selves and objects, a process achieved by using signs of various kinds. Such signs of objectification, however, are always elements of complex vocabularies, each of which is able to allow a minded organism to identify itself and being identified by others. This is identity. Identities are embedded in these discursive structures. An individual and his or her social circles use elements from these structures to name a self and be named by it."

[279] I refer here to Max Weber's classic discussion of charisma in *The Sociology of Religion* (1964), and therefore I mean the quality of an individual personality which sets him apart from ordinary men, and the signs, qualities, and powers, that cause the individual concerned to be treated as a leader.

other the self-representation process triggered by the *gter ston*, the individual himself. The *gter* theory remains an implicit, embodied form of charismatic knowledge. It is manifested, as my case study attempts to show, in the ritual capacity of *gter ston* to imbue their concrete surroundings with their sacred persona, and extend their spiritual domain through infinite giving. These actions create a moral space of love and amity, sacralising local neighborhoods through ritual practice and sacred exchanges, protecting devotees, taming nature, and enacting an alternative ethical order.

THE POETICS OF SELF AND ITS REPRESENTATION

Given the rich and textured quality of religious experiences such as treasure discovery in Tibet and the fact that discoverers are concerned with a dramatic presentation of self, one would expect to find that treasure retrievals would be a story they tell themselves about themselves. While reflecting on the meaning of discoveries of treasure items, one is lead to ask not only whose interests are being served and what social function fulfilled, but also what story is being told through a performance of spiritual virtuosity and supernatural powers.

Set against the textured aesthetic of Tibetan Buddhist hermitages and monasteries, the intricate regime of day to day life, the charged relationship between supporting lamas (*chos bdag*), patrons (*byin bdag*), Treasure Masters (*gter ston*), disciples, and the symbolic world brought to life by the *gter ston*, the actual act of gter retrieval is a one-dimensional, abbreviated event. This is not to say that it is insignificant or marginal in any sense. *Gter ston* take revelations very seriously even today. Moreover for many Tibetans revelations are synonymous with high blessing. It is one of the most visible and often public aspects of the gter activity itself. It is the focal point in the matrix of higher teaching transmission though gter items, for it is then that the *gter ston* can make a name for himself as both an active *gter ston* and as one who has lived up to the ideals of a rigorous way of religious life.

In the context of his mountain hermitage, retreat or monastic centre, the treasure master's identity is subsumed within the larger rubric of asceticism and contemplative practice. His individuality — his public identity and unique biography — is less important than the fact that he lives by a strict code and subscribes to certain values. A recurrent theme in the following paper is that of world renunciation as a moral value subscribed to by the treasure master (at least the ones described in this paper). Many *gter ston* turn their backs on worldly pleasure and sensory satisfaction being concerned with a disciplinary way of life in their quest for self-realization. Contemporary *gter ston* whose lives and works I am studying, seem to see themselves as renunciants and ascetics in objective terms as a generic category with certain distinguishing characteristic traits. This is a crucial point for the argument that follows. The ascetic or renunciant of which the *gter ston* speak is a figment of his ideological imagination. He is not a particular renunciant, but an amalgam constructed to fit, analogically, with the *gter ston*'s conception of his own identity and iconic notion of self.

The thesis taking shape in this study is that *gter ston* co-opt the values inherent in a life of asocial world renunciation and transpose these values onto their unique life path. This transposition has important implications. The gter ston is, unlike the monk, an individual-outside-the-world whose orientation is egalitarian in a devotional and disciplined sense rather than hierarchical, an orientation towards principles closer to nationalism rather than principles of social prestige if not position.

While *gter ston* recognize the moral virtue of world renunciation, they are confronted with a paradox that manifests itself in various ways. The problem that seems to be raised for the *gter ston* in particular, and for lay Tantric practitioners in general, is how to live a moral life while trying to subscribe to values, which define social life as basically immoral and unhealthy. Can a *gter ston* live with his wife, or consort, and be celibate? Can he claim possessions and still be dissociated from prestige and social status? Can he subscribe to a certain way of presenting himself and be immune from concerns of pride and conceit? I think that in the case of Tibetan religious systems we could easily accept that the notion of worldly asceticism is not intrinsically paradoxical. There is a devotional component in the gter ston's activity, whereby aspects of ascetic ideals are given legitimate, worldly form. What the *gter* ideology does, in my opinion, is to force the issue of asceticism in relation to the householder religiosity, into a sharp dichotomy of either this worldly moral and physical weakness—where emotion and wealth, among other things, are false consciousness—or otherworldly spiritual values and self realization, where pure consciousness is asocial.

CASE STUDY: GTER CHEN BDE CHEN 'OD GSAL RDO RJE

Gter chen Bde chen 'Od gsal Rdo rje is an interesting example of a contemporary treasure discoverer. He is a tantric practitioner and master, and a visionary treasure finder belonging to the 'ancient', or Rnying ma, tradition of Tibetan Buddhism. Heir and promulgator of one of Tibet's most arcane knowledge, wisdom, and tantric-based practices, he is a representative figure of visionary and contemplative movements in present-day Tibet.[280]

Born in 1920 to a nomadic family of northern Khams, his birth was welcomed by a series of auspicious signs and many people went to his birthplace to witness the event. As a boy he immediately showed signs of wit and initiative. When he was only seven he responded to an inner impulse and wandered alone through solitary plains and woods while tending herds of yaks on the slopes of the mountains near his parents' encampment. He loved this experience and took it as a great opportunity to isolate himself and contemplate nature and its phenomena. At the same age he began to experience intense dreaming and visionary activity. In his visions he saw deities and demons, whom he later came to identify as Padmasambhava, King Khri srong Lde btsan, his son Mu Khri Btsan po, Shanta-rakshita, Ye shes Mtsho rgyal, Rgyal ba Mchog dbyang, and Vai-rocana. But his claims to communicate with demons and deities soon caused agitation and discomfort among his fellow children. Adults, annoyed by the child's unusual behaviour, frequenting solitary places, sky burial sites, forests and lake banks started to consider him mad and treated him accordingly. He was repeatedly harassed, and finally compelled to flee from family's encampment. He thus renounced all worldly ties and at the age of thirteen left his parents and set out on a journey. He wandered for many months alone until he eventually came under the care and guidance of *mkhan po* Bkra shis Chos 'phel, who became his first master and who instructed him

---

[280] Most of the data provided herein have been elaborated from personal communications of Gter chen Bde chen 'Od gsal Rdo rje himself and his autobiography (Bde chen, 1998).

in reading and writing, and in the *Na ro mkha' spyod* (the Vajrayogini *sadhana* according to Naropa). Following his teacher's advice, he left for a long pilgrimage in Central Tibet (Dbus and Tsang), in order to remove obscurations, and met many of the highest lamas of that time.

He also went on pilgrimage to Bhutan and India in the 40s. He pursued an eclectic and nonsectarian education studying with teachers and exponents of the main schools of Tibetan Buddhism in different parts of the country. He thus studied with Grub dbang Bde chen Rdo rje, Rig 'dzin Nyag bla Byang chub Rdo rje and the XVI Karmapa Rig pa'i Rdo rje, among others, and they prophesied the young man's future as a great teacher and *gter ston*.

The depth of Gter chen Bde chen 'Od gsal Rdo rje's image increases when we consider the series of claims that he has asserted concerning his past life. His visionary experiences have allowed him to discover his previous past lives as Rgyal ba Mchog dbyang and Grub Mchog Dpal gyi Seng ge, two of the main disciples of Padma-sambhava. Masters such as Mkhyen sprul Bde chen Gling pa, Mkhan mchog Grub brnyes 'Jam dpal Nor bu, and Don rgyud Nyi ma have confirmed these incarnations.

In Tibetan Tantric Buddhism visions of deities are a measure of spiritual mastery and basis for religious authority. Although pure visions and appearances (*dag snang*) share some common modalities with *gter ma*, and some Tibetan scholars do consider them almost on the same level since a few *gter ma* teachings have been revealed through visions, technically speaking they are not the same (cf. Tulku Thondup, 1984:63; 1995:104). A vision is not a mind-mandate transmission but a teaching given directly by an enlightened being, a teacher, Buddha, or deities. However the authoritativeness of these teachings springs from the tantric practitioner's own encounters with the deities. The *yogin* meets the deity face-to-face and receives teachings or, in the case of earth treasures, (*sa gter*) instructions on how, when, and where a new *gter* item will appear.

In my analysis of treasure discovery I find some considerable similarities to Weber's 'exemplary prophecy'[281], according to which

---

[281] "[...] wherein the prophet is the living receptacle of a static, immanent, and abstract essence [...] Technical disciplines such as meditation and withdrawal from the world, over and above moral righteousness, are the road taken to reach this end. In popular understanding the saint is a magical being; a God on earth who can

the prophet is the receptacle of a superior message, and through
discipline becomes a magical being. In the specific case of treasure
discoverers we also face a pattern similar to the formation of the
individual's charismatic self proposed by Weber.[282] Actually the role
of *gter ston* can be explained as a spontaneous charismatic calling
based on a mind-mandate transmission (*gtad rgya*), received by
Padmasamhava during one of the *gter ston*'s past lives under
particularly intense meditation states and visionary activity. In
addition the individual has distinguished his life through a series of
positive acts and superior behaviours that construct a self-image
reconciling ideas of moral, devotion, and ritual superiority with an
emphasis on idealising compassion in his love and services for other
human beings.

During fieldwork periods in areas of Central Tibet (TAR) and
northeastern Tibet (Khams), I have realised that besides the normal-
ised and commonly accepted background, formation, shaping, and
development of individual selves as treasure discoverers, there are
other important factors in the process of each treausre discoverer's
unique growth. These include a series of ritualistic practices related
to an intense connection or link with the Tibetan soil and landscape,
which eventually triggers a positive and continuous receptivity
towards visionary intuitions. These practices are long-term meditative procedures and pilgrimage journeys in sacred and powerful
places, which enrich the practitioner in experience, devotion, and
mystic spontaneity and help him to achieve a higher social status.
The pilgrimage is seen as a highly meritorious action and a form of
purification that deserves social esteem and public recognition (cf.
Huber, 1994:45). This status-building period can exist as a two-fold
development stage in the career of a treasure finder. Gter chen Bde
chen 'Od gsal Rdo rje began his discoveries by unearthing material
earth treasures first, and then retrieving mental ones later. The *gter
ston*'s experience and age also affect this process. Gter chen Bkra
shis Rgyal mtshan and Ven. Bsam gling Tshe bzang Rin po che,
stepbrothers and two of Gter chen Bde chen 'Od gsal Rdo rje's

---

intercede to help ordinary human beings escape their round of suffering and
delusion. Exemplary religion is the natural home of charisma, since it rests upon the
recognition of a spiritually gifted individual's oneness with the sacred" (Lindholm,
1998:210).
    [282] Please refer to note above.

disciples, are also *gter ston* and they both have so far discovered only earth treasures due to their young age. Gter chen Bkra shis Rgyal mtshan is the elder of the two and only recently has unearthed a *sgrom bu*, or treasure casket, which opened and revealed a mental treasure to its discoverer. According to these *gter ston*, mental treasures are much more important than earth treasures.

A treasure discoverer's authority is also built up in accordance with previous discoverers' activities and authorities. His behaviour and spiritual identity are constructed according to specific patterns previously identified as proper and suitable to certain ways of life and personal message. Typically the treasure discoverer, whether clerical or layman, has not only received training in the formal Buddhist doctrine, but in most cases, he has been educated and trained in treasure lineage, and is able various elaborate sets of rituals and meditations. In the case of Gter chen Bde chen 'Od gsal Rdo rje, his main teachers have been Grub dbang Bde chen Rdo rje and Nya bla Byang chub Rdo rje. Nevertheless, a would-be-treasure finder is supposed to possess certain qualities and powers of a well-established charismatic persona independently of his training. Many of the *gter ston* of the past are well known for their unearthly feats and deeds. Skills in subduing nature, taming elements, and super-normal physical acts have always been, and still remain elements that contribute to the popular imagery of the construction of *gter ston* personalities. Their meditative achievements and religious virtue is fundamental, but the performance of miracles and pranks also play an important role in constituting the treasure discoverer's self-conception and public image. Gter chen Bde chen 'Od gsal Rdo rje is famous for a few miraculous acts. He is believed to have risen end floated in the air, left bodily prints in rocks, bent and twisted a thick sword blade, and produced precious medicine pills. The skill needed produce these pills came to him during the time of the Cultural Revolution as memories from his past life. In fact, one of his previous lives was that of Lha rje Kun dga' Nyi ma, King Gesar's personal physician and assistant in many a battlefield *(gdug pa spun bdun,* 1993:34-5). Treasure Finders' magical skills and supernatural powers are still admired by Tibetans in China. Even in a recently published and well-known Tibet guidebook a few lines are devoted to Mkhan po 'Jigs Phun's residence and activity:

> Khenpo Jikpun is well known for obtaining the 'bird-dogs' of Tibet, a
> tiny dog which is reputably found in the nest of cliff-nesting birds, and
> has the power to detect poison in food! (Gyurme Dorje, 1999:611)

In the act of representing himself, Gter chen Bde chen 'Od gsal Rdo
rje as a lay *gter ston* adopts an anusual way of dressing in order to
characterise his adherence to a strictly disciplined ascetic life style. It
is well known that Indian, as well as Tibetan, yogins have adopted
visual and decorative elements in their attire and clothing distinguishing their adherence to one tradition or another. The way hair is
grown and clustered on the head, different kind of garments, jewels
and decorative items, paraphernalia and ritualistic tools, are all
elements that play a major role in the presentation of the *gter ston's*
image to the lay community. Among Gter chen Bde chen 'Od gsal
Rdo rje's revealed teachings is a mental treasure (*dgongs gter*) that
focuses on the list of specific tools and items which are supposed to
characterise a *gter ston's* outlook. *Rta mgrin yang gsang rdo rje me
char gyi tsol med gsang sngags myur lam*, is the title of the brief text
which describes the *Dpa' chas bco lnga* (the Fifteen Objects of
Bravery), fifteen ornaments and tools appointed by Padmasambhava.
This *gter ston* and a few among his closest disciples who are also
gter ston themselves, have adopted the attributes described n this text
as distinctive emblems of their outlook, practice, and results. These
include a plaited tuft of hair on the top of the head (*dbu kra ral pa
thod du bcing pa*) as a sign of mastering the mantras of a great tantric
practitioner; a white cotton robe (*ras dkar*) as a sign of the production of the inner heat from the *rtsa rlung*; a pair of white conch-shell
hanging ear-rings (*thung gi snyan rgyan*) as a sign of turning the
wheel of Dharma of both ritual and divine sciences; ornaments made
out of human bones and fastened around six parts of the body (*rus
pa'i rgyan drug*) as a sign of being the chief of Dakinis; a golden
crossed *vajra* (*rdo rje rgya gram*) around the neck as a sign of
accomplishment of the four religious services;[283] a clear mirror
hanging on the breast (*thugs dkar gsal ba'i me long*) as a sign of
profound knowledge of both samsara and nirvana; a rosary made of
red *raksha* berries as beads (*do shal*) as a sign of development in
tantric ability; a ribbon to support the body during meditation (*sgom*

---

[283] *Zhi rgyas dbang drag gi 'phrin las*: worship, abundant service, religious
service to obtain power, and terrific methods in coercing a deity by spells.

'*ching*) in five different colours of the rainbow, as a sign of the crossed-legged posture of meditation; a nine-spiked vajra (*rdo rje rtse dgu*), as a sign of the appearances of perception of the nine vehicles; a ritual dagger (*phur pa*) as a sign of domination over the *dam sri* entities; a raven-shaped hat (*bya rog prog zhu*), as a sign of submission of the external world to one's own power; a large cloak (*ber chen*), as a sign of the ability to submit all deities to one's own service; a sling-shot ('*ur thig*), as a sign of the ability to crush evil spirits into powder; the bow and arrow of method and wisdom (*thabs shes mda' gzhu*), as a sign of support from the allied defenders of the Dharma; a pair of fish-head pointed felt boots (*srin lham nya mgo*), as a sign of the offerings received from wordly deities and demons ('Od gsal Rdo rje, 1998:5b-6b).

Gter chen Bde chen 'Od gsal Rdo rje's activity and position in the religious world of Tibetan Buddhism is also characterised by strict adherence to a certain life style and religious practice that emulates a well-established way of life of past hermits and tantric practitioners of the Rnying ma school of Tibetan Buddhism. Isolated on a mountain slope, his residence hut is made of stone, wood, and turf. With no running water, or electricity, the daily chores are shared by a few monks and nuns who alternate chores with their daily practice. The local inhabitants of the nearby villages have built most of the compound and the furniture decorating it with private funding and donated labor. This has resulted in the construction of a series of retreat huts and buildings for monks and nuns. They also come regularly to pay visits to the lama and his disciples, offering alms, requesting advice and blessings, name for newborns, forecasting and divinations. Benefactors (*sbyin bdag*) thus also play a decisive role in the relationship between the retreat center and lay community. The inhabitants from the nearby peasant and semi-nomadic villages frequently give food and materials, produce garments and build huts and furniture for Gter chen Bde chen 'Od gsal Rdo rje, his entourage, and the hermitage itself as tokens of their esteem and as a way to gain religious merit.

Gter chen Bde chen 'Od gsal Rdo rje is the exponent of an ancient way of religious life. He represents a conscious attempt to transmit the revealed teachings and maintain the pure *gter ma* legacy and tradition without much interest in establishing an insitutionalised network of devotees and disciples beyond those living around the hermitage itself.

Gter chen Bde chen 'Od gsal Rdo rje is not intentionally spreading or forcing his own image as a *gter ston* beyond the community itself. As Germano has shown in his outstanding study, for example, *mkhan po* 'Jigs med Phun tshogs' visionary and treasure revealing activity must be seen in its social and historical background as a sign of religious revival and cultural identity emphasising ecumenical and monastic-centered ethics (Germano, 1998:72). On the contrary Gter chen Bde chen 'Od gsal Rdo rje's life style and visionary treasure tradition reflect a classic tantric paradigm of religious life within an ordinary lay community typical of the Rnying ma order. Separated from any monastic discipline-centered ethics and political or nationalistic activism, Gter chen Bde chen 'Od gsal Rdo rje is closer to the traditional figure of Tibetan s*ngags pa* families and lay tantric married practitioners (*ser khyim*), a national hero struggling for the religious and cultural revival of his country. His activities differ from those of *mkhan po* 'Jigs phun. In fact *mkhan po* 'Jigs phun's revelation and networking activities seem to be polarised around his attempt to establish a renewed monastic disciplined order. Through the revelation of *gter ma* and his quest for a traditional life style, Gter chen Bde chen 'Od gsal Rdo rje has made measured choices in order to harness the energising force of rNyingma Buddhism and channel it towards an ideological countermovement against modernity.

Gter chen Bde chen 'Od gsal Rdo rje's Buddhist and specifically tantric identity, as well as that of his followers, is deeply characterised by a path of accumulation of wisdom through meditation practice. The central expression of his religious and cultural identity is therefore asceticism and meditation practice. The adherence to a certain set of rules for personal representation such as a specific and codified style of attire with traditional Tibetan garments and symbolic ornaments and accessories, can be seen as an attempt to establish a more authentic way of religious life style that advocates the past as ultimate model. This life style promotes a detachment or semi-detachment from urban areas and the maintenance of the teachings into a carefully circumscribed entourage of disciples and lay practitioners. Gter chen Bde chen 'Od gsal Rdo rje, as a true exponent and representative of the old model of ascetic practitioner, is a yogin who prefers silence and a secluded life to the fame and success of open and public activity. Finally, another feature of his traditional attitude is the belief that women are of crucial importance as consorts (*rig ma*) for male visionaries. Thus, in his opinion, the practice of sexual yoga contributes to the success of a treasure revealer's activity. Gter chen Bde chen 'Od gsal Rdo rje's consort, Bkra shis Mtsho mo, is his tantric partner, caretaker, and above all his scribe.

Gter chen Bde chen 'Od gsal Rdo rje has never taken any vows. Many of his disciples and resident followers are monks and nuns belonging to different traditions who are attached to monasteries of the area. Most of them bear full vows. However, Gter chen Bde chen 'Od gsal Rdo rje though conducting a relatively secluded life as a tantric practitioner, has never adhered to any strict vow or monastic conduct.

Conclusions

Gter chen Bde chen 'Od gsal Rdo rje's activity is not centered in any monastic institution. His religious power and prestige is based on personal ability and achievements. The master's accomplishments have been and remain of central importance in establishing and developing eventually a lineage (see Gyatsho, 1998).

Within the Tibetan religious world visions and personal virtuosity of the master, are fundamental methods adopted in the process of self-representation. Gter chen Bde chen 'Od gsal Rdo rje's crafts in distinctive visions and his mastery of what has been sanctioned by tradition have characterised his experience and shaped his identity. As we have just seen his identity as a treasure discoverer entailed past lives as Rgyal ba Mchog dbyang and Grub mchog Dpal kyi Seng ge, two of Padmasambhava's twenty five disciples. His personal charisma has been enriched by the identification with Lha rje Kun dga' Nyi ma, the personal physician and assistant of King Gesar of Gling. These arcane claims add considerable depth to the image of Gter chen Bde chen 'Od gsal Rdo rje. Nowadays the notion that someone could have been appointed in a past life to retrieve a hidden treasure from the earth or from his mind is still accepted in the Tibetan religious milieu both in the Diaspora and in Tibet itself. In Tibet, however, it assumes stronger connotations than in the Diaspora evidence of the quest for a link between the present and the past of Tibet, for renewal and revival of the teachings, and for the presence of an enlightened being who has been chosen for this mission and task. In his attempt to continue an archaic tradition such as treasure discovery, Gter chen Bde chen 'Od gsal Rdo rje persists in a process of interpretation and negotiation of meaning between historical preconception and practical circumstances.

The success of Gter chen Bde chen 'Od gsal Rdo rje's and other contemporary *gter ston* religious revival and cultural identity is not due to their success in reproducing a nostalgic and romantic institution, but rather because "their view concerning their present status and situation is ideologically compatible to other main events in their long history" (Klieger, 1992:16). In this continuity Gter chen Bde chen 'Od gsal Rdo rje finds the way to define his existence as a Tibetan, working and operating in his country, for the welfare of his fellow countrymen.

BIBLIOGRAPHY

WORKS IN TIBETAN

Bde chen, 'Od gsal Rdo rje. 1998. *Rig 'dzin nus ldan rdo rje'i rnam thar bsdus pa dri med rdo rje'i zlos gar bzhugs*. Khams (Qinghai). Original manuscript in the author's possession.

—— n.d. *Rta mgrin yang gsang rdo rje me char gyi rtsol med gsang sngags myur lam bzhus*. Original manuscript in the author's possession.

Xizang Renmin Chubanshe. 1993. *Gdug pa spun bdun*. Lhasa, 34-5.

WORKS IN WESTERN LANGUAGES

Aris, Michael. 1988. *Hidden Treasures and Secret Lives: A Study of Pemalingpa and the Sixth Dalai Lama*. Delhi: Motilal Banarsidass.

Butters, Chris and Padma Tshewang (eds.). 1995. *The Treasure Revealer of Bhutan: Pemalingpa, the Treasure Tradition and its Critics*. Kathmandu: EMR.

Dargyay, Eva M. 1979 (1977). *The Rise of the Esoteric Buddhism in Tibet*. Delhi: Motilal Banarsidass.

Germano, David. 1998. "Re-membering the Dismembered Body of Tibet: Contemporary Visionary Movements in the People's Republic of China," in M.C. Goldstein and M.T. Kapstein (eds.), *Buddhism in Contemporary Tibet: Religious Revival and Cultural Identity*. Berkeley: University of California Press, 53–94.

Gyatso, Janet. 1998. *Apparitions of the Self: The Autobiography of a Tibetan Visionary*. Princeton: Princeton University Press.

Gyurme, Dorje. 1999. *Tibet Handbook with Bhutan*. Bath: Footprint Handbooks.

Hanna, Span. 1994. "Vast as the Sky: The Terma Tradition in Modern Tibet," in G. Samuel (ed.), *Tantra and Popular Religion in Tibet*. New Delhi: International Academy of Indian Culture and Aditya Prakashan, 1–13.

Huber, Toni. 1994. "Putting the *gnas* Back into the *gnas-skor*: Rethinking Tibetan Buddhist Pilgrimage Practice," in *Tibet Journal*, XVI(2).

Klieger, P. Christiaan. 1992. *Tibetan Nationalism: The Role of Patronage in Accomplishment of National Identity*. Meerut: Archana.

Lopez, Alan. 1992. *Reality Construction in an Eastern Mystical Cult*. New York: Garland.

Mayer, Robert. 1996. *The Phur-pa bcu-gnyis: A Scripture from the rNying-ma'i rGyud-'bum*. Doctoral disseration, Leiden University.

Norbu, Namkhai. 1986. *The Crystal and the Way of Light: Sutra, Tantra and Dzog-chen*. J. Shane (ed.). London: Routledge & Kegan Paul.

Perinbanayagam, R.S. 2000. *The Presence of Self*. Lanham: Rowman & Littlefield.

Prats, Ramon. 1982. *Contributo allo Studio Biografico dei Primi gTer-ston*. Napoli: Istituto Universitario Orientale.

Thondup, Tulku Rinpoche. 1986. *Hidden Teachings of Tibet: An Explanation of the Terma Tradition of the Nyingma School of Buddhism*. Harold Talbott (ed.). London: Wisdom Publications.

CHAPTER TEN

WILL THE REAL TIBETAN PLEASE STAND UP!
IDENTITY POLITICS IN THE TIBETAN DIASPORA

EMILY YEH (UNIVERSITY OF CALIFORNIA — BERKELEY)

In January 2000, I attended a pre-Losar party sponsored by the Tibetan Association of Northern California with a friend whom I shall call Drolgar, a Chinese-educated Tibetan woman who had recently come to the US to continue her studies. Walking up to the bar, she asked to buy two soft drinks in her flawless Lhasa-dialect Tibetan. The two Tibetan women behind the bar, both exiles from India, looked at each other in disbelief, one saying to the other loudly in Tibetan, "Oh! She's Tibetan! I thought she was Chinese." Embarrassed, we both took our drinks and walked quickly away. Several months earlier, the two of us had attended another party, this time at the home of a mutual Tibetan friend in Berkeley. Towards the end of the evening, one of the women, who was born in Kham but had lived for many years in India, called across the room, "You know, I really did think you were a Chinese woman when I met you today. You really do look like a *rgya mo*."[284] The same woman had commented to me earlier on how much she thought I looked like a Tibetan. According to another Lhasa woman, now that I had learned to speak the Tibetan language, I had "become the same as a Tibetan." These and other incidents of mistaken Han-Tibetan identity finally led to a long conversation in which Drolgar asked me plaintively, "I feel I am really Tibetan inside but all the other Tibetans think I am Chinese. How can I make myself more Tibetan?" She went on to explain that when she met other Tibetans she immediately and intuitively recognised them as Tibetan. But, she wondered, if she could step outside her own body and meet herself, would she get that

---

[284] Note that in this paper I use 'Chinese' interchangeably with 'Han Chinese'. I understand the problems with this usage, but do so for the sake of convenience. All names have been changed.

sense of Tibetan-ness which she felt to be her true essence, or would she see a Chinese woman as so many other Tibetans do?

The conversation made me uncomfortable: how could I, a Chinese-American, try to answer a Tibetan woman's question about how to be more Tibetan, especially given deeply held and often politically strategic beliefs in the existence of an essential Tibetan identity, as well as in the highly polarised context of exile in which all things 'Chinese' become the 'Other' against which (at least some) Tibetan self-presentations are made. My usual glib explanation about why I can sometimes 'pass' — long hair, turquoise earrings, a lot of time in the sun — seemed suddenly offensive, as if I were suggesting that there was no more to fulfilling a deeply held desire to be recognised as Tibetan (with all its implications) than surface adornment. While a completely essentialist notion of identity is clearly untenable, so too is one in which identity is a voluntaristically chosen act, like picking a set of clothes to wear in the morning. How can one ensure that other people recognise and accept one's identity as the one that one believes it to be, especially when categories by which identities are named take on multiple meanings? As Lisa Malkki (1997:71) states in her study of Hutu refugees,

> identity is always mobile and processual, partly self-construction, partly categorisation by others, partly a condition, a status, a label, a weapon, a fund of memories, and so on. It is a creolised aggregate composed through bricolage.

This formulation of identity is a useful starting point for raising questions about Tibetan communities and identity both in exile and in Tibet. What are the relevant markers of Tibetan identity and how do they differ in different sites of Tibetan identity-formation, particularly in the homeland of Tibet itself, in refugee communities in South Asia, and in the proverbial melting pot of the United States? What role does "categorisation by others" play in identity and the social life of Tibetan communities? How is Tibetan-ness understood, experienced, contested, or enacted by differently situated Tibetans and how does this bear on political position, relationships to all things 'Chinese', or the problematics of recognition or 'passing'? In this paper I address these questions vis-à-vis the experiences of the

Tibetan community[285] in the Bay Area of California, US. To a lesser extent, I also address the cultural politics of Tibetan identity in India, in Lhasa, and in 'inland China' (*neidi*) in order to compare different sites in which Tibetan identity is claimed and performed.[286] In doing so, I wish to step back from a focus on 'the Tibetans' as an unproblematic collective to ask instead about the fissures or fragments encompassed within the category 'Tibetan'.

Although it may well be impossible to talk about representations of Tibetan culture without discussing the way Tibetans are imagined by the West, (McLagan, 1997:69; see also Klieger, 1997; Bishop, 1989; and Lopez, 1998), I try specifically to address Tibetan presentations of self to other Tibetans, rather than to Western supporters. I believe this is possible and necessary even if there is "a whole set of multicultural and transnational mechanisms through which 'authentic' Tibetan-ness is scripted by Chinese and Westerners and is internalized by Tibetans in performances ..." (Adams, 1996:511). That is, while mimesis, a complex mirroring relationship through which representations come to affect who and what the represented consider themselves to be, must thus shape Tibetan subjectivities (see discussion of racialised images and 'passing' below), an exclusive focus on western representation and consumption of Tibetan culture obscures certain everyday practices which are also partially constitutive of identity. By focusing on some seemingly mundane details of social relationships, I discuss a variety of alternative Tibetan subject positions, all of which are valid and all of which struggle with questions of authenticity.

The relatively new Tibetan communities in the US such as the one in the Bay Area are especially interesting places to consider such cultural politics, given much greater freedom from both state and

---

[285] By 'Tibetan community' I mean only the sum total of all people residing in the Bay Area who consider themselves to be Tibetan. I do not mean to posit a priori any particular sense of group belonging, mutuality, or closeness, as much of the sociality takes place within smaller subsets.

[286] This paper is based on semi-structured and unstructured interviews conducted with twenty Tibetans living in the Bay Area; as well as observations and experiences gathered from three years of social interactions with Tibetans in the Bay Area and one year of living in Lhasa as a student. Tibetans from all three 'categories' discussed in the paper were interviewed in approximately equal numbers. Some interviews were conducted only in Tibetan; others in various combinations of Tibetan, Chinese, and English.

community pressure than is experienced within Tibetan communities in India, Nepal, and certainly China. Among the nearly 500 Tibetans now residing in the Bay Area, many have come to the US as participants or family members of participants of the US-Tibetan Resettlement Program. At the time of the program there was great concern in Dharamsala that the immigrants would become 'less Tibetan', and as a result there has been a conscious effort on the part of at least some of the 'America 1000' to propagate the cause of a free Tibet (Korom, 1997a:7). Others, however, have arrived as students, through private sponsorships, or through extended kinship networks unrelated to the resettlement program. Some understand themselves primarily to be refugees or exiles, while a few view themselves as foreign students from China. Many hope to become citizens and settle in the US; the stigma — the dismayed suspicion that one has given up hope—often attached to seeking citizenship in South Asia seems not to apply in the West. Others dream of earning money for a few years and then returning to do business or retire in India, Nepal, or even Tibet. Very few, however, have been in the US long enough to have become American citizens, or to conceive of themselves in American melting pot ethnic labels such as 'Tibetan-American' or 'Asian-American'.

In any case, there is a unique mixture of those who were born and raised in exile (that is, refugees in India or Nepal); those who left Tibet in the 1980–90s and experienced being 'new arrivals' in India; and a smaller number of homeland Tibetans—Tibetans who have arrived directly from Tibet, most of whom have been relatively well educated in the Chinese school system. Indeed, I find these three groups, based place of socialisation and subject-formation to be quite important in shaping aesthetic sensibilities as well as determining who forms friendships and other social relationships with whom.[287] Generational differences are also of great importance, as different cohorts are marked by history in very different ways. Here I focus primarily on a younger generation of people between the ages of roughly 20–40. It should be understood that like all such analytical classifications, these groups are in no way absolute. Some people such as those who have come straight from the homeland but without

---

[287] Social relations, identities, and bodies are of course gendered; unfortunately, I do not have space to discuss the gendered nature of Tibetan-ness in this paper (see Makley, 1999).

much formal education, or exiles from India who have spent years in Taiwan, do not fit neatly into these categories. Furthermore, most Tibetans do not articulate their social relationships in these terms, even if they are lived in practice. Instead of a community struggling over its own boundaries and identities, what gets projected instead — often in the service of a larger political cause — is a self-perceived homogenous community. My purpose here in discussing differences is emphatically not to undermine Tibetan goals, aspirations, and struggles but simply to open up space for franker discussion about the changing meanings of Tibetan-ness.

Because I am interested in everyday social interactions that take place in contexts not specifically meant for non-Tibetan participants (rather than large demonstrations, exhibits, etc.), my own role as a non-Tibetan observer must be acknowledged. Thus, in the first part of the paper, after addressing racialised and misrecognised identities, I draw upon my own embodied experiences of success and failure in 'passing' to reflect upon the contradictory nature of identity as well as the effects of my own otherness. In the second part, I examine different ways in which Tibetan subjects are constituted in different places, particularly through the question of 'Sinicised' Tibetans and the relationship between language use and politics.

RACE AND (MIS)RECOGNITION

I began with the story of Drolgar not because her experience is typical, but because it opens up questions about the "increasingly racialised politics ... between Chinese and Tibetan identity" (Adams, 1996:516) both within the PRC and in exile, where the manners, clothing, and tastes of 'new arrivals' are criticised for being 'too Chinese' (Diehl, 1997:126). There are two phenomena at work here, one of which might be called recognition in the first instance — that is, being recognised as Tibetan at first sight; and the second of which is related to authenticity — judgements that a person known to be (at least racially) Tibetan, still seems somehow 'un-Tibetan' The two are related insofar as the different markers of identity including physical characteristics, mannerisms, and behaviour are often very difficult to disentangle.

Of the Tibetans whom I interviewed who are occasionally — or in some cases, commonly — mistaken for being Han, most were either from Khams or A mdo, or had spent long periods of time living in large Chinese cities, or both. For example, one Khampa businessman told me:

> It's very strange, but no one ever believes I'm Tibetan. I was once wearing a chuba (*phyu pa*) while doing business at the border (Dram). After I finished and was walking away, I heard the Tibetans whispering to each other that they did not think I was Tibetan, even though I was speaking Tibetan to them the whole time. They thought I was a Han who was raised in Tibet.

Another Tibetan man who was originally from Lhasa but now works in Beijing, complained to me that when he returns to Lhasa and goes to Nang ma, he often hears people whispering to each other as he enters the door, "here comes a *rgya mi*."

I suggest there are two reasons for mis-recognition, both based on the drawing the boundaries of Tibetan-ness too tightly. First, the circulation of racial images about what Tibetans should look like—both in the context of the PRC and through the 'Tibet movement' in the west—does not necessarily match the actual phenotypical characteristics of some Tibetans, especially those from eastern regions.[288] In popular culture of the PRC, the most frequently invoked characteristics of Tibetans, like those for other minority *minzu*, are those that tend to exaggerate their contrast with the Han (Blum, 1992:268). Minorities are both exoticised and eroticised to form the majority Han's constitutive outside, through a logic which has been termed both 'oriental orientalism' (Gladney, 1994) and 'internal orientalism' (Schein, 1997). Tibetans are said to be barbarians (*yeman*), dirty, superstitious, and violent (Blum, 1992:271). Moreover, they are thought to be dark (*hei*), and to not speak Chinese. According to one woman from A mdo,

> the Han [in Xining] were always saying to me: "Your skin is so white! You speak Chinese so well! You're just like us Han, not like one of those other Tibetans at all." They thought they were complimenting me, that I should be happy to look like a Han. But it didn't make me happy.

In his study of racial prejudice in China, Dikotter (1992:x) states that "the phenotype of most minorities was not significantly at variance

---

[288] The whole question of intermarriage vis-à-vis Han/Tibetan identity is a complex one that I do not explore here.

with that of the Han Chinese: there was a physical continuity that precluded the elaboration of racial theories." Yet popular imagination, if not official state discourse, of Tibetans as an 'internal other' within China is in fact couched at least partially in racialised terms; phenotypical similarity exaggerates rather than eliminates sensitivity to physical characteristics.[289] Tibetans engaged in building or consolidating a national identity from a number of regional affiliations are actively defining boundaries, some of which may mimetically internalise such external definitions. Nor is this process limited to the PRC. Tibetans in exile are exoticised through images of religious piety and victimhood (Adams, 1996) found in glossy coffee table photo books, brochures, web pages, and booklets for humanitarian as well as political organisations. They are also exoticised through the selection of images that emphasise the cultural as well as phenotypical uniqueness of Tibetans, especially their differences from the Han. If only a subset of the full range of Tibetans is ever represented, this may partially explain whysome Tibetans seem to 'not look Tibetan' to others. I hasten to add that there is nothing at all unusual about judging ethnicity by physical markers; it is a natural way of navigating and making sense of the world. It is of interest here because Tibetans in exile have been socialised into thinking of themselves as a homogenous group through symbols and rituals that separate 'us' Tibetans from the Chinese (Shakya, 1993:11), that is, because of the politicised nature of 'Chinese' as opposed to 'Tibetan' identity.

Boundaries around what is considered 'Tibetan' tend to get drawn too tightly around what is familiar from the context of exile not only on physical bases, but also on cultural markers such as dress, behaviour, and mannerisms, such that something as simple as seeing a young woman wear glasses becomes weighed as evidence in favor of Chinese rather than Tibetan categorisation. Of course, nobody thinks it is inappropriate for young women to wear glasses; rather, because is unfamiliar, it seems to be un-Tibetan.

---

[289] Dikotter (34) does state that the Manchu court was "progressively turning towards a rigid taxonomy of culturally-distinct races (*zu*) within China." Nevertheless his discussion of ways in which race is constructed as various types of biological essence is mainly limited to "physically discontinuous peoples, mainly Westerners and Africans" (x).

Interestingly, many of the same people who claim that they are often mistaken for being Chinese also insist emphatically that they can immediately tell a Tibetan when they see one, whether on the streets of Lhasa, Dharamsala, or Berkeley. In fact, all but one Tibetan with whom I spoke insisted that they were able to know intuitively whether or not someone was Tibetan, with nearly 100% accuracy. However, taking apart this claim of intuition-based recognition proved difficult; most emphasised a 'feeling', a combination of physical appearance, mannerisms and behaviour, ranging from 'way of walking' to 'way of speaking', which were difficult to disaggregate further.

For some, Tibetan-ness is at its core characterised by an emanation of compassion (*snying rje; byang chub kyi sems*), which was said to be a daily, lifelong practice with much deeper significance than its English translation, 'compassion'. It was also described as being at the core of being a *nang ba*, much more so than more overt, public actions such as visiting monasteries or participating in large religious ceremonies. As such, certain modes of behaviour and composure were thought to be outward manifestations or bodily inscriptions of this *snying rje* at the center of Tibetan identity. Nevertheless, convictions that Tibetan-ness, as an outward sign of an inward essence, could be unproblematically recognised by fellow Tibetans were not borne out by actual experience.

Mis-recognition often, though not always, reinforced judgements of inauthenticity because of the complex interplay of different types of identity markers. These relevant markers clearly do not originate only from external representations. As Louisa Schein (2000:62) has written in reference to the Miao,

> [the Miao] have embraced some of these [external] definitions in a dialogic accommodation ... [yet] The defining of the Miao is not reducible to a form of knowledge/power in which external agents script and draw the boundaries of Miao identity for them.

Indeed, for Tibetans the self-definitions most emphasised (e.g. speaking the Tibetan language, exhibiting *snying rje*, as well as *ngo tsha* in certain contexts) are neither dominant Chinese representations (i.e. *hei/zang*) nor western ones (i.e. extreme piety). Physical markers are also understood differently; rather than opposing black (*hei*) with white as is done in Chinese discourse, many Tibetans talk about redness, especially of the cheeks, as a marker of Tibetan-ness as opposed to being 'lacking any colour' (Chinese).[290]

Homeland Tibetans readily agree that there are differences between themselves and the long-term exiles, but do not necessarily see themselves as any less Tibetan. One such man, Tsewang, defended his own extensive engagement with Chinese culture by criticising the long-term exiles for mistakenly "treating Tibetan culture like an object or thing which can be put on a table, bounded, defined, moved around." On the other hand, authenticity is clearly a concern among Chinese-educated Tibetans as well, becoming visible for example in Tsewang's statement to another Chinese-educated Tibetan, "For a long time I thought you were just a Chinese girl, but now I see that you are truly Tibetan inside." Tsewang claimed that it was easy to tell which Tibetans had spent many years working in large Chinese cities because the places where one lives are inscribed on one's body, through habits, gestures, and other subtle but unmistakable ways. Contradictorily, however, he felt himself to be exempt from this bodily inscription of many years of life in eastern China— even though in the Bay Area younger exiles easily classified him as one of those very 'Sinicised' Tibetans. Concerns about authenticity are often displaced from oneself onto others, either peers, or more often, the next generation. In particular, urban Tibetans in the PRC worry about children today who 'grow up wanting to be Han'.

Ironically, the strong sense of Tibetan-ness experienced by at least some Tibetan youth who grow up integrated with urban Chinese society is engendered by the very politics of passing as Chinese. In traditional usage, 'passing' refers to the practice of assuming the identity of another type, class, or group of persons in order to be recognised as a member of that group, for social, economic, or political reasons.[291]

Recent efforts to re-theorise passing in terms of performativity[292] critique the implicit connotations of inauthenticity or deception in

---

[290] According to Stein (1972:40), Tibetans traditionally imagined and described themselves as 'red-faced' and "from their monkey ancestor the first inhabitants inherited ... red faces ...."

[291] In the US in particular, passing has historically denoted the practice of light-skinned people of African descent assuming a white identity (Caughie, 1999:20).

[292] Here performativity refers to a theory of identity as something that the subject does; "the subject is the incoherent and mobilised imbrication of identifications; it is constituted in and through the iterability of its performance ... Performance as

traditional formulations, arguing that this assumes and reinforces the binary logic of identity that gave rise to the practice in the first place. Thus Caughie (1999:25) claims that by deploying the term 'passing' in close relationship to performativity, she rejects the presumption of a real authentic model or original. The insistence on the existence of a real, authentic Tibetan identity is at stake in the debates over language, appearance, and politics, which I discuss in this paper. However, like Venturino (1997:100), I find the reluctance to "theorize essentialist rhetoric on its own terms ... inadequate for critical analyses of how Tibetans and others (re)construct Tibetan culture." For the Tibetans I interviewed, 'passing' as Chinese was not only unintentional but also undesirable, a possibility not generally considered in efforts to celebrate hybridity and the contingent, fragmented nature of identity.

In particular, I am familiar with several Tibetans from eastern regions who speak perfect Chinese and have, by all outward appearances, assimilated. While they admit that some of their outward characteristics may be somewhat 'Chinese', they also passionately believe that their minds (*sems*), and thus their essences, are Tibetan. As such they wish to be recognised and welcomed into the community of Tibetans who share the same cultural and religious values. Yet they may discover that being Tibetan is no guarantee for passing as Tibetan, a position that simultaneously takes seriously the rhetoric of essentialism and also examines the problems it may encounter. As

---

bounded 'act' is distinguished from performativity insofar as the latter consists in a reiteration of norms which precede, constrain, and exceed the performer." Formation of the subject, by contrast, implies more of a hailing of the subject into being, as in Althusser's interpellation, without the stress on the reiteration of performativity (Butler, 1993:121, 131, 234). I wish to draw upon Butler's insights into the role of reiteration, which leaves open the possibility of gaps, fissures, and instabilities in the reiterative practices; but I also wish to take much more seriously claims of the essentiality of identity. That is, categorical differences such as ethnicity and race may be argued "to acquire their inexorability through an accumulation of verifying performances or to have their essential aura eroded by crossover performances" (Schein, 1999:371); my discussion of misrecognition, passing, and alternative Tibetan subject positions all show how some aspects of an essential aura are eroded; but they do not necessarily undo all aspects of essential identity claims, particularly those couched in spiritual or religious terms (e.g. *snying rje*). Essentialist claims of Tibetan identity need to be theorised more on their own terms.

Caughie (1999:255) notes in reference to an ex-coloured man's situation in a James Weldon Johnson novel,

> When he finds out that he is colored, not white, he sets out to become a Negro by learning what it means to be that identity. He reads literature, history, studies music and dialect, and observes and imitates other blacks. [The book shows that] being something is no guarantee that one will or will not pass as that identity.

It is through this type of process that at least some urban Tibetan youth strive to become more Tibetan. On the one hand, they are sometimes discriminated against because of their Tibetan *minzu* label, and subject to negative stereotypes hand they themselves are also sometimes complimented for being different from other Tibetans. According to Drolma, who grew up in Xining:

> When I was young I didn't think there was any difference between Tibetan and Han. I didn't think it was a big deal being Tibetan, since we were just another minzu. But other people kept wanting to make me different. When I go out with my friends in the city and dress like a city girl, no one believes I am Tibetan. They always ask me "which one of your parents is Han, your father or your mother?" ... They congratulate me for not being like a Tibetan ... Whenever a rural Tibetan gets on a city bus people hold their noses and walk away and say rude things. Once I took my cousin from the countryside to a hospital in Xining. All of the doctors sat around and tried to ignore her, each telling the other to go and look at the dirty Tibetan ... I started to feel like, okay, I am Tibetan. I'm not at all like you Han people. Then after I finished junior high I decided to go back to another school to learn Tibetan for several years. I volunteered to teach for a year in a nomadic area ... Now I'm proud of being Tibetan ... I think it's very important for us to keep our Tibetan culture.

Pride and awareness of Tibetan identity are thus constituted in very different ways among Tibetan youth in the PRC and Tibetan youth in exile. For the latter, Tibetan-ness as an essential identity distinct from Chinese-ness is part of the formal and informal educational system which emphasises the 'mythico-history' (Malkki, 1995) of the lost territory of the Tibetan nation. For Tibetan youth who are educated in China, by contrast, the process of identification is often rooted ironically in their own adoption of Chinese patterns of speech, dress, food, and other ways of life; that is, in the specters of their own inauthenticity.

These various contestations over what Tibetans should look and act like reveal an ongoing process of active negotiation, definition, and construction of Tibetan identity. Despite western or Chinese scripts that may demand a certain politics of difference between Tibetans and other groups (Adams, 1996), struggles over Tibetan identity take place as much among Tibetans themselves as between Tibetans and westerners or Chinese. I next briefly consider my own transgressions of the unstable boundaries of Tibetan-ness to reflect upon the complexity of identity as neither pure essentialism nor a free flow of signifiers.

NOTES ON 'PASSING'

Over the last several years, I've chosen to do a few simple things such as keep my hair long and wear Tibetan jewelry, yet I no more voluntaristically chose to begin 'passing' as a Tibetan than I chose to be identified as a Japanese tourist the very first time I went to Lhasa as a tourist, nearly a decade ago. 'Passing' involves more subtle and unconscious transformations, similar to those Charlene Makley (1999:xx) describes about the course of her research in Labrang:

> It was the entire context those earrings indexed of my entering into gendered interactions on Tibetan terms. It was in the subtle socio-linguistic clues and gestures associated with gendered Tibetan-ness I gradually took on ... As my body became marked with local gendered emblems (earrings, hairstyle, amulets and on festival days full traditional dress) and my practices and expectations became shaped by local mores, gender confusion about me subsided and I got grateful approval instead.

Reflecting upon my own experience, I found changes in my own sense of aesthetics and ideals of identification. Indeed, after a year of living in Lhasa, I found myself unconsciously adopting relevant visible markers of Tibetan-ness and very much wanting to be identified as Tibetan. My closer friends, who were not particularly fond of the Han in Lhasa, often impressed upon me their pride in all things Tibetan; thus I was perhaps trying to reflect back to them an image of myself I thought they wanted to see. Every taxi ride in which I successfully 'passed' as Tibetan was a secret victory; every identification as Chinese, a source of disappointment. Although the desire to pass was occasionally a simple practical matter, it more often grew out of a desire to feel accepted, to become one of 'us'. At the same time, however, I was and am acutely aware of my own 'real' identity not just as non-Tibetan but as ethnically Chinese-American; my discomfort with 'deception' made me want to reveal this fact as soon as I had established that I had successfully passed as Tibetan.

This led to some rather interesting problems. One incident stands out in particular. I was having dinner in a small, dimly lit restaurant when I struck up a conversation with a particularly talkative and somewhat intoxicated Tibetan man. He assumed I was Tibetan and I did not disabuse him of the idea at first, though after a while I decided that I should tell him I was American. Rather than express-ing curiosity or enthusiasm for America, however, he expressed only disbelief, telling me I was obviously Tibetan, not American. I was suddenly overcome with a desire not to tell him that I was Chinese; we had, after all, been discussing 'the Chinese' in a rather unflatter-ing way. I could not even bring myself to tell him that my parents were from Taiwan, my usual explanation for such situations. I continued to insist that I was American, and he began to get agitated and then angry until I finally understood that he assumed I was a Tibetan-American, too proud to admit my Tibetan roots. Back in California, I called a friend hoping to talk to her mother, who had arrived recently from Lhasa for a visit. I heard my friend saying in the background to her mother, "that *rgya mo*, you know, Emily, wants to talk to you."

How, then, does being a Chinese-American shape my interactions with Tibetans in Tibet and in exile? In the PRC, where race is conflated with culture and language to a greater extent than in the US, I was more often mistaken for being a Tibetan at first sight than I am at home. In the US, a country of immigrants where experience and socialisation take on a greater role in judgements of identity, I am more often told that I've "become just like a Tibetan" after people learn of my Chinese-American ethnicity. In both settings, looking like an insider facilitates being considered one, being told things "we usually don't tell the foreigners." Like all researchers, however, I cannot escape my own 'layered otherness', a position that is both productive and constraining (Makley, 1999:38). Because of the particular interstices that my sometimes deliberately blurry identity opens up, in the Bay Area I am closer to the Tibetans who have come recently from the homeland than I am to those born in exile. With the former I can discuss my parents' native places, my former workplace in Beijing, as well as mundane details of Tibet's concrete geography; whereas the latter expect more that I be a regular 'Tibet supporter'; not fitting the mold, they tend to see my views as being much more biased against their position than I believe to be the case. I turn next to explore the cultural politics of Tibetan-ness in greater detail.

THE POLITICS OF LANGUAGE AND THE LANGUAGE OF POLITICS

Scholarly attention to contemporary Tibetan culture has tended to focus on the dialectical relationships between Tibetans in exile, western supporters of a free Tibet, and western consumption of Tibetan culture (Korom, 1997a, b). Questions have been asked, for example, about how foreign images of Tibetans influence Tibetan identity, and how Tibetans creatively engage with Western discourses to produce Tibetan-ness (McLagan, 1997). The already 'scripted differences' meant to keep Tibetans distinct from Chinese, Chinese distinct from Westerners, and Westerners distinct from Tibetans have also been explored (Adams, 1996). However, despite occasional mention of the dialectical relationship between Tibetans in Tibet and Tibetans in exile (Korom, 1997a:3, and Strøm, 1997), fissures and faultlines within the 'Tibetan community' have not been fully discussed. Exceptions (Diehl, 1997 and 1998; Calkowski, 1997; and Harris, 1997) have for the most part addressed various arts, crafts, literature, and performance traditions, where the politics of cultural preservation has often included the dismissal of new or syncretic forms of expression. Harris' account of Gongkar Gyatso's struggles as an artist in Dharamsala because he does not produce thangka paintings, and Diehl's account of 'new arrivals' whose old folk songs were disparaged in Dharamsala for sounding 'too Chinese', both demonstrate that questions of authenticity are not posed only from the outside (cf. Korom, 1997:7). Disagreements over whether or not Tibetans should watch Chinese soap operas at home may be partially engendered through a long dialectical relationship with western supporters and western ideas about what Tibetans should be, but an exclusive focus on relationships with the west obscures social dynamics within the Tibetan community itself.

Tibetans who have left Tibet for India since the early 1980s, almost always referred to as 'new arrivals' (*gsar 'byor*), are often looked down upon by 'old arrivals' and younger Tibetans raised in exile for being *kacha* ('raw' in Hindi), a reference to their unfashionable clothing, haircuts, and musical tastes (Diehl, 1998:77). To the style-conscious younger generation in particular, the new arrivals "who wear those pants with really skinny ankles and don't slick their hair back" are *kacha*. In addition, many exile Tibetans complain that the new arrivals "have bad behaviour (*spyod pa sdug chag*)" and "love to fight."[293] This was considered especially bad because of the self-understanding of Tibetans as refugees, temporary guests of the Indian state who do not really belong there. Bad behaviour on the part of the new arrivals is believed to engender Indian resentment towards the Tibetan population as a whole, to give them an undeservedly bad reputation.[294]

Thus while *gsar 'byor* literally means only 'new arrival', several Tibetans told me that it also had connotations ranging from 'ignorant' to 'bad smelling' to 'someone who enjoys picking fights'. Others insisted, however, that they attached no special meanings to the term and that it was the new arrivals themselves who thought that it was a derogatory term, perhaps out of their own insecurity. Regardless, the experience of the United States has led to much less overt discrimination between 'old' and 'new', since the new arrivals are no longer dependent upon the old ones, and everyone is busy fending for himself or herself. More pointedly, several former 'new arrivals' insisted that the Tibetans originally from Tibet were as a group much more successful in the US than the refugees from India, despite their being educationally and financially disadvantaged (the

---

[293] See also Strøm (1997:41), who found that in India, monks from Tibet were characterised by exiles as being wild and unruly. However, Strøm also found that the same monks were described as being very diligent and good students. The people with whom I spoke agreed that many *gsar 'byor* often study much harder than the young exiles, who are much more *drep do*, but attributed this largely to their lack of financial means and close friends with whom to hang around.

[294] When relaxation of the border policy first allowed a small trickle of Tibetans to visit India, the newcomers were actually treated quite well by the exile community. It was only after a few years, as the trickle turned into a flood, that things started to turn sour. Tibetans said this was because there was "all kinds of people" (*mi gang byung ma byung*) among the 'new arrivals', including a small number of riff-raff who did unfortunate things like steal and get into fights a lot.

latter, of course, do not necessarily agree). As one such man told me, "My boss at the hotel saw that I was doing a very good job at work, so I convinced him to hire four other Tibetans who were looking for jobs, all from exile. Those guys from India certainly can't make fun of me for being a *gsar 'byor* anymore!" Nevertheless I often hear Tibetans from exile refer to the others as *gsar 'byor*.

Perhaps the most contentious issue that continues to arise in the mix of Tibetans from a variety of places, however, is that of politics and language. New arrivals in Dharamsala are crucial to the exile community as sources of the latest information about the situation in Tibet. Yet when exile Tibetans, especially the younger generation, find themselves face to face with the new arrivals and their unfamiliar (and hence, 'Chinese') habits, the image of their fellow Tibetans as uncorrupted (Strøm, 1997:37) quickly gives way to a belief that they have been brainwashed by their upbringing under Chinese rule. Occasional arrests in Dharamsala of 'new arrivals' allegedly spying for the China bolster such feelings of deep suspicion (Diehl, 1998:77).

Suspicion of the new arrivals is often based on the fact that they speak Chinese. Many Tibetans who went to India in the 1980s recounted their frustrations at arriving in Dharamsala unable to read or write Tibetan. This was especially a problem for Tibetans who were not from the Lhasa area; generally able only to speak their local dialect of Tibetan (and thus unable to communicate easily with most exiles), they were often chastised for speaking Chinese to each other:

> When I first arrived in India, I constantly had to explain that just because I sometimes read a newspaper in Chinese or spoke in Chinese didn't mean that I didn't understand about politics. I always had to explain that one must consider the contents of a book or what someone is saying, not just what language it's in.

Whereas mixing Hindi and English words into Tibetan sentences is hip and fashionable among exile youth, the mixing of Chinese words is considered inexcusable.

In the Bay Area, Tibetans born and raised in exile tend to continue to view Chinese as the language of the enemy, though community pressure is certainly much more muted here. The former new arrivals may or may not often speak Chinese themselves (depending on the extent to which Chinese was spoken in their hometowns in Tibet), but are quite a lot more tolerant of Chinese-speaking Tibetans than are the long-term exiles. They also tend to be closer friends with Tibetans from the homeland than those who have spent their entire lives in exile.

If Tibetan identity in exile has been founded on anti-Chinese ideology (Shakya, 1993:11), former new arrivals are generally careful to separate Chinese culture from the state, including disarticulating the long-term exiles' assumption of a necessary connection between the use of Chinese language and incorrect politics. Often this is done through affirmations of personal commitment to *rang bstan* politics. Dawa, for example, grew up around Lhasa but fled to India after several of his relatives were killed in demonstrations in the late 1980s. He also happens to be very fond of watching Chinese soap operas and movies, a hobby that led to some tension when a new roommate from exile complained that he couldn't understand why Dawa had to watch so much Chinese television. Dawa defended himself by insisting that only content, not language, was important, and by citing his dead relatives, as well as his own experience of fleeing over freezing mountain passes to India—two proofs of his correct Tibetan politics which the exile roommate could not contest.

Other former new arrivals take a different tact, criticising the exiles' aversion to Chinese as a sign of their political naiveté. According to Ngodrup, a Tibetan from Kham who had gone to school in India before returning to Tibet (where he met a sponsor who brought him to the US),

> It is narrow minded for Tibetans not to learn Chinese in exile. If you want to engage in diplomacy and really make change in Tibet, then you have to learn Chinese. These exiles in India are not fighting ... they are retreating. They will not be able to accomplish their goals unless they engage with China, and for that more Tibetans in exile should learn Chinese.

Ngodrup himself had been the object of some suspicion when he first arrived in the US from Tibet:

> They were suspicious because they think that leaving Tibet is just like escaping from Alcatrez.[295] They think that anyone who is actually able to leave must have really good connections with the Chinese government.

---

[295] An infamous former prison in the San Francisco Bay.

Despite their sometimes very strong convictions, Tibetans like Ngodrup tend to be less involved in exile political organisations in the Bay Area than the long-term exiles.

Among Tibetans from the homeland there is a wide variety of political opinion, probably much wider than in the long-term exile community. Some believe strongly in the desirability and long-term possibility of *rang bstan*, while others hope mainly that policies will loosen up enough to provide equitable economic development without a complete loss of Tibetan language and culture. As one man, who felt himself to be rather more cosmopolitan than most of the long-term exiles, put it: "in this age of transnationalism and the internet, when the world is getting smaller and smaller every day, it doesn't make sense to still be talking independence anymore." However, his particular 'citizen of the world' view of transnationalism and hybridity is a distinct minority among Tibetans from China, not to mention exile.[296] Unlike the Tibetans from exile for many of whom political protest is a constitutive part of who they are, Tibetans from Tibet often profess that they have no interest in politics. Their studied lack of interest in 'politics' and low priority given to attending protests, rallies, and meetings is engendered by a variety of factors, including concern for close family members in Tibet, plans to return, and the feeling that many of the long-term exiles don't know what Tibet is really like these days. Furthermore, for some homeland Tibetans speaking Chinese is just as convenient as speaking Tibetan (or, at least, the versions of Lhasa-dialect Tibetan that have become lingua franca in exile). They tend to find the linguistic double standard, whereby mixing Hindi and English with Tibetan is acceptable but Chinese is not, to be irritating if not hypocritical.

Another Tibetan woman described her own inability to read and write Tibetan as "a victory for the Chinese government." She explained that she believed in *rang bstan*, and was a *nang ba,* but also had nothing against Chinese language, people, or culture per se.

---

[296] I agree with Venturino (1997:108) in cautioning that "it is important to question the logic that demands that formerly 'essentialist' culture progress into transnational, hybridised entities ... Tibetan claims to an essential identity, while demonstrably imaginary, constructed, and teleological, are no less essential in that they serve as foundational claims that operate politically, socially, and for many, spiritually."

She thought that the long-term exiles should understand how impossible it would be to forget her seventeen years of Chinese education; on the other hand, they should see that this did not make her *sems* any less Tibetan. Most importantly, however, she felt that for the time being she simply wanted to make a better life for herself in the US rather than spend time thinking about politics. While many of the long-term exiles have essentially the same goals in the US—to make money to send home, or to provide a better life for their children—many find it much more difficult to articulate their goals without also articulating their explicit support for the 'Tibetan cause'.

MULTIPLE SITES OF TIBETAN IDENTITY FORMATION AND PERFORMATIVITY: QUESTIONS OF AUTHENTICITY

Historically, practices such as long distance trade and pilgrimage gave a relative coherence to Tibetan culture and identity, including a sense of shared history, a common literary language, aspects of genealogy, myth, and religion, as well as folkloric notions such as Tibetans as *tsampa*-eaters (Kapstein, 1998:115–17, 140–45). However, Tibetan identity as a national identity emerged only in response to Tibet's incorporation into the PRC; prior to this century, Tibetans conceived of themselves primarily in relation to their religious and regional affiliations (Stoddard, 1994:125). In exile, the Tibetan government has actively worked to forge a single Tibetan identity which overrides regional and sectarian differences (Nowak, 1984:65); and indeed, younger exiles in the Bay Area are noticeably much less concerned with their regional origins than are the older generation of exiles or their counterparts (no matter what age) born in Tibet.

Whether in exile, in the United States, or in Tibet itself, Tibetans are quick to point out their unity rather than their differences: "we are all the same, we are all Tibetan." As Kapstein (1998:144) notes, a Tibetan identity is one that is emphasised most when dealing with non-Tibetans. Other affiliations come into play among Tibetans themselves; shifting senses of identity depend in part on the interlocutor, on who is doing the asking. I have tried to show that, within the relatively new Tibetan community in the Bay Area, place of subject-formation—which shapes dress, attitude, language use, and desires—is an important (though not the only) axis along which Tibetan identity is negotiated.

Discussing the Tibetan performing arts, Calkowski (1997) notes that artists sanctioned by the PRC base their claims to cultural authenticity upon their emanation from the aboriginal land, i.e. on a sense of spatial propriety, whereas artists in exile explicitly frame their performances as traditional, that is on a sense of temporal authority. Younger Tibetans born in exile are constituted as Tibetans by their education and upbringing, which emphasises that they are being taught the traditional, and hence the 'real' (un-Sinicised) Tibetan ways. For them, the notion of being refugees is a foundational principle of what and who they are (Strøm, 1997:35). These young refugees, many of whom have adopted rap as a style of speaking and dress in the United States, nevertheless hold tightly to a 'mythico-history' (Malkki, 1995:54f.) of Tibet, a moral ordering of the world that heroises the past of the Tibetans as a people distinct from all others. History of 'Tibet as it was' is not just a list of past events but a powerful narrative which emphasises, among other things, intense nationalism and cultural uniqueness (Nowak, 1984).

The distinct identity that binds the younger generation with the older is the shared experience of exile (Venturino, 1997:104), and the memories of others' experiences that they have been taught. Thus when I spoke with one nineteen year-old Tibetan 'gangsta rapper' about what he thought it meant to be Tibetan, he referenced the memory of the older exiles' culturally unique clothing styles as if it was his own memory:

> Back before 1959 when we were still in Tibet, we used to wear chubas every day. The fact that we wear chubas is part of what makes us Tibetan ... We don't wear chubas in the US because we Tibetans are very easily embarrassed (*ngo tsha*) if we stick out in a crowd, not because they're not important.

On the other hand, he was convinced that if some urban Tibetans in the homeland no longer wear chubas, it is either because they are forced not to dress that way, or because of undue Chinese influence in

Figure 10.1:   Tibetan Merchants at Annual Himalayan Fair, Berkeley, California. P.C. Klieger.

Figure 10.2: Family at Annual Himalayan Fair, Berkeley, California. E. Yeh.

their lifestyles. That is, his own adoption of African-American rap fashion rather than a chuba reflected not inauthenticity, but a truly Tibetan trait of sensitivity to *ngo tsha* (see Nowak, 1984:77). Tibetans in Tibet, however, must genuinely want to wear chubas; if not, they are either under undue compulsion, or have been Sinified.

However, the situation in the Bay Area is not simply one in which the Tibetans from exile consider themselves to be 'more Tibetan' than all Tibetans from contemporary Tibet. While the new arrivals may be 'too Chinese', many believe this is because the Tibetans they are able to meet are mostly urban; they locate the site of authenticity further in the countryside, especially in pastoral areas. At least some of the younger exiles also privately express doubts about their own knowledge base, as well as a strong desire to go to see Tibet as it is, for themselves. Anxiety about the degree and speed to which children and teenagers have assimilated is also quite pervasive.

Whereas younger Tibetans raised in exile tend to define their Tibetan-ness in mythico-historical terms, Tibetans who emigrated to India in the 1980s enjoy a spatial authority of being from the homeland itself, of knowing its concrete geography (unlike many of the younger exiles; see Strøm, 1997). However, having also been in India before arriving in the US, they have to some extent gained the temporal authority of exile, despite concerns about their 'Sinicisation'. Nevertheless, some are clearly concerned about the ways they and their peers have been changed from what they were, particularly linguistically. Several Khampas from rural areas remarked to me that they could no longer speak their home dialect well; but neither could they speak Lhasa *ge* well; moreover they had forgotten most of their Chinese, and were not particularly proficient in English. They felt that their families back in Kham represented the 'true' Tibetans whereas they themselves were in a highly displaced, liminal position of being not-quite-anything-in-particular. Furthermore, as a group these former new arrivals articulate with 'Tibetan-ness' a particular set of cultural habits which are much more similar to those of the homeland Tibetans; thus they are also socially closer in the Bay Area.

For Tibetans like Drolgar who come to the Bay Area directly from Tibet, being Tibetan is no more incompatible with speaking Chinese and singing Chinese songs than it is with speaking English or enjoying Hindi movies. If some of these Tibetans are genuinely concerned with the way their own Tibetan-ness has changed from outside influences, or more commonly, if they are concerned with the authenticity of the younger generation of Tibetans in the PRC, they see this as no different from the Indian and western influences observable in the styles, mannerisms, and language of Tibetans from exile. Like the exiles, as well as the former new arrivals, many of these urban Tibetans tend to locate the figure of the authentic Tibetan in rural areas, particularly in the Drog pa. Furthermore, many younger Tibetans who have been educated and raised in urban China come to first identify and then perform their own Tibetan-ness through a contradictory process in which their simultaneous similarity to and difference from the Han is precisely what engenders their desire to become 'real' Tibetans, to inhabit and embody the identity category 'Tibetan'. These processes of Tibetan subject-formation within the PRC are in stark contrast to the experience of exile in India, where constant repetition and verbalisation of the mythico-history of Tibet is a primary way in which identity is constituted and performed. As I have tried to show, these differences carry over into the cultural politics of Tibetan identity in the Bay Area, where performances of Tibetan-ness such as Drolgar's are often not accepted or recognised by other Tibetans, who circumscribe the limits of Tibetan-ness to that which is familiar from the context of south Asian exile.

BIBLIOGRAPHY

Adams, Vincanne. 1996. "Karaoke as Modern Lhasa, Tibet: Western Encounters with Cultural Politics," *Cultural Anthropology*, 11(4):510–546.
Bishop, Peter. 1989. *The Myth of Shangri-La: Tibet, Travel Writing and the Western Creation of Sacred Landscape*. Berkeley: University of California Press.
Blum, Susan. 1992. "Ethnic Diversity in Southwest China: Perceptions of Self and Other," *Ethnic Groups*, 9:267–79.
Butler, Judith. 1993. *Bodies that Matter: On the Discursive Limits of 'Sex'*. New York: Routledge.
Calkowski, Marcia. 1991. "A Day at the Tibetan Opera: Actualized Performance and Spectacular Discourse," *American Ethnologist*, 18(4):643–57.
—— 1997. "The Tibetan Diaspora and the Politics of Performance," in Frank Korom (ed.), *Tibetan Culture in the Diaspora*. Papers Presented at a Panel of the 7th Seminar of the International Association for Tibetan Studies, Graz, 1995. Wien: Verlag Der Osterreichischen Akademie der Wissenschaften, 51–59.
Caughie, Pamela L. 1999. *Passing & Pedagogy: The Dynamics of Responsibility*. Chicago: University of Illinois Press.
Diehl, Keila. 1997. "When Tibetan Refugees Rock, Paradigms Roll: Echoes from Dharmasala's Musical Soundscape," in Frank Korom (ed.) *Constructing Tibetan Culture: Contemporary Perspectives*. Quebec: World Heritage Press, 98–122.
—— 1998. *Echoes from Dharamsala: Music in the Lives of Tibetan Refugees in North India*. University of Texas at Austin Ph.D. dissertation.
Dikotter, Frank. 1992. *The Discourse of Race in Modern China*. Stanford: Stanford University Press.
Gladney, Dru. 1994. "Representing Nationality in China: Refiguring Majority/Minority Identities," *Journal of Asian Studies*, 53(1):92–123.
Harris, Clare. 1997. "Struggling with Shangri-La: A Tibetan Artist in Exile," in Frank Korom (ed.), *Constructing Tibetan Culture: Contemporary Perspectives*. Quebec: World Heritage Press, 160–77.
Kapstein, Matthew. 1998. "A Pilgrimage of Rebirth Reborn: The 1992 Celebration of the Drigung Powa Chenmo", and "Concluding Reflections," in Melvyn Goldstein and Matthew Kapstein, (eds.), *Buddhism in Contemporary Tibet: Religious Revival and Cultural Identity*. Berkeley: University of California Press, 95–120, 139–51.
Klieger, P. Christiaan. 1997. "Shangri-La and Hyperreality: A Collision in Tibet Refugee Expression", in Frank Korom (ed.), *Tibetan Culture in the Diaspora*. Papers Presented at a Panel of the 7th Seminar of the

International Association for Tibetan Studies, Graz, 1995. Wien: Verlag Der Osterreichischen Akademie der Wissenschaften, 59–69.

Korom, Frank J. 1997a. "Introduction," in Frank Korom (ed.), *Constructing Tibetan Culture: Contemporary Perspectives*. Quebec: World Heritage Press.

— 1997b. "Introduction: Place, Space and Identity: The Cultural, Economic, and Aesthetic Politics of Tibetan Diaspora," in Frank Korom (ed.), *Tibetan Culture in the Diaspora*. Papers Presented at a Panel of the 7th Seminar of the International Association for Tibetan Studies, Graz, 1995. Wien: Verlag Der Osterreichischen Akademie der Wissenschaften.

Lopez, Donald S. Jr. 1998. *Prisoners of Shangri-La: Tibetan Buddhism and the West*. Chicago: University of Chicago Press.

Makley, Charlene. 1999. *Embodying the Sacred: Gender and Monastic Revitalization in China's Tibet*. University of Michigan Ph.D. dissertation.

Malkki, Lisa. 1995. *Purity and Exile: Violence, Memory and National Cosmology among Hutu Refugees in Tanzania*. Chicago: University of Chicago Press.

— 1997. "National Geographic: The Rooting of Peoples and the Territorialization of National Identity among Scholars and Refugees," in Akhil Gupta and James Ferguson (eds.), *Cultural, Power, Place*. Durham: Duke University Press, 52–75.

McLagan, Meg. 1997. "Mystical Visions in Manhattan: Deploying Culture in the Year of Tibet," in Frank J. Korom (ed.), *Tibetan Culture in the Diaspora*. Papers Presented at a Panel of the 7th Seminar of the International Association for Tibetan Studies, Graz, 1995. Wien: Verlag Der Osterreichischen Akademie der Wissenschaften, 69–91.

Nowak, Margaret. 1984. *Tibetan Refugees: Youth and the New Generation of Meaning*. New Jersey: Rutgers University Press.

Schein, Louisa. 1997. "Gender and internal orientalism in China," *Modern China*, 23 (1):69–99.

— 1999. "Performing Modernity," *Cultural Anthropology*, 13(3):361–95.

— 2000. *Minority Rules: The Miao and the Feminine in China's Cultural Politics*. Durham, N.C.: Duke University Press.

Shakya, Tsering. 1993. "Whither the Tsampa Eaters?" *Himal*. Sept./Oct., 8–11.

Stein, R.A. 1972. *Tibetan Civilization*. Stanford: Stanford University Press.

Stoddard, Heather. 1994. "Tibetan Publications and National Identity," in Robert Barnett (ed.), *Resistance and Reform in Tibet*. Bloomington: Indiana University Press,121–57.

Strøm, Axel Kristian. 1997. "Between Tibet and the West: On Traditionality, Modernity and the Development of Monastic Institutions in the Tibetan Diaspora," in Frank Korom (ed.), *Tibetan Culture in the*

Diaspora. Papers Presented at a Panel of the 7th Seminar of the International Association for Tibetan Studies, Graz, 1995. Wien: Verlag
Der Osterreichischen Akademie der Wissenschaften, 33–51.

Venturino, Steven. 1997. "Reading Negotiations in the Tibetan Diaspora,"
in Frank Korom (ed.), *Constructing Tibetan Culture: Contemporary
Perspectives*. Quebec: World Heritage Press, 98–122.

AUTHORS' BIODATA

Dibyesh Anand is a doctoral candidate at the University of Bristol in the United Kingdom. Born in Bihar, India, he is currently studying the Tibetan freedom movement, identity, and nationalism within the field of Political Science.

Georges Dreyfus is Professor of Religion at Williams College in the United States and holds the Geshe Lharampa degree from the Council of Religious and Cultural Affairs of the Dalai Lama's establishment in India. He is the author of *The Sound of Two Hands Clapping: the Education of a Tibetan Buddhist Monk* (University of California, 2002*), Les Deux Vérités selon les Quatre Ecoles* (Vajra Yogini: 2000), *Recognizing Reality: Dharmakirti's Philosophy and its Tibetan Interpretations*, (SUNY: 1997), and other books and articles on Tibetan religion and nationalism.

Nellie (P.C.M.) Grent studied Youth Welfare Service and Cultural Anthropology at the University of Amsterdam, Netherlands. She has written papers on Tibetan women, nuns, and youth. She trained at the Library of Tibetan Works and Archives in Dharamsala and is currently working at the Library of the University of Amsterdam. For several years she was employed as the co-ordinator of the Tibet Library and Archive in Amsterdam. At present she is studying Information Service and Management, specialising in libraries and archives

P. Christiaan Klieger is an anthropologist who has worked among Tibetans since 1978. He is the author of *Tibetan Nationalism* (Archana, 1992) and many articles on Tibetan identity. His latest book, *Tibet-o-Rama* (Green Arrow, 2002), is a reflexive ethnography dealing with fieldwork among Tibetan refugees and in the homeland. He is presently with the California Academy of Sciences in San Francisco, and has recently returned from fieldwork in the remote Hkakabo Razi region of northernmost Myanmar (Burma), home of the Rawang peoples.

Laurie Hovell McMillin has travelled among Tibetan communities since 1982. She teaches in the Rhetoric and Composition Program at

Oberlin College in the United States. Her book, *English in Tibet, Tibet in English: Self-Presentation in Tibet and the Diaspora*, was published by Palgrave in 2001.

Lara Maconi is a doctoral candidate in Tibetan Studies at Langues 'O INALCO in Paris where she is also assistant researcher-teacher. Graduated in Chinese Studies from Ca' Foscari University in Venice, her personal research deals with Tibetan contemporary literature written in Chinese. She collaborates with the literary magazine: *Neige d'aout, Lyrisme et extreme orient*.

Jan Magnusson, PhL, works at the Research Department of the School of Social Work, Lund University, Sweden. His research interests include the Tibetan diaspora, especially its internal and external political and cultural dynamics. He is also one of the founders of the recently established Swedish South Asian Studies Network (SASNET).

Antonio Terrone holds a MA in Oriental Languages and Civilizations from the Oriental Institute of Napoli University and is a Ph.D. candidate at the Research School CNWS of Leiden University. He is currently working on a research project concerning the *gter ma* tradition and the life and works of active Treasure Masters in the Tibetan regions of the People's Republic of China (PCR. He has studied in Dharmasala, Beijing, and Lhasa.

Emily Yeh is a doctoral candidate at the Energy and Resources Group, University of California—Berkeley. She is currently working on dissertation fieldwork on the recent social history of agricultural production and landscape practices in Lhasa.